International Socialism 120

Autumn 2008

Contributors

Anne Alexander is a writer and researcher on the Middle East.

Colin Barker has been associated with *International Socialism* since the early 1960s.

Ian Birchall is writing a biography of Tony Cliff.

Paul Blackledge is the author of *Reflections on the Marxist Theory of History* and recently coedited a collection of writings by Alasdair MacIntyre.

Pepijn Brandon is a researcher at the history department of the University of Amsterdam, where he is working on a project on war, capitalism and state formation in the Dutch Republic.

Alex Callinicos is the author of *The Resources of Critique, An Anti-Capitalist Manifesto* and *The New Mandarins of American Power*.

Helen Davies works in social care in London.

Andy Durgan is the author of *The Spanish Civil War*.

Neil Faulkner is an archaeologist and the author of *Rome: Empire of the Eagles*.

Donny Gluckstein is the author of *The Paris Commune: A Revolutionary Democracy*.

Mike Gonzalez is the author of *Che Guevara and the Cuban Revolution*.

Andrew Kliman is the author of *Reclaiming Marx's "Capital": A Refutation of the Myth of Inconsistency* and teaches economics at Pace University in New York.

Kim Kwang-il is a member of the South Korean socialist organisation All Together.

Owen Miller is a research associate at the School of Oriental and African Studies centre of Korean studies.

Jonathan Neale is the author of *Stop Global Warming: Change the World* and *What's Wrong with America?*.

John Newsinger is the author of a book on the IWW, *The Flames of Discontent: The Wobblies and Class War America*, to be published in 2009.

John Rose is the author of *The Myths of Zionism*.

Colin Wilson is currently doing research for a book on sexuality and imperialism.

Andy Zebrowski is a member of the Marxist group Pracownicza Demokracja (Workers' Democracy) in Poland and writes for the monthly of the same name.

Four unknowns and a certainty

The biggest financial crisis for 79 years, followed by the most expensive nationalisation of all time; a combination of recession and inflation with completely unpredictable effects; a new explosive flashpoint of international tension, this time on the Black Sea midway between Europe and the Middle East; the unknown outcome of the most passionate US election campaign for four decades; a crisis of the New Labour government in Britain from which there seems to be no way out. Those who preside over the system face unknowns on every side—as do those of us who fight them. There is, however, one certainty about the next few months. There will be sudden turns in the political situation, nationally and internationally, which will create new challenges—and new opportunities—for the left.

New twists to the double crisis

The first big unknown is the way the "double crisis" of the financial crunch and inflation will pan out. The instability was shown graphically as we were producing these notes. The US government stepped in to take over the two giant mortgage corporations Fannie Mae and Freddie Mac—probably the biggest nationalisation in world history—in order to stop a catastrophic collapse of the financial system. Just seven days later it allowed one of the US's biggest investment banks, Lehman Brothers, to go bust, causing such a reaction that the US government then promised to absorb an estimated $700 billion in bad debt from across the system.

It is in the nature of capitalist economic crises to be unpredictable. Feeding statistics into supposedly elaborate mathematical models produces daily economic forecasts. They are invariably wrong. The models produced in July last year could not predict the credit crunch that suddenly broke out in August 2007, so today they cannot predict what things will be like in three or four weeks time—let alone in the coming years.

Back in the spring, when it was already clear that things were going badly in the US, there was a lot of talk of the "decoupling" of the different major economies—some of it from the same people who had previously claimed they were seamlessly welded together. Don't worry, they said, the US is not as important as it used to be, Germany is growing, and China and India are storming ahead. Then in August a couple of favourable economic figures led them to say that the US was not doing too badly and that the problem was that Germany was contracting, and maybe things were not going as well as expected in China and India. Since then there has been an unexpectedly sharp rise in American unemployment, the panic move over Fanny Mae and Freddy Mac, fears that nationalisation is going to cost hedge funds billions through credit derivatives, the collapse of Lehman Brothers, the nationalisation of the giant insurer AIG, warnings by the former head of the Federal Reserve Alan Greenspan that more banks would go bust, the $700 billion "bad bank" buy up...who knows what the situation will be by the time you read this?

Some things, however, are clear:

● What is happening is more than simply a financial storm. It reflects deeper imbalances in the system. We have given our own analyses of these in the four most recent issues of this journal. We have also carried commentary from slightly different perspectives by Costas Lapavitsas and Fred Moseley, as well as a piece critical of our analysis by Jim Kincaid. In this issue Andrew Kliman writes on the very important implications, as he sees it, of the US state's attempt to manage the crisis.

● The political impact of what is happening is bound to be enormous. Recessions lead to splits within capitalist classes between those who are going to lose a lot and those who, losing little in the short term, hope to gain in the long term. Meanwhile the impact on the mass of the population can also lead to sudden explosions of bitterness—as with the militant demonstrations during Margaret Thatcher's first two years in office (1979-81) or the pit closure revolt of 1992. But if the explosions do not produce positive change, a sense of hopelessness can increase receptiveness to the message of racists and fascists.

● Inflation can also lead to explosions of anger, as with the rash of riots in the Global South over food price rises. These have the potential to take a structured, more stable, form than reactions against joblessness, because workers can look to collective struggles through industrial action to keep wages in line with price rises.

● The combination of recession and inflation is particularly worrying to governments and ruling classes. They fear that any moves to limit the impact of recession on businesses by cutting interest rates will stoke up inflation and with it class struggle that can take on a political edge. That is why there are so many references in the media to crisis of the mid-1970s and "stagflation". That is also why our rulers are divided on how to react today, with the US Federal Reserve lowering interest rates in an effort to ward off recession while the Bank of England and European Central Bank are keeping them high for fear of inflation, causing huge problems for Spain and Italy.

● What is happening has enormous ideological implications. Since the 1980s our rulers have sought to justify capitalism through an appeal to neoliberal ideology, in particular the allegedly miraculous properties of free markets in "liberating entrepreneurial spirit". But while they tried to impose neoliberalism on workers at home and weaker governments abroad, the ideology always contradicted reality in the established industrial economies. Here the interaction of states and corporations remained very marked— through defence contracts; tax subsidies; investment grants; the state's promotion of national corporate interests in the World Trade Organisation, the International Monetary Fund and the European Union; and so on. In the past this contradiction between ideology and reality was a hidden one. Now the nationalisations and the billions shoved into the banking system bring it into popular view just as people are demanding state action to protect them from the dual crisis. This can give old socialist arguments about the insanity of capitalism a popular resonance unimaginable a decade ago.

The British dimension

Back in March the OECD argued that Britain was experiencing "solid growth". Now, in a complete reversal of its position, the OECD sees Britain as the worst placed among the world's major economies to withstand the impact of a global slowdown—and the only one it forecasts to be in recession this year.[1] The warnings are echoed by Charlie Bean, deputy director of the Bank of England ("The malaise could drag on for some considerable time"); David Blanchflower, of the Monetary Policy Committee (two million may be unemployed by Christmas according to

---

1:   See, for instance, "OECD Say UK Is Worst Placed In G7 To Withstand Global Downturn", *Independent*, 3 September 2008.

the ILO measurement); and, to everyone's surprise, by chancellor Alistair Darling ("The economic times we are facing are arguably the worst they've been in 60 years").

It remains to be seen how accurate these predictions are. But the impact of the double crisis is already visible in Britain. House sales and new building are at record lows, repossessions are rising, food prices were up 12.5 percent in the year to August and unemployment was up 20,000 in July, with the total claiming dole at 864,700. The ILO measurement of joblessness puts the figure far higher at 1.67 million (5.4 percent).[2] There is widespread fear of what the future holds—and price rises are already leading workers to cut back on expenditure. Reports tell of a switch to supermarkets' "own brands", a decline in organic food sales, a fall in car use and fewer cheap flight bookings. Increases in gas and electricity prices announced in August will add considerably to the number of households in fuel poverty—already 4.5 million in April.

Such things cannot avoid affecting the whole political mood in Britain. Over the decade and a half after 1993 inflation and recession were no more than bad memories for people, with the exception of those stuck in abandoned industrial and mining areas. For young people entering the workforce or in education today they are not even memories—they have never been experienced. Now they are suddenly realities worrying old and young alike. The impact can already been seen in the misery and backstabbing on the New Labour front bench. But it is unlikely to end there.

New Labour pains

"The smell of death around this government is so overpowering it seems to have anaesthetised them all... The imaginary Blair/Brown ideological distinction has now been exposed as the sham it always was... The sad truth is that he [Brown] opposed Blair, not Blair policies... Unseating a prime minister is very high risk—but a dying party should be ready to take dangerous medicine if that's the last chance left".[3]

2:    www.hrmguide.co.uk/jobmarket/unemployment.htm
3:    Polly Toynbee, "Unseating Gordon Brown May Be Labour's Last Chance", *Guardian*, 6 September 2008.

It is a sign of the depth of New Labour's crisis that such things are written by Polly Toynbee, a social democrat so opposed to real radicalism that she joined the SDP split from Labour 25 years ago and then went on to enthuse first for Tony Blair and then, until just a year ago, for Brown.

New Labour's sickness is not, of course, new. Writing quarterly comment on its condition over the past three years has been like writing sick notes for a patient with a near incurable illness. Fifteen months ago the Brown medicine promised recovery from the Blair disease. Now that medicine is blamed for a greatly worsened condition. The problem is not Brown's personality. It is that New Labour, faced with the double crisis, has neither the desire nor the capacity to relate to the section of the working class that has constituted its voting base.

Brown's wing of New Labour claims to be able to relate to its traditional support among the manual working class because of Brown's ability to share a pint of beer with union leaders. Yet his spell as chancellor saw the destruction of a third of the remaining jobs in manufacturing industry and, in the past three years, a decline in manual workers' living standards (see box: "The decline in working class incomes"). The Blair wing, with its would-be kingmaker Charles Clarke and its new pretender David Miliband, claims to appeal to "middle England". But a big section of those on or a little above the median income are white-collared, salaried workers alienated from New Labour by its encouragement of marketisation, job testing, targets, privatisation and managerial bullying, with the added ingredient of a public sector pay norm half the official level of inflation. It is hardly surprising that the four million decline in New Labour's vote between 1997 and 2005 is now turning into a collapse, as shown in recent by-elections and opinion polls (see box: "The decline in working class votes").

The immediate beneficiaries in England are the Tories. But that, as we have emphasised before, does not signify a great popular swing to the right. The Tories have had to position themselves to the left of their old policies in order to pick up support and, significantly, in Scotland it has been the SNP that has gained from Labour. It has been able to do so by picking up some of the social democratic policies that New Labour has abandoned. The devolved Scottish government has gained working class popularity with real, although minor, reforms, while leaving it to the New Labour British government to implement the unpopular policies needed to keep capital happy. Nonetheless, the fact that the Tories are gaining support does have important political implications. It further demoralises activists who have looked to Labour in the past, creating a sense of hopelessness.

Such developments will necessarily lead to counter-developments.

The decline in working class incomes

"Between 2004-5 and 2006-7 incomes fell for the poorest third of households, including skilled manual workers, unskilled workers and the out of work poor," according to the Institute for Fiscal Studies. "Even in the middle of the income distribution spectrum, income growth has been agonisingly weak since 2001. Having grown by 15 percent more than inflation between 1996-7 and 2001-2, the income of the median household grew by only 4 percent in the five years between 2001-2 and 2006-7, the most recent year of data."

What is left to spend after essential bills have been paid has been even harder hit. According to a uSwitch survey, "The typical household in Britain has seen disposable income drop by 15 percent... Disposable income now represents 28 percent of average household income, down from 35 percent a year ago."

Gas prices have risen by 28 percent, electricity 20 percent, petrol 28 percent, and food and drink 25 percent. The average family is also spending 6 percent more on mortgage repayments as a result of higher interest rates. This was equivalent to a fall of about £40 a week for a working couple on the median income. Those living in traditional working class areas have been hardest hit. "People living in Newcastle are spending 77 percent of their net income on bills—far more than the 35 percent spent by those in Surrey or Buckinghamshire."

New Labour's disastrous performance is increasing a widespread sense among those who regard themselves as on the left that there is even less to be gained from relying on it than in the past. This has been very marked at trade union conferences, including September's TUC conference. Speeches critical of the government were the norm. Tony Woodley, joint general secretary of Unite, Britain's biggest union, was derisive about New Labour's refusal to put a windfall tax on energy companies to deal with fuel poverty: "This can't be addressed by lagging the loft as some crackpots around the prime minister want us to consider. Without help with fuel bills now, we'll be lagging the coffins of the elderly if we have a cold winter".[4] His union voted for a resolution from the rail workers' and seafarers' RMT for nationalisation of the utilities.

4: Quoted in the *Financial Times*, 10 September 2008.

The decline in working class votes

In 1997 Labour had a 37 points lead over the Tories among semi-skilled and unskilled workers—the opinion pollsters' "D" and "E" groups. By 2005 the lead had fallen to 12 points; in June this year it was a statistically insignificant one point according to Populus.

The "C2" group voted Labour by two to one in 1997. The Tories now have a seven point lead. This group is usually described as "skilled workers", although it includes foremen and the manual self employed.

Two other groups were important in the Labour election victories over the past 11 years: routine white collar workers ("C1") and the salaried workers classified as "professional" in the "A" and "B" groups. Historically most members of these groups thought of themselves as middle class, with more than half voting Tory. For instance, a majority of teachers voted Tory in 1979 and only 35 percent voted Labour. But in 1997 60 percent voted Labour and only 20 percent Tory. Labour has now lost out among these groups as well, without, however, the Tories regaining their traditionally massive lead.

But bitter criticism of New Labour is not the same as a clear political and ideological alternative to it. The same delegates who voted for left wing resolutions deeply critical of the government listened politely to Alistair Darling when he spoke. The leaders of the biggest unions still take it for granted that they fund New Labour. And when it came to a vote on an amendment that would have committed the TUC to organising united industrial action over pay, the Unite delegation voted for it on a show of hands but then abstained when it came to the decisive card vote, ensuring the resolution was defeated.

It was left to unions not affiliated to Labour, the civil servants' PCS, the RMT, the firefighters' FBU, and the journalists' NUJ, to launch a more radical Trade Union Coordinating Group, convened by left Labour MP John McDonnell. It indicated that its support for MPs would go to those who endorse union demands, which would mean a few of the Labour ones but also some in parties like the SNP and the Welsh nationalist Plaid Cymru.

Each time in the past century, when there has been a crisis of Labourism, political forces have emerged that have attempted to provide a focus—the Independent Labour Party on the one hand and supporters of Stafford Cripps on the other in the early 1930s, the supporters of Aneurin

Bevan in the early 1950s and those of Tony Benn in the early 1980s. Today it is difficult to see such forces emerging as they did in the past from within the confines of Labour.

McDonnell is now virtually alone on the Labour parliamentary left in pushing for a political alternative to New Labour. He failed to get sufficient nominations from other MPs even to stand in last year's leadership election and indicated at a TUC fringe meeting that he does not see any possibility of an alternative emerging before the general election—which will probably not be for another 18 months. As for what happens after that, his expectations are pessimistic. He says a viable socialist electoral alternative must fulfil three criteria: it must be democratic so that socialists are allowed to organise in it, it must get support from working class people, and it must be broad enough to attract enough votes to gain a substantial parliamentary presence in the British "first past the post" system. Labour, he argues, hardly fulfils the first criterion. But a party with clear socialist policies would not fulfil his third. McDonnell makes the point that even in proportional representation elections the dice is strongly loaded in favour of the existing parties. His implication is that electoral activity outside the Labour Party is not going to get very far in the foreseeable future.

A little to the right of McDonnell are John Cruddas, who did manage to get enough nominations to stand for Labour deputy leader last year, and the Compass group. They make lots of noises about New Labour having cut itself off from the working class, and they got some publicity with a petition signed by about 100 MPs calling for a windfall tax. But they define themselves as "centre-left" (Cruddas even voted for the Iraq war) and they do not pose anything like a clear public alternative. Their limited impact was shown by the dismal support for their fringe meeting at the TUC.

In all these respects things are very different from the fag end of the last Labour government in the late 1970s when Tony Benn, although a willing prisoner within the government, did provide a limited focus for activists outside. This time there is a clear vacuum on the left with a great deal of discontent looking for a focus that does not yet exist. We were involved in trying to provide such a focus, through Respect and then the Left List in England and Wales, and the Scottish Socialist Party and then Solidarity in Scotland. These attempts were absolutely justified. Nevertheless, we have to be honest and accept that our very poor election results in May show we cannot provide a sufficiently prominent focus for the time being.

The political vacuum will not remain empty indefinitely. The widespread feeling that there is no political representation for the working class will find expression at some point. A smattering of former Labour activists are standing and winning council seats as independents to the left of Labour—for instance in Barrow, where the Barrow Socialist People's Party has four seats. But such local moves are a very long way from congealing into a national force as has happened, for instance, in Germany (see Alex Callinicos's article in this issue). Activists who worked with Respect and then the Left List have a role to play in encouraging the networks that can help promote such a focus. But we have to recognise that we are very unlikely to achieve it in the near future.

The electoral path has never been the only one for socialists—and for revolutionary socialists it has never been the most important one. In the current situation it is important to grasp this. Struggles will arise over wages, housing, fuel poverty, the health service, and against racism and war. Inevitably many of these will break out when people least expect them. There cannot be a single plan, drawn up in advance, on how to react. What will matter will be the capacity to respond pragmatically to movements and struggles that suddenly arise locally or nationally—and to try to draw them together into single strand of resistance with an anti-capitalist consciousness.

One central issue in the short and medium term is going to be pay. This has already caused a small but significant increase in the level of industrial struggle. Strike figures have been rising for the past two years, even if they are nowhere near the level of the 1970s, and a survey of 450 firms shows that "a quarter have been hit by strikes over the past 12 months".[5] The government was finding the second year of its 2 percent public sector pay limit more difficult than the first, even before the recent upsurge in food and energy prices. The civil service workers' PCS and the teachers' NUT are balloting for further industrial action this autumn, and the strategy of the left in the two unions is to unite their actions so as to give real force to a successful TUC resolution for a national demonstration and days of action. Meanwhile, the capacity of pay to be a catalyst for action in parts of the private sector has been shown by a succession of strikes—and big picket lines—among bus workers in London.

5: "Pay Policy Sees Strikes Increasing", *Financial Times*, 15 September 2008.

Dented hegemony and Georgia's nasty little war

The media has been full of talk of a "new Cold War" since the brief war between Russia and Georgia. It is more accurate to talk of the latest episode of the "war on terror"—that is, of the US's attempt to use military might to assert global hegemony. The setbacks for its project in Iraq, Afghanistan and Lebanon explain its arming of its Georgian client Mikheil Saakashvili—and the hypocritical anguish with which those who connive in rendition kidnappings have screamed about human rights in the Caucasus when he got a beating.

The Russian angle is very different to that presented in the liberal as well as conservative media. When the Eastern Bloc collapsed in 1989-91 the political representatives of the American ruling class believed it removed a smaller, but heavily armed, rival imperialism that had been an obstacle to their global economic and military hegemony. This was supposed to give them a free hand to eliminate anyone else who might stand in their way—invading Panama to kidnap their former agent Manuel Noriega in December 1989, bombing Baghdad (with Soviet acquiescence) to bring another recent ally to order in 1991, playing their own part in tearing the Balkans apart by promoting Bosnian independence in 1992 and then bombing the Serbian capital, Belgrade, in 1999.

But key figures still felt they were far from achieving the global dominance they had expected. The Iranian regime that had humiliated them in the late 1970s remained in power. Their troops were forced to withdraw from Somalia in 1994. The world's fastest growing economy, that of China, was open to US multinationals but it was not beholden to the US state. And there was the underlying worry that the European ruling classes would assert their own interests more forcefully now they no longer feared Russia would exploit US weakness.

Henry Kissinger could be blunt about the problem:

> The end of the Cold War has created what some observers have called a "unipolar" or "one superpower" world. But the US is actually in no better position to dictate the global agenda unilaterally than it was at the beginning of the Cold War... The United States will face economic competition of a kind it never experienced during the Cold War...domination of a single power of either Europe or Asia...remains a good definition of strategic danger to America... Such a grouping would have the capacity to outstrip America

economically… China is on the road to superpower status… China's Gross National Product will approach that of the United States by the end of the second decade of the 21st century.[6]

Similar concerns among Bill Clinton's advisors in the mid-1990s led to a conscious strategy of expanding US influence into countries once under Russian influence in the Eurasian landmass. Those in Europe were encouraged to join Nato and the European Union; the Central Asian former Soviet Republics were encouraged to accept US bases. The US's aims were to counter any tendencies towards independence from "old Europe" (particularly the enlarged Germany), to pre-empt any growth of Chinese influence, to pen in Russia if it showed any signs of reviving as a "regional" power, and to have the means at hand to crush wayward smaller powers in the oil rich Middle East, especially Iraq and Iran.

The Bush presidency gave influence to neocons who believed their predecessors (and even cabinet colleagues such as Colin Powell) were too soft when applying this strategy. That was the message behind the "Project for a New American Century" and the motivation for an attack on Iraq. This was to be the decisive move that would establish a century of unchallengeable hegemony.

Paying for a failed gamble

That strategy has backfired completely. The US's ability to achieve what it wants elsewhere in the world has been damaged by the way its troops have been tied down in Iraq, with the chairman of the joint chiefs of staff worrying whether "the military could provide the 10,000 extra troops" requested by commanders in Afghanistan. The military "surge" in Iraq over the past 18 months may have achieved more than some of us expected but not much more. It has brought some limited stability but not clear victory. General Petraeus, who was sent in to oversee the surge, could still warn before the summer, "We haven't turned any corners. We haven't seen any lights at the end of a tunnel. The progress, while real, is fragile and is reversible".[7] And he repeated the warning, in a more subdued tone, at the beginning of September: "innumerable challenges are out there still. Make no bones about it".[8]

The real "challenge" is that any stabilisation has depended on the

---

6: Henry Kissinger, *Diplomacy* (1994), p809.

7: Quoted by *Voice of America*, 10 April 2008.

8: "US Says Troops Could Quit Baghdad Soon", *Financial Times*, 3 September 2008.

attitude of Iraqi groups that do not accept long-term occupation or control of the oil by US firms. They are also deeply antagonistic to one another. The "Awakening Councils" of Sunni former resistance groups took American arms and money in order to eliminate the threat to their own position from Al Qaida in Iraq. But they are deeply hostile to the US's firmest allies, the Kurdish Peshmerga. The Mahdi Army of radical Shia cleric Muqtata al-Sadr may be avoiding military confrontation with US troops, but that is because its leader, currently in Iran, ordered it to do so to avoid dissipating its strength.[9]

Even the corrupt politicians who have worked with the US occupation for five years have been wary of agreeing to the US's goals. They have blocked US companies from getting long-term contracts for Iraqi oil, while "in the race among global oil majors to re-enter Iraq, China scored the first win".[10] Patrick Cockburn, writing on negotiations for a new security accord between the US and the Iraqi government, argues:

> The new accord is very different from the one the US proposed as recently as March which would simply have continued the US occupation… If it is implemented as expected the US will cease to be the predominant military power in Iraq from next summer.[11]

A lot of things could upset this arrangement, which would leave an Iraqi government asserting its independence by balancing between US and Iranian pressures. But the very fact that it is under consideration represents a blow to the dream of US hegemony.

That hegemony is also under pressure elsewhere. Jonathan Neale's account of Afghanistan's 30 years of wars in this issue shows how close the US and its allies are to facing the same fate that beset the USSR's occupation. The Ethiopian government is threatening to withdraw its troops from Somalia because of the degree of resistance to its US-backed invasion. Iran is refusing to make a humiliating climbdown in the face of US sanctions and threats. Central Asian republics that used to court the US are now courting Russia again.

Such blows to US hegemony explain its determination to turn a

---

9: "Crucial to the success of the government against the Mahdi Army has been the support of Iran. It is they who arranged for the Shia militiamen to go home"—Patrick Cockburn, *Counterpunch*, 3 September 2008.

10: Forbes.com, 28 August 2008.

11: Patrick Cockburn, "The Big Questions about Iraq", *Counterpunch*, 26 August 2008, www.counterpunch.org/patrick08262008.html

small war into a major international crisis. They also explain the Russian government's response.

Putin's goal

For most of the past two decades Russia's rulers felt they could do little to reassert their interests in the face of growing US pressure around their borders. They had lost control of half the former USSR and industrial production had fallen 50 percent in the rump Russian Federation. Former state capitalist *nomenklaturists* transmogrified into private capitalist oligarchs roamed wild, and the armed forces had faced difficulty dealing with resistance from the mere 1.1 million inhabitants of Chechnya.

Things have begun to change since the late 1990s. Putin was able to marshal enough military brutality to finally crush resistance in Chechnya, and reassert fighting discipline within what is still one of the world's most powerful militaries. He was able to exile some of the oligarchs and draw others into his camp. The global rises in oil and gas prices enabled the economy to escape from slump and become one of the fastest growing in the world. They also enabled Russia to exert pressure on, as well as be pressurised by, the states of the European Union.

Now dents to US power in Iraq and Afghanistan have provided Russia with the chance to respond to US challenges close to its borders, just as they have made it easier for China to pursue its own imperial projects in Africa, for Iran to defy the US, and for Venezuela to challenge US power in Latin America. No wonder the US political establishment and their hangers on this side of the Atlantic are so upset.

The two wings of New Labour have responded as you might expect. David Miliband has been running round Europe with Brown's support calling for the building of a new alliance against Russia. Editorialists and liberal commentators have denounced ethnic cleansing with references to Hungary in 1956 and Hitler's move across Czechoslovakia's borders in 1938. There has been ethnic cleansing on *both* sides, just as both sides have been exploiting experiences of national oppression, of Georgians by Russians under Tsarism and Stalinism, and, more recently, of Ossetians and Abkhazians by Georgians. Putin *has* exploited the situation because he wants to extend the influence of the Russian state beyond its own borders, in the Ukraine as well as the Caucasus. But the comparison of the diminished Russia of today with the USSR or Germany when they were the world's second economic and military powers is absurd. Putin's imperialism is a mini-imperialism, on nothing like the scale of that practised by those who have occupied Iraq and Afghanistan.

Further flashpoints

The US's aim is to try to rescue something out of the Georgian debacle by raising fears about Russia in order to try to get the European powers to accept its global agenda. This might work with those Eastern European states with memories of domination by a much more powerful Russia— although even with those there are problems, as is shown by a split in the Ukrainian government between the two figures who stage-managed the country's supposed "Orange Revolution" four years ago, with the president accusing the prime minister of plotting an "anti-constitutional coup".[12] It is not working with Germany, France or even Berlusconi's Italy. They are dependent on Russian energy and their big firms want to benefit from Russian economic growth. They are prepared to make a lot of noise over Georgia in order to strengthen their position to bargain with Putin, but posturing in public is accompanied by efforts at conciliation in private. Singing to the US's tune is not the same as dancing to it.

The US's problems should not, however, be a cause for complacency on anyone's part. It will attempt to recoup its position and still has immense resources for trying to do so. The tactical advance it has made in Latin America with its attacks on the Farc guerillas in Colombia show its continued capacity (see Mike Gonzalez's article in this issue). As we have repeatedly stressed in this journal, a beast that is wounded but still alive is a dangerous beast. The next flashpoint in the war on terror probably won't be in Georgia. The front could shift to Iran, Pakistan, Africa or somewhere else entirely. But there will be a next flashpoint—with the usual piles of corpses and thousands of devastated lives. We have to be prepared to respond. And we must always remember an old slogan, especially when there is a clash between a big imperialism and the little imperialisms that will not bow down to it: "The main enemy is at home."

12: *Financial Times*, 4 September 2008.

Latin America and the future of the Farc

Mike Gonzalez

In February this year the Colombian army launched a cross-border raid on a Revolutionary Armed Forces of Colombia (Farc) camp within Ecuador, killing 18 people. One of the victims was the organisation's second in command, Raúl Reyes. The Colombian president, Alvaro Uribe, claimed the raid as a major victory in the 46-year war with the guerrilla organisation and announced that in the course of the attack three laptop computers had been found containing hundreds of thousands of confidential files. Uribe was unmoved by the furious protests of Ecuador's President Correa, for whom this barefaced intrusion into Ecuador's territory was a grim reminder of his country's relative weakness in the face of a Colombian state whose role in the region continues to be as a stalking horse for US imperial intentions.

The raid and its murderous consequences raised a number of unanswered questions that perplexed the left across the world. Why had the second in command of this powerful guerrilla army allowed himself to be killed while he slept with no sign of armed vigilance and without his gun by his side? The raid was brief and devastating and conducted with precision electronic equipment that had clearly pinpointed the guerrilla camp and the people in it. Was it possible that laptop computers and USBs containing so much information could have been captured so easily by the Colombian state or held together and in such insecure conditions by an organisation that had so much experience of the murderous intents of successive Colombian governments? Was this really just a successful military operation or in fact the result of internal betrayals supplying a major intelligence network?

Uribe's indifference to Correa's protests and his obvious sense of having won a major propaganda victory over Hugo Chavez gave an inkling of the confidence he clearly felt and of the unstinting support he could expect (and got) from Washington in justifying and defending his actions. He had violated national sovereignty, raided the territory of a neighbouring state, paid civilian assassins to supplement the work of the 200,000-strong Colombian army (to murder a second Farc leader, Ivan Marquez), and enjoyed the full support of the intelligence services and counter-insurgency commands of Israel and the Pentagon as well as his own. In the aftermath of the raid it became clear too that a number of people at the highest levels of the government of Ecuador were also involved. Correa sacked his head of military intelligence, replaced his defence minister and accepted the resignation of the heads of all three armed services in the weeks that followed.

Clearly, this was no ordinary operation. Its purposes were far reaching and strategic. It was a critical moment in the Colombian state's war with the Farc, and its impact on that organisation should not be underestimated. It was also calculated to undermine the role of Hugo Chavez in Latin America and to discredit him—serving the interests of Colombia, whose government was competing for regional hegemony as a representative of the long term interests of the US and global capital. More broadly, it was designed to change the balance of forces across Latin America at a time when the rejection of the Free Trade Area of the Americas (the FTAA) by the majority of Latin American governments, and the emergence of an independent economic block around Venezuela and Bolivia, could represent a serious challenge to the neoliberal project.

All of these ends would be served by a defeat of the Farc. And beyond that, and whatever the criticism that might be aimed at the Farc's strategic vision, Colombia remains a country where thousands of peasant and trade union activists are murdered every year by a state ruled by drug traffickers and their satraps. Thirty congressional deputies are currently under arrest for involvement with the paramilitary death squads directly linked to the drug barons, and a senator was recently exposed for accepting bribes in exchange for votes. But that is no more than the norm. The presidential campaigns of Uribe, like many by his predecessors, were financed by drug money.

The reality of a Colombia dominated by a military financed to the tune of $7 billion over the past ten years by the United States is the clear explanation for the continuing existence of the Farc. They are persistently described in the Western media as "narcoterrorists" whose activities and 10,000 or so members under arms are thus represented as little more than another form of criminality. But the Farc were formed in the late 1940s after a savage repressive assault on what was called the Independent Republic of Marquetalia—effectively a mass seizure of land by small peasants and agricultural workers led by the Colombian Communist Party. One of its leaders, Manuel Marulanda "Tirofijo" (Sureshot), set up the Farc after the raid as an organisation of rural self-defence. Marulanda died earlier this year at the age of 80. He had led the organisation throughout but the Farc's role had undoubtedly changed. Over the years it had suffered corruption, desertion and some level of disillusion among its supporters. The guerrillas' increasing use of kidnapping as a political weapon caused controversy and dissent among sections of the left. It brought down vicious reprisals against the ordinary population while disarming them politically.

Yet wherever the Farc has failed to maintain its hegemony, the brutal paramilitary death squads have continued to terrorise rural populations, seize their land and control local communities with an iron hand.

The Colombian state, far from acting against the paramilitaries, incorporated them into its repressive machinery—with the explicit support and approval of Bill Clinton's Plan Colombia of 1999. This gave their activities legitimacy, and the so-called "war on drugs" allowed large-scale military operations against a rural population. The accusations of "narcoterrorism" allowed that "war" to morph imperceptibly into the "war on terror" of the early 21st century. Against that background the Farc's survival is explained by the necessity of some form of self-defence.

The raid on the camp in Ecuador came at a time when the release of hostages, including the high profile former presidential candidate Ingrid Betancourt, was being actively negotiated through the mediation of Hugo Chavez. He had been photographed in the mountains with them and was later seen smilingly negotiating with Uribe. The main intermediary in those negotiations was Raúl Reyes, the man murdered in Ecuador.

It has been argued, convincingly I think, that the involvement of Chavez and Bernard Kouchner, the French foreign minister, as well as several other high profile European mediators, led the Farc leaders into a false sense of security, causing them to let down their guard—persuaded, perhaps, by those amiable photo opportunities, that the Colombian government had somehow changed its spots. Yet the Farc knew from bitter experience that no Colombian state would allow them to score either a political or a military victory and that peace negotiations now, as in the past, would be likely to serve that state only as a screen behind which to prepare a deadly assault.

In the late 1980s the Farc negotiated with the then government to come in from the cold. The Unión Patriótica (UP) was formed to present candidates for the elections of 1990 and won major victories at all levels. The Colombian ruling class avenged itself, unmasking the peace initiative and murdering 5,000 UP members, including all its major leaders. Ten years later the Farc again embarked on a peace initiative, holding extensive public debates and developing strategies for democratisation. Once again the initiative was suddenly removed from the Colombian presidency and the process stopped on direct instructions from Washington. The US's alternative strategy was set out soon afterwards in Plan Colombia, which saw the Colombian state as the bridgehead for US regional hegemony as well as an important testing ground for neoliberal economic strategies. Colombia became the bulwark against a rising tide of protest at the impact of ten years of globalisation.

The new initiative brokered by Chavez had much to do in the first instance with the increasing presence within Venezuela of the paramilitaries and the deepening instability that this implied on Venezuela's huge and porous land border with Colombia along the Andes mountains. The Farc clearly did represent a kind of buffer against that intervention, but it was uncertain and unstable, particularly destabilising in Venezuela's economically important state of Zulia. Chavez called on the Colombians to recognise the Farc as insurgents rather than terrorists, but by the same token he echoed the Cuban government in arguing that the time for armed struggle had passed and that resistance should move into the political terrain.

In the abstract, that is a convincing position to adopt when recent years have shown that the great political leaps forward occur as a result of organised mass activity—as they have in Bolivia, Ecuador and Venezuela. In practice, however, there was absolutely no reason to believe the Colombian government's avowed commitment to a democratic process it had corrupted, undermined and ignored, attacking and repressing social movements, trade unions and collective resistance. It would seem that Chavez fell into a trap laid for him by the Colombians and their US and Israeli advisers. The release of hostages was at an advanced stage of negotiation when the Ecuador raid happened. But when the hostages were eventually released three months later through military action it was presented as an achievement of Uribe's government. The Farc had in fact been actively preparing their release but had always insisted that the release must be part of a prisoner exchange for some or all of the 500 Farc prisoners in Colombian jails. None, of course, have been released.

Uribe paid a visit to Caracas for discussions with Hugo Chavez some weeks ago. There were major protests outside the Miraflores presidential palace, denounced by Chavez as "counter-revolutionary". The disbelief among many of the most active and committed supporters of the Bolivarian revolution was palpable. The Farc, after all, now described themselves as a Bolivarian revolution so how could their bitter enemy be received as a statesman in the birthplace of Bolivarianism?

The answer is diplomacy and *realpolitik*. The assault on the Farc and the manner of the release of Betancourt and the other hostages were political setbacks for Chavez. Venezuela's border with Colombia is all the more vulnerable as the Farc is so severely weakened. Correa has cooled towards Chavez too and has stepped back from participating in his Bolivarian Alternative for the Americas (Alba). He has also announced, however, that the US military base at Manta in Ecuador (established, paradoxically, as part of Plan Colombia) will be closed when its contract ends. There are strong rumours that a new base will be built within Colombia, near the Venezuelan border.

In the short term, the severe setback for the Farc has forced Chavez and Correa into negotiations with a Colombian government which represents not only US military interests but is also the spearhead for neoliberalism. Over ten years Colombia, a rich agricultural country, has become a net food importer as more and more of its agricultural land is given over to export agriculture or biofuels. And despite its long coastline and fertile rivers it now imports its fish from Argentina and Vietnam. This is in addition to the impact of cocaine production. It is also rich in oil and gas. Barrack Obama's stated intention to lessen US dependence on Middle Eastern oil is a virtual declaration of intent to control oil and gas supplies in Latin America by any means necessary. And John McCain has direct connections with supporters of the paramilitaries. Colombia is an important oil producer, as is Ecuador. The US actively engaged in the so-called autonomy movements in eastern Bolivia whose objective is to undermine Evo Morales's nationalisation policies. And the major prize, of course, is Venezuela.

The political issue is complex but clear. The Farc will continue to exist and to fight, but from a position of extreme weakness. Venezuela and Ecuador will not support the organisation though its weakness makes both vulnerable on their borders. Uribe will drive home his advantage by every means possible while pursuing a remorseless campaign to destroy the Farc. And for the Farc, history has shown what they can expect if they listen to the pleas to come down from the mountains and join the democratic process. Colombian democracy is a blood-soaked thing.

The attack on the Farc is a setback for the revolutionary movement in Latin America as a whole. The ground will not be recovered by more hostage taking or the arming or rearming of this or that guerrilla group. Seizing the initiative back from imperialism and its servants will be the result of a shift of power to the mass organisations like those that brought down governments in Bolivia and Ecuador, and defeated a right wing coup and a bosses' strike in Venezuela. And the forging of a common political instrument that links and increasingly coordinates those struggles is the common task of the grassroots movements across the continent.

Michelle Bachelet, the president of Chile, has called for Ingrid Betancourt to be given the Nobel Peace Prize; the Argentinian peace campaigner Pérez Esquivel, himself a Nobel peace laureate, has asked what she has done to promote peace. Betancourt's memoirs are now in bookshops across the world, produced at dizzying speed. Her sponsors include the French, Spanish and Colombian governments. Sympathy for a long-term hostage should never blind us to how she is being used and by whom. It is not peace, freedom or democracy that they have in mind.

Korea's summer of discontent

South Korean socialist Kim Kwang-il spoke to Owen Miller about the country's recent protest movement

This summer the biggest mass movement since the 1980s erupted in South Korea as hundreds of thousands came onto the streets to protest against the recently elected right wing government of Lee Myung-bak. Ostensibly the crowds were protesting against the government's decision to resume imports of US beef which had been banned due to fears of "mad cow disease", but their anger and slogans were directed at everything from education privatisation to Lee's plans to construct an environmentally disastrous "grand canal" down the length of the country. The movement began online and then in May escalated into daily candlelight vigils in central Seoul. From late May people began to march, attempting to take their protests directly to the presidential residence, still carrying candles as a symbol of their defiance against the government. Since the middle of August the government has gone on the counter-attack, arresting and intimidating scores of activists.

Kim Kwang-il is a member of the steering committee of All Together, the South Korean sister organisation of the Socialist Workers Party. He has also been a leading figure in this summer's protest movement and, along with a number of other leaders, he has been barricaded in a protest camp at Seoul's central Buddhist temple—Chogyesa—since the police issued arrest warrants for the protest organisers in June. He and six others are unable to leave the grounds of the temple, which is surrounded by riot police who search everyone leaving or entering. This interview was conducted via email on 8 September.

The right wing Grand National Party has recently come back to power in South Korea with the victory of Lee Myung-bak. The Korean right characterises the past ten years as the "lost decade". How would you describe the decade of "centre-left" or "social-liberal" governments under Kim Dae-jung and Roh Moo-hyun?

When the right wingers talk about the "lost decade" they are only half right. For them the handing over of power to liberal forces 50 years after the establishment of South Korea's authoritarian government in 1948 was an unbearable insult. So in 2004 the Grand National Party, as the political party representing the Korean right, attempted to impeach President Roh Moo-hyun. This attempt was defeated by massive street protests.

But having said this, it is certainly not the case that the Kim Dae-jung or Roh Moo-hyun governments fundamentally challenged the values of the right. In fact, as members of the South Korean ruling class they remained faithful followers of neoliberal and pro-imperialist policies.

When Kim Dae-jung came to power in 1998 it was the period of Korea's so-called "IMF crisis", and he pushed ahead with restructuring and intensified worker layoffs. Kim Dae-jung may have received the Nobel Peace Prize but the repressive National Security Law (NSL) remained in place. During the Kim Dae-jung government South Korea's International Socialists, such as myself, were punished and imprisoned under the NSL simply for selling a socialist newspaper! And Kim Dae-jung sent Korean troops to Afghanistan immediately after George Bush's invasion.

The Roh Moo-hyun administration was exactly the same. When he came to power the first thing he did was to send troops to Iraq. Last year he sent Korean special forces troops to Lebanon as well. Because I organised demonstrations against the dispatch of troops I was convicted by his government. The Roh Moo-hyun government also pursued neoliberal policies. In order to conclude the recent free trade agreement (FTA) with the US the Roh Moo-hyun administration used repressive measures against the anti-FTA protest movement that were second only to those of the current Lee Myung-bak government.

The resumption of US beef imports that was the spark for the candlelight protest movement was actually a concession that was promised by the Roh Moo-hyun government in order to reach agreement on the trade treaty with the US. The Roh Moo-hyun government also imprisoned more workers than any other Korean government, including the military dictatorships of the 1970s and 1980s, while the proportion of casual workers in the economy rose sharply.

It is not really appropriate to call these people "centre-left" or "social-liberals". Both their social base and their political platform are different to the traditional reformist parties. Although they have been supported by social movement leaders, including some of the mainstream NGOs and a section of the nationalist left, their principal base is among the populist liberals who form a part of the capitalist class.

It was the betrayals of the liberals and the sense of disgust and disappointment these gave rise to that opened the door for the election of a right wing government.

Lee Myung-bak—the former CEO of the construction subsidiary of conglomerate Hyundai and nicknamed the "Bulldozer"—won a convincing victory last December. How did this come about? Did it represent a significant shift to the right?
The recent huge protests show that the election of a right wing government in Korea does not mean Korean society as a whole has moved to the right, despite the pessimistic analysis offered by a considerable number of activists on the left.

First, the turnout in the presidential election was extremely low, which means that mistrust and disillusionment with mainstream politics are very high. Lee Myung-bak actually polled the lowest number of votes of any elected Korean president. Second, due to the sense of betrayal and disillusion with ten years of liberal populist governments, particularly the five years of the Roh Moo-hyun administration, voters could not bring themselves to vote for Roh Moo-hyun's successor.

If you look at various opinion polls you can see that public support for progressive values has not diminished at all. The movement in Korea has also not suffered a decisive defeat.

However, a considerable number of social movement leaders have been gripped by a sense of defeat, fear and lack of morale. As a result, the majority of social movement forces were bewildered when the candlelight protest movement first erupted on 2 May, and just stood back and watched. So they ended up joining the movement late.

Fortunately, because All Together correctly understood that the election of a right wing government did not mean the Korean people had become more conservative, we joined the demonstrations right from day one.

In Europe too the right has been able to make gains as a result of the sense of disillusion that has accompanied the betrayals by "social-liberal" governments. But this is very unstable. We need to understand that popular consciousness is very contradictory. You can see this to a great extent with the participation in the candlelight protest movement by people who voted for Lee Myung-bak at the last election.

What was the immediate background to the massive wave of protests against the Lee Myung-bak government that began in May?

The start of the demonstrations back in May was the combined result of a whole series of issues that had been thrown up since Lee Myung-bak was elected. From the moment he was elected Lee began announcing a whole host of blatantly right wing neoliberal, anti-democratic and pro-imperialist policies. It was like a policy tsunami—so much so that you became irritated every time you looked at a newspaper or news bulletin. Every day you got up in the morning to find that another right wing policy initiative had been announced in the media.

The gradually worsening economic situation was also behind the sudden explosion of demonstrations. Lee Myung-bak's core promise in the presidential election was that he would "revive the economy". This was his so-called "747 pledge" in which he promised to achieve economic growth of 7 percent, average per capita income of 40,000 US dollars, and raise South Korea to the world's seventh largest economy. Of course this was nothing more than rhetoric that completely ignored the world economic crisis. After Lee took power the economic indicators became gradually worse while the suffering of the exploited grew.

Popular anger gradually built and then on 19 April, when Lee travelled to the US and made an agreement with Bush to allow imports of American beef, this anger exploded. This agreement drastically eased the regulations dealing with the risk of beef infected with BSE. At first the protests against this agreement centred around internet communities. An online petition set up by a high school student attracted more than a million signatures in no time.

In the early stages of the candlelight protests the active participation of young people was particularly noticeable and this reflected their anger against Lee Myung-bak's education privatisation plans. Middle and high school education in Korea is extremely oppressive and there is intense competition to do well in university entrance exams. However, the Lee government's plans to destroy public eduction would clearly drive young people into even more oppressive conditions. One of the slogans that the young people brought to the demonstrations was "Let's eat a little, let's sleep a little". It's a slogan that shows clearly the sort of position they are in where they have to go to school before dawn and then study at cram schools until late in the evening.

This anger and sense of crisis exploded into the open in the candlelight demonstrations. On the first day the sight of 20,000 people filling the streets was a real shock. On that day everyone was surprised at the scale and the confidence of the demonstration: the internet-based group that had called the demo, the participants themselves and the police.

The demonstrations were not simply limited to opposition to the resumption of US beef imports. From the very first day opposition was directed towards the government's plans to destroy public education, its proposed "Grand Canal" plan aimed at providing profits for the construction sector, as well as plans for the privatisation of health insurance. As time went on the dynamic between these various demands became clearer.

To put it another way, the candlelight demonstrations shared the values of the international anti-neoliberal movement, as embodied in the slogan "People before profit". So this struggle stands shoulder to shoulder with the struggles against neoliberalism all over the world, from Latin America to Europe.

When I joined the protests in May there was already an amazing feeling of power among the protesters but also a sense that no one knew exactly what was happening or where it was going—neither the organised left nor the police nor the government, nor even the crowds themselves. Why do you think these protests surprised and disorientated everyone in this way?
The new movement was overtaken by a sense of euphoria when the protests exploded without any warning and then demonstrated their staying power. People felt confident that the movement could be victorious without any major ordeals or complications. During this phase it was natural that a sort of "spontaneism" would gain strength. It was also the case that the protests had not started with calls from the organised social movement forces. The social movement forces entered the new protest movement late and in a rather timid fashion, and they also compromised with the spontaneism of the movement.

The candlelight rallies that started at Chonggye Square in central Seoul on 2 May gradually grew in size and from 24 May began to take to the streets. This was the turning point that really broadened the movement. The protesters no longer stayed in the square but wanted to charge out into the streets.

At this time the reformist majority in the People's Countermeasure Committee on Mad Cow Disease hesitated either to take the responsibility for organising street protests or to bring up the question of the direction of the movement. They felt a heavy burden of responsibility. In this situation it was All Together, alongside a number of other groups, that began to lead the demonstrations and this gave rise to some criticism within the candlelight protest movement. People claimed that the left should not intervene in the demonstrations because this would damage their spontaneity. Some of the spontaneists attempted to seize megaphones from those leading the marches and even tried to crowd around the speaker cars that were at the front of the demonstrations to prevent them from moving. They habitually obstructed discussions about the form that the marches should take, so there were repeated situations in which it was difficult to make any decision about where the march would go and where we would hold a closing rally.

However, the situation changed again. On 31 May the established social movement forces found their confidence again, readied their ranks and participated in the demonstration in large numbers. As they led that demonstration the atmosphere was reversed. You could see how the realisation of the need for the organisation and experience of the social movement forces spread among the protesters when they came within spitting distance of the Blue House [the presidential residence] and were faced with repression in the form of massive police violence and widespread arrests.

What is the mood among Korean workers at the moment and how has it been affected by this summer's protests?
The biggest weakness of the candlelight protests has been precisely the inadequate participation of the organised working class, though it is true that the transportation union actively resisted the transportation and distribution of US beef and the Korea Confederation of Democratic Unions [KCTU, the left union federation] organised a strike for a few hours.

The reasons for the labour movement's lacklustre response to this new movement were similar to the causes of the South Korean social movements' unenthusiastic participation in the early stages of the protests. The victory of the Lee Myung-bak government lowered morale in the union movement and created a sense of insecurity. In fact the leadership of the KCTU thought that it would require a year of preparation to take on the Lee government head to head.

As a result, the sudden eruption of the candlelight protests was a shock to both the leadership of the unions and the rank and file union members. As the demonstrations expanded a section of the more advanced activists made efforts to organise the movement, but they were unable to counter the majority tendency in the unions.

Another cause lies in the "workerism" of the Korean unions. The unions have never been enthusiastic about political protests that go beyond economic disputes.

As one leading All Together member, Choi Il-bung, has recently noted, "When their expectations in Kim Dae-jung, Roh Moo-hyun and the other populist politicians came to nothing, KCTU members reacted with a tendency towards workerism that was expressed in their lack of positive participation in the candlelight rallies."

For example, at the height of the candlelight protest movement the trade unionists organised rallies and marches at which they pushed their own economic demands and on occasion these demonstrations ended without getting to the place where the candlelight rally was being held so only some of the participants actually joined the candlelight protesters.

The Lee Myung-bak government also tried to force a separation of politics and economics by announcing that it would take a hard line against political strikes by workers.

The majority reformist leadership of the candlelight protest movement also failed to positively call for the mobilisation and participation of the organised working class.

However, the candlelight protests that have shaken Korea this summer have left the organised working class with the confidence that it is possible to confront and fight the Lee Myung-bak government. And they have also highlighted the importance of political protest movements that go beyond labour disputes. The candlelight protests have provided some important lessons for organised workers about the battles that are likely to lie ahead in the developing economic crisis. But it is only when those lessons have been learnt and absorbed that they can actually become weapons in the struggle.

There seems to be a lull in the movement at the moment. Has the government been successful in suppressing the movement? Do you think this is the end of the current phase of resistance to the right wing government?
The movement began on 2 May and continued for more than three months until 15 August. That date saw the hundredth demonstration. The protests continued every single day and there were a number of occasions on which the numbers of demonstrators ran into hundreds of thousands. On 10 June at least one million people came onto the streets nationwide and on 5 July too there were 400,000 to 500,000 people on the streets in Seoul alone. These were the first demonstrations on such a scale in 20 years.

It is true that there is a lull in the movement at the moment, though small protests are continuing. The biggest reason for this is the repression. Because even legal rallies have become impossible these days, people are unable to gather. So far a total of 1,530 people have been arrested by the police and 49 people are being detained. There are a further 29 of us currently on the police's wanted list, including myself and the others at the Chogyesa Temple protest camp. The police are now investigating internet community sites and are serving summonses to people simply for having written anti-government comments online.

The movement also has strategic problems. It reached its climax on 10 June. This day was chosen with the intention of reviving the memory of the great struggle of 10 June 1987 and, although it was a weekday, the demonstration brought some 700,000 people onto the streets in Seoul alone. This was the moment when the leadership of the movement needed to give some clear direction. But the majority of the reformists in the leadership evaded the question of an anti-government struggle—ie a political struggle—and gradually tried to limit the movement to opposition to the import of US beef.

Although there is currently something of a lull in the movement this does not mean to say that the Lee Myung-bak government has been successful. His approval rating barely scrapes 20 percent—and this after only 200 days in office!

Two recent episodes have illustrated the continued instability of the government. In an attempt to further curtail the movement the government recently detained seven activists from a radical left group called the Socialist Workers League of Korea under the repressive National Security Law, but the warrants for their arrests were thrown out of court because the outcry was so great.

[In another case] Lee Myung-bak came up against opposition to his plans to privatise water services from the Grand National Party, his own party, because they were afraid that this plan might give rise to another round of candlelight protests.

When it seemed that the candlelight protests were burning themselves out the Lee Myung-bak government had to hold back its urge to push forward with its neoliberal policies. But in reality it is just refuelling for the struggle ahead. The Korean people have behind them the experience of a massive struggle and will not simply stand aside and watch. As the economic crisis gets worse the stakes of the struggle are also getting higher.

Afghanistan: the case against the "good war"

Jonathan Neale

Afghanistan is one of the poorest countries on earth. More than a million Afghans have died in 30 years of war, and almost everyone has lost someone close to them. Now George Bush, John McCain, Gordon Brown and Nicolas Sarkozy, and even Barack Obama, call for more troops to be sent, more planes and more death.

In every country in Europe majorities in opinion polls are against participation in the Afghan war. Yet the media still present it as a good war. Iraq, they now admit, was a crime or wrong or maybe just a mistake. But Afghanistan is a war on terrorists, we are told; on fanatics, *jihadis*, sexists, savages; on people who are not "modern" and therefore deserve to die.

This article will argue differently. My central points are these:

● First, there was almost no resistance when the Americans first invaded Afghanistan in 2001 and for the three years afterwards. The resistance has been produced by the occupation.

● Second, that resistance is led by the right wing Taliban because they are the only organised force who have been root and branch opposed to the occupation. It is also because back in the 1980s Communists and feminists supported another invasion, by the Soviet Union. Soviet troops killed between half a million and a million Afghans, and discredited the left and feminists for at least a generation.

● Third, the resistance is spreading, growing and winning. As a result, the occupying powers are coming under intense pressure to launch a massive air war against villagers and to invade Pakistan.

Afghanistan

● Fourth, there are no easy outcomes for Afghans in this situation, but the best one is a victory for the resistance.[1]

The origins of the 30 years war

I will begin with the Communists.[2] One afternoon in the autumn of 1971 I stood on the side of the unpaved main street in Lashkargah, the capital of Helmand province, and watched a protest by high school boys who took turns standing on a wooden box. They didn't give speeches. The boy on the box would just shout a slogan loudly, and his mates would cheer. Most of the boys who took a turn had only one slogan: "Death to the *khans*."

These children were brave. Khan is the Pushtu word for the man who is a big landowner and local power. These boys were not calling for the end to an abstract social category. They were calling for the physical killing of the men who held power in their villages, who ruled the lives of their fathers and mothers. Only 30 boys, or a bit fewer, had the courage to stand in that crowd. But around the edges of the street many adult men stood and watched, silently, never looking away, betraying nothing on their faces. There were a couple of policemen watching. More important, the secret police were in every urban crowd, and feared for good reason. There were informers in every village too. If you lived in a village and knew people, a flicker across their faces would tell you when one of the local informers entered the room.

No one said anything. No one smiled. If they did, the khan would know. But the silence spoke approval.

Those boys were part of a national movement of students and educated people led by the Communists. They had good reasons to want to overthrow the established order.[3] Until 1974 Afghanistan was ruled by a king, Zahir Shah. There was a parliament and elections, but more dictatorship than democracy. Real power lay in the hands of the big landowners

1: This article is based on several sources: my fieldwork in Afghanistan from 1971 to 1973; wide reading since then; many conversations over the past 13 years with Nancy (Tapper) Lindisfarne; and many conversations with Afghans over the years. Most good books and articles on Afghanistan rely heavily on such conversations, which cannot be footnoted, and so do I. Where I assert something without a reference, that is where it comes from. Many of the topics covered here are dealt with in more detail in Neale, 1981, 1988, 2001 and 2003.

2: The best book on the Afghan Communists is Anwar, 1988. Male, 1982, Emadi, 1990, Bradsher, 1985, and Cordovez and Harrison, 1995, are also very useful.

3: The best sources on Afghan society in the 1960s and 1970s are the ethnographies by anthropologists, particularly Doubleday, 1988, Canfield, 1973, Shahrani, 1979, Azoy, 1982, Jones, 1974, and Barfield, 1981, and especially Tapper, 1991, which is also the essential book for understanding gender in Afghan society.

with mud forts in the countryside and their own armed retainers. The central government largely did their bidding and not the other way round.

These khans[4] ruled through fear and force. Central power was weak. Judges ruled for whoever gave the largest bribe. Land ownership was partly a matter of tradition—"This is my land because everyone knows we have always had it." But when a family looked weak, the strong would move in and take what they had. The best of the khans tried to be fair, but many were murderers several times over. Everyone had guns, and it was good to have several brothers.

Indeed in a situation where tenure and justice were so fragile, and where power came from force, it paid to demonstrate that force from time to time. And there were always potential challengers to every khan—men who could and would take his power if they could. But by 1970 the central government had chosen and backed one leading khan in most valleys of the country, and that gave people some stability. It also meant that the state was a joint enterprise between those men, the king and the army.

Afghanistan was a desperately poor country. There were, and are, no reliable statistics. The land was arid, often mountain or desert. Only about 2 percent could be farmed with irrigation. The main exports were hash, raisins and lambskin hats. Roughly 90 percent of people lived in the villages. Below the khans were small landowners, who worked their own land. More than half of villagers did not have enough land or animals of their own and had to make at least some of their income from sharecropping or herding. Exploitation was fierce. A sharecropper took between a fifth and a third of the crop, the landlord all the rest. Shepherds made a similar income.

Most families made just enough to eat. Across the country in 1972 the wage for a day's labour was 20 afghanis and for a month 500 afghanis. Twenty afghanis would buy ten nan breads a day—three for the father, three for the mother and two each for two children. That was enough to live, but there was no money left over for other food, or anything else.

Most poor people—and most people were poor—lived at a similar level. I did two years of fieldwork as an anthropologist from 1971 to 1973, and the people I knew best were poor pastoralists who had lost their flocks and now made yoghurt. Their lives were not unrepresentative. Most of them got two sets of adult clothes in their lives—one when they first grew up and one when they married. A bicycle was a sign of moderate wealth.

4:    These powerful landlords were also called *beg*, *arbab*, *malik*, *padshah* and other names in different parts of the country.

Out of 30 households in the camp, three were wealthy enough to afford to offer me a fried egg in hospitality. And they reminded me of it: "You ate his egg," they said to me. Out of 30 households, 29 ate meat once a year. An average household had one teapot and one cup.

People talked much of modesty, and the books will tell you that Afghans secluded their women. But in an average village of, say, 200 households usually only three or four families could afford that. The other 196 or 197 houses needed the labour of their women in the fields, with the animals and to fetch water. People also talked much of the feud and Pushtun traditional law. Khans could and did feud, for they could afford to hide behind the walls of a fort and only venture out with bodyguards. The vast majority of men had to work in the fields and could not afford enemies.

The books, and the rich, said the lives of Afghans were ruled by honour. I heard the poor people I knew use the word for honour only once and the word for shame every day.

The government and the society were rotten, and everyone knew it. The first time I entered Afghanistan I watched a woman and a customs officer bargain at the top of their voices about the level of bribe she would pay him. The doctors and nurses stole the medicines and sold them in the bazaar.

I used my status to find a bed for a poor friend in the only TB hospital in Kabul, a public institution. When I visited the other patients, men from every group in the country crowded round his bed and chatted. My friend told me his family had to bribe the nurses to give him the food the government had paid for. I asked if they all had to do this.

"Yes," they said.

"Why?" I asked.

One patient said, *"Afghanistan, Zulumistan"*—in English, "Afghanistan, Tyrannistan"—and they all laughed.

Everyone hated the government. My poor friends, who were Pushtuns, were proud that the king and the generals were Pushtuns, but they still hated the government. So did the Communists

The royal government relied on foreign aid from the US and the Soviet Union to cover two thirds of the budget. The king and the khans did not want economic development—that would threaten their power. In any case, the prevailing corruption made it very difficult.[5] So the foreign money was spent mainly on education, an expanded civil service with nothing to do and the army. This spending created a new class of educated people. This was a small class. There were about 20,000 university

---

5: For the structural limits of development in the 1970s, see Fry, 1974.

graduates in a population of 15 million in 1978. But the old elite had been so small that most of the new educated class came from middle peasant families. They were not the landless poor, but they were often the first child in the family to finish high school. They brought with them to the city their parents' hatred of the khans and the government. Their education gave them a desperation about the country's poverty and a yearning for "modernisation".

There were two political wings of this new class. The Communists looked to ideas from the Soviet Union. The Islamists looked to the ideas of the Muslim Brotherhood in Egypt, and not to the more mystical and laid back traditions of Afghan Islam. They saw tradition as the problem, education as the answer, and revolutionary change as a necessity. In the early 1970s the Communists and the Islamists fought each other at Kabul University and in the city high schools. The Communists won because they had far more support, and the Islamist student leaders fled to exile in Pakistan.

Geography and ethnicity

Let's pause for a moment to look at the geography and ethnic make-up of Afghanistan. I did not start with ethnicity, because it has never been as important as class. Social organisation is broadly similar in all ethnic groups, and the key traditional division is between the landowner who took 67 to 80 percent of the crop and the sharecropper who did the work.

However, ethnicity, language and geography do matter in the story that follows. Reliable statistics do not exist. But 40 to 50 percent of the population are Pushtuns. They speak Pushtu and live in the south and east. Kandahar is their largest city. In the central mountains live the Hazaras, the poorest of Afghan farmers and the most likely to migrate to the cities for work. They speak Farsi (Persian), are mostly Shiah and are about a tenth of the population. Another tenth are Uzbeks, who speak a Turkic language and live in the plains of the north east. About a fifth of the population are Tajiks, largely in the west around Herat and in the north east. Tajiks are not an ethnic group as such and have never united politically. The word simply means a Farsi speaking villager with no other ethnic loyalty.

Kabul, the capital, is a mixed city. Many in the upper reaches of government have traditionally been Pushtun. But Farsi is the dominant language in Kabul and widely regarded as more cultured than Pushtu.[6]

6:   Farsi is also sometimes referred to as *Dari* in official settings, in order to pretend it is not the same language spoken in Iran.

Afghan politics, though, was not organised around ethnic lines. The key dividing lines were religion, Communism and attitudes to the royal family. There were many from each ethnic group on every side.

Revolution from above

In 1972 a devastating famine swept the north and centre of the country. The king's government did nothing, and senior officials stole the food aid. So when the king's cousin Mohammed Daoud staged a coup in 1974 to create an Islamic socialist republic, no one fought for the old order. At first Daoud's dictatorship leaned towards the Soviet Union in foreign policy and the Communists supported him. By early 1978, though, Daoud was swinging back towards the US and he had the main Communist leaders arrested.

The Communists immediately launched a coup based on army and air force officers, many of them trained in the Soviet Union. Like the other Communists, most of the officers were educated men from modest backgrounds. Hardly anyone was willing to die for Daoud, the royal family or the old order. But this absence of resistance was not the same as support for the coup. The new Communist government had support in the cities but very little in the countryside, where 90 percent of Afghans lived. Afghanistan had conscription, and the enlisted ranks were a mirror of the country. The Communists did not even try to build among ordinary soldiers. This was to prove their fatal weakness.

The Communists were, however, revolutionaries. They wanted to change everything, to break the power of the landowners and to liberate women. Their first decrees on land reform and women's rights were largely symbolic, but no one was in any doubt what the symbolism meant.

Small rural uprisings began, at first in places where government power had always been tenuous such as Nuristan in the east and Pakhtia in the south east. These uprisings spread. They were usually led by local village mullahs rather than by educated Islamists. The mullahs argued that the Communists were atheists, tools of the Russians, and wanted to destroy the modesty of women.

Because the Communists did not have real support in the countryside, their first step was to send educated government officials in Western dress down to the villages in jeeps. The villagers saw them as the same sort of men as the old oppressive government. When sending officials failed, the answer was arrests and torture. This was cruel but could be targeted. However, arrest, torture and executions only stoked hatred and further resistance. The next step for the government was bombing from the air, an indiscriminate attack on all the peasants. That in turn only widened the revolt. Within 18 months the rebellions covered much of the countryside. Everyone knew the Communist government would fall soon.

The Communists were brave and dedicated men and women. They wanted to end the old oppression and to free women. Indeed many of them were women and, like the men, they were prepared to die. But they had tried to make a revolution from the top down, not from the bottom up, and they were paying for that. They went for a coup from the top because the prevailing idea on the left internationally in the 1960s and 1970s was that socialism meant dictatorship. To be a Communist in those days was to believe that poor countries needed a dictatorship to develop. Sometimes the dictator was brutal, like Joseph Stalin, and sometimes relatively gentle, like Fidel Castro. But Communism was dictatorship: top-down rule.

Many of the Afghan Communists had been educated, in part, in the Soviet Union. For them it was simple. They wanted a modern, developed, civilised country like the Soviet Union. And that meant, obviously, the sort of dictatorship they saw there. Some Afghan Communists had lived elsewhere. Taraki, the first Communist president, had worked in India. Amin, the second, had studied at Columbia University in New York. In both places, as in Europe and Latin America, most radicals felt that Communism meant dictatorship. This was also widely believed in Third World nationalist circles, where dictatorship was again largely taken for granted. Mustafa Kemal Atatürk, Gamal Abdel Nasser, Castro and Sukarno were widely admired dictators.

There were socialists who believed in democracy and revolution from the bottom up, and who said that this had been the politics of Marx and Lenin. This journal comes from that tradition. But we were a small voice on the global left then, hardly heard in the poorest countries.

The Afghan Communists, though, were digging their own grave. It is sometimes possible to stage a coup with minority support and to rule with a minority. But it is another thing to change the whole structure of a society—the major economic relationships and the family. Change on that scale requires a passionate majority. So within 18 months the ring was closing around Kabul and the Communists.

As they lost popular support, the Communists began killing each other. There had always been two factions in Afghan Communism. The *Khalk* (People) group were more radical. They wanted to push the revolution, land reform and women's liberation to the end. They were by and large from poorer rural backgrounds, and most spoke Pushtu. The *Parcham* (Flag) group were from richer homes, more often from the cities, and more likely to speak Farsi. They wanted to hold back the revolution and negotiate with the mullahs.

What made the disagreement between the People and Flag groups bitter was that neither had a solution. The Flag were right that pushing the revolution to the end without popular support would accomplish nothing. The People were right that the rebellion would not be fooled by concessions. Without any solutions, their hopes drowning in cruelty, the two factions turned on each other. The People purged the Flag, arresting, torturing and executing many thousands. Then the People split and began to kill each other. The Communist terror concentrated on Communists.

Occupation and resistance

On Christmas Day 1979 Soviet tanks began rolling over the border.[7] The reasons for the invasion were, for the Soviet Union, clear and compelling. Afghanistan was a Muslim country with a Communist government. It lay just south of the majority Muslim republics of the Soviet Union with their immense oil wealth. If the Communist government of Afghanistan fell to a Muslim uprising, the example might easily spread north. Moreover, many of the Soviet elite thought they could negotiate with tribal elders and moderate forces. In their eyes the trouble with the Afghan Communists was that they were revolutionaries—they wanted to change everything. The Soviet elite were conservative men of power.

The Soviet tanks and planes quickly secured the cities. They deposed the People faction and installed Babrak Karmal from the Flag faction. The Flag police began rounding up the People leaders. Some men and women left prison, and others filled their cells.

The mullahs had been saying that the Communists were Russian puppets. Now everyone could see that this was true. The Communists lost the majority of their support in the cities. The urban demonstrations started in Farsi speaking, Iranian influenced, Herat in the east. Men and boys climbed onto their roofs at night and shouted, all across the city together, "God is Great". No one dared shoot or bomb them for that.[8]

The shouting protests spread to Pushtu speaking Kandahar in the south and then to Farsi speaking Kabul. The civil servants, long a Communist base, went on strike against the Soviet occupation. The

---

7:   Nowadays it is difficult to find anyone from the old Soviet elite who admits to responsibility for the invasion of Afghanistan or sees any reason for it. They all blame it on Leonid Brezhnev and say they warned against the invasion. And indeed the experts on Afghanistan and the military probably did make such warnings. See Cordovez and Harrison, 1995.

8:   Kakar, 1992, has a good description of these demonstrations, in which he participated.

students at the girl's high school in Kabul had been at the forefront of the fight for women's rights. Now they massed in the playground, afraid to demonstrate on the streets, and shouted, as women had when the British invaded in 1878, calling upon the men of Afghanistan to show that they were men and not girls.

The Communists were deeply torn. Their revolution was at an end. The Soviet "advisers" took control of every ministry and stopped all reforms. The Communists faced a choice of collaborating with the invader or giving in to bloody "Islamist" reaction. Some simply left, but most decided to go with the Russians.

The Soviet war lasted for the next seven years. The Soviet armed forces held the cities and patrolled the highways with tanks. But in the countryside they came under sustained attack. Here their main tactics were land mines, helicopter gunships, bombers and free fire zones. There are no reliable numbers for the Afghan dead. The usual figure of one million is probably too high. It may only have been half a million from a population of 15 million.[9] Roughly another million were wounded and disabled for life. Four million became refugees in Pakistan, another two million in Iran, and at least another two million fled to the relative safety of the Afghan cities. In other words, about two thirds of the population were killed, wounded or forced to flee.

To put this into comparative perspective, it is as if Britain in the 1980s had suffered two million dead, four million badly wounded and 32 million refugees. Imagine for a moment that this devastation was due to foreign invasion, and that the socialists and feminists had almost all supported the invasion. How popular do you think feminism or socialism would be in Britain?

In Afghanistan too, feminist and socialist politics don't get much support even a generation later. The key thing to remember is that this is *not* because Afghans have always been right wing and patriarchal. After all, the Communists won every seat in Kabul in an election in the 1960s. It is because of what the left did to ordinary Afghans.

The resistance to the Russians was unlike any of the armed national liberation movements of the 20th century. The movements in Vietnam, Algeria, Angola and the rest were all led by a political party and had a more or less integrated army. The Afghan resistance was a whole people in revolt. But they fought local community by local community (*qaum* in Pushtu and Farsi). Sometimes that community was a village or a few villages together

---

9:    The most careful work on the numbers of dead is Khalidi, 1991.

in a valley; sometimes it was an ethnic group or a faction, only part of a village. Each qaum fought on its own.[10] If a main road ran through the village or valley of the qaum, then they attacked Russian convoys and saw terrible fighting. While the men, women and children of the community might walk hundreds of miles to Pakistan to find refuge or get weapons, they rarely walked far to fight.

The ideas of the resistance were the ideas of Afghan Islam. These were different from the ideas the Islamist students had imported from Egypt. Instead people knew they fought for god and religion. They also knew that the Afghans had fought and won three wars against the British in the name of Islam: the First Afghan War (1838-42), the Second Afghan War (1878-80), and the Third Afghan War (1919). The cruelty of the occupation, the torture and the bombing did the rest.

The resistance called themselves the *mujahedin*, those who do *jihad*. This did not make them fanatics. It meant they were resisting a foreign invasion.

The situation was complicated, however, by the existence of seven Islamist political parties based in Peshawar, the capital of Pakistan's largely Pushtun North West Frontier Province. These seven parties were all funded and armed by an alliance of the CIA, Saudi intelligence and the Pakistan armed forces Inter Services Intelligence (ISI). The CIA and the Saudis provided money and weapons. The Pakistani ISI kept tight control of distribution and favoured some of the exiled parties over others.[11] For the US government and the CIA, the motive was partly to bleed the Soviet Union and partly revenge for Vietnam. For Saudi intelligence, it was keeping Communism at bay. Pakistan in the 1980s was a military dictatorship under General Zia. In return for supporting the Afghan resistance, Zia got American support, essential to continuing his regime. The ISI and Saudi intelligence were also supportive of Islamism. The CIA was not, but could not find anyone else to work through in Afghanistan.

The leaders of the seven parties all took a hefty personal cut and then sent some of the money and more of the weapons on to the resistance inside Afghanistan. The largest share of the money went to the most radical party, led by Gulbuddin Hekmatyar, a Pushtun who had been a student of engineering at Kabul University. The other big party was led by Rabbani, a former professor of theology at Kabul University, and Massoud, a student

---

10: Of the many books on the Afghan resistance to the Soviet Union, start with Dorronsoro, 2005, Roy, 1986, and Bonner, 1987.
11: The best source on the CIA role is Crile, 2003.

Islamist. Both men were Tajiks.[12] There were also three smaller Islamist parties, and two small parties that represented the old elite of landowners and the royal family.

Inside Afghanistan each community allied itself to one of the seven parties in Peshawar. These allegiances were not primarily ideological or ethnic. The leader of one community was often a rival (not an enemy) of the leaders of the neighbouring communities. So he would ally himself to a different political party from them. As alliances shifted within the country, moreover, people would shift their allegiances from one party to another. This produced a sort of patchwork quilt pattern of allegiances.

In other words, the Afghan resistance was both a people in revolt and a group of American clients. But the fact of revolt was more important. Hundreds of thousands of Afghans died in the war, and they did not give their lives for American hegemony. And the relationship between the Islamists and the CIA was always an uneasy alliance. On a global level, the US was opposed to Islamism—in the 1980s Iran was a major enemy. In one telling incident, plans to bring the leaders of the seven parties to Washington had to be cancelled because Hekmatyar refused to shake President Reagan's hand.

During the seven-year war against the Soviets—the Fourth Afghan War—class relations in the villages were transformed. The old Afghan elite, the big landlords and their allies in the cities, simply fled and never returned. Many had the money and contacts to become Afghan-Americans. This left a vacuum in the cities. There a new class of educated people was taking power, a new bourgeoisie. Both the Communists and the Islamists belonged to this class. The question was which wing of this class would win.

In the countryside the changes were equally profound but different. The old landlords left and have never come back. Many poorer families also fled as refugees. But often a household would leave one man, even in very dangerous circumstances, to hold onto their land, because suddenly no one really knew who had a valid claim over much of the land. There were new strongmen—the local "commanders" of the resistance in each community. In some ways these men modelled themselves on the old khans. They were different in that their legitimacy came from their leadership in the resistance. But their claim to land was also weaker because newer. Moreover, there were no courts at all. So like the khans before them the commandants had to demonstrate their power over land by using violence against the

---

12: There were also several more parties, many with Iranian links, active in the central mountains of the Hazarajat.

weak and against anyone who challenged them. Precisely because every-thing was in flux, these demonstrations of power had to be more brutal. Some ethnic groups and communities had also fled from particular areas, and some had been pushed out. Here too a clear threat of violence was necessary to hold the new claims.

The CIA and the Pakistani ISI also encouraged a massive expansion of opium and heroin production in Afghanistan. The crops helped Afghan farmers survive, and selling the drugs raised money for the political parties. But since then the drug trade has thrived in both Afghanistan and Pakistan. This makes both countries more unsafe and chaotic places, and regional leaders compete for drug money. In Pakistan drug money has also corrupted the main political parties, the army and the intelligence service. And it is one thing to live under a state where politicians take bribes. It is another to live in a state where secret policemen and generals are narcotics bosses.[13]

Then in 1988 the mujahedin won. The Russians left Afghanistan. Within a year the old order would begin to crumble in the Soviet Union, and the Afghan resistance had helped bring that about. Crucially for the present situation, the mujahedin had *defeated* the Soviet invasion. The Afghans had won the Fourth Afghan War, like the previous three. Moreover, they had done so under the banner of Islam. The Afghan peas-ants had paid an enormous price, but they had won. Among other things, this means that most Afghans now believe they can defeat the Americans if they have to, but the cost will be very high.

As soon as the Soviet tanks left, the CIA and Washington dumped the seven parties based in Peshawar, and cut off all money and weapons. The result was chaos. The Russians had left behind a compromise regime led by Mohammad Najibullah, the former head of the Communist secret police. The seven Islamist political parties all moved to take control of the cities. But the mujahedin had fought to defend their own communities, and were not about to march on Kabul, while many of the city dwellers who had rejected the Soviet occupation now found Najibullah preferable to the Islamist parties. After Kabul did eventually fall in 1992, there was no central authority. The Islamist political parties covered themselves in shame. It became clear that they were only interested in fighting each other for power. One party would ally with another, then change sides, betraying their old friends, and then change sides and betray again. Kabul had sur-vived the Soviet occupation without being bombed. Now the city was

---

13: For Pakistan see Asad and Harris, 2003, a brave, wise and important book, and for Afghanistan, MacDonald, 2007.

flattened as competing Islamist parties shelled the working class areas. Kabul looked like a German or Japanese city after the Second World War.

On a local level the Islamist commandants replicated what was happening at the national level. Only force could demonstrate power, but that force had to be continually demonstrated. For ordinary Afghans this was a time of deep insecurity and demoralisation. Many had been prepared to fight and die for Communism. Many more had been prepared to fight the invaders and die in the name of Islam. But as people watched the Islamists, there was nothing left to believe in beyond a person's own family and their own relationship with god. Any larger morality was a con. And people lived in deep insecurity as national war and local conflicts swept back and forth over their homes. Moreover, the Islamists, their local followers or the local commandants could at any moment come and take your land, your shop, your husband, your son or your daughter. People lived continuously in fear and uncertainty, and in bitter disillusion.

The rise of the Taliban

The Taliban were a consequence of seven years of war against the Soviets and seven years of civil war among the mujahedin. They are often described as a bunch of medieval fanatics. They are "traditional", we are told, and the current regime in Kabul is, by contrast, "modernising". But there has never been a regime like the Taliban in any Muslim country anywhere in the world, ever. They are something new, a product of the modern world.[14]

The Taliban came into being in 1994 under the patronage of the ISI in Pakistan, and with the quiet support of the US. The Pakistani military had found the Islamist parties useless in gaining control of Afghanistan. The US wanted law and order in a united Afghanistan so they could run an oil pipeline down from Central Asia, without having to route it through Iran or Russia.

The Taliban began as an army. They attacked Afghanistan from Pakistan. Many of their officers had served in the Pakistani army.[15] The soldiers were boys from the religious schools in the Afghan refugee camps in Pakistan. Taliban simply means "the students". The boys had spent most of their lives not in traditional villages but in that very 20th century institution, the refugee camp.

14: A point made strongly by Dorronsoro, 2005, the best history of Afghanistan over the past 30 years. For the Taliban see also Rashid, 2002, Rubin, 2002, Marsden, 1998, Maley, 1998, and Griffin, 1998.
15: At first quite a number were also former Khalk Communist army officers, but these were soon purged.

The leadership of the Taliban were different again. They were Afghan village mullahs, men with limited formal education. They had never attended university and did not come from big landowning families; they were men of low social status and had little in common with the educated Islamists. They did have a deep hatred of foreign Christians, but there was nothing medieval about that hatred. It was learned in a long war with bomber planes and helicopter gunships. And in no Muslim country, at any point in history, had men like these mullahs ever run a government.

Their religious strictness was not traditional in Afghanistan—nor were their long beards. When I lived in rural Afghanistan in the 1970s I had a short, trimmed beard. Every other man with a beard was either a white haired elder or a mullah, and all of them trimmed their beards neat and short. I was regularly ridiculed in public for my beard, which was immodest and un-Islamic, and it would have been quite unacceptable to grow it long.

At first the Taliban seemed to sweep all before them. They promised law and order, peace and honesty. After 16 years of war and insecurity many Afghans were willing to accept that promise, all the more so because they were known to have American and Pakistani support, and so might be able to deliver peace. But the Taliban also had two other organising bases to their ideology. One was an Islam that concentrated on enforcing the law and modesty. Modesty meant keeping women in seclusion in the cities—most rural women still had to work in the fields. It meant keeping girls out of school in the cities, though in the Pushtun areas villagers insisted on educating their daughters. Crucially, the Taliban promised that their leaders and soldiers would not molest boys and girls as the mujahedin commanders had often done.

The Taliban were driven to emphasise their Islamic credentials partly because everyone knew they were in fact clients of the Pakistani and American governments. Their public executions in football stadiums were barbaric but also welcome to many Afghans. The Taliban enforced law and order, they were more honest than the commanders and people hoped for security. Their odd and un-Afghan Islam went too far for most people. So they had little passionate support but a good deal of toleration in Pushtun areas from people who felt they were better than the alternatives.

However, the central ideology of the Taliban was Pushtun chauvinism. The Taliban were exclusively Pushtun. Since the 1920s Afghan politics had always been polarised on religious and class grounds. The Communists, for instance, had always included Pushtuns, Tajiks, Uzbeks and people from other groups, and so had the Islamists. The various factions, too, had been mixed. Ethnicity was not trivial, but it was not the main basis of politics. Now that Communist and Islamist politics had betrayed people, ethnicity was all that was left for political organising.

The Taliban took the Pushtun south and east, and even Kabul, within two years. When they tried to take Mazar, the main city in the north, the Hazaras there rose up against them. The Hazaras were the poorest, most oppressed group and provided a large proportion of urban workers. They had also had a century of fights with Pushtun herders over land. The Taliban eventually re-established control, but their grip on the north was never firm after that. This ended their appeal to the Americans, who needed a secure government for the pipeline they wanted to put through the north west of the country. The Americans withdrew support. And Osama Bin Laden came home.

The Bin Laden family were a dominant presence in the construction industry in Saudi Arabia. In the 1980s Osama had worked in Pakistan coordinating foreign volunteers and aid for Saudi government intelligence. He often crossed the border into Afghanistan and in a sense went native, adopting the Afghan cause as his own. This did not make him a nationalist—it made him a radical Islamist.

With the Soviet withdrawal Bin Laden left Afghanistan. But then, almost immediately, came the First Gulf War. Bin Laden's first instinct was to support the alliance of Kuwait, Saudi Arabia and the US against Iraq. Two things changed his mind. One was the stationing of US troops in Saudi Arabia itself, which looked too much like a Christian occupation of the Holy Land. The other was the sheer cruelty of the US bombing of Iraq and massacres of soldiers. Bin Laden came to the conclusion that there was no fundamental difference between the Soviet forces in Afghanistan and the American forces in the Middle East.

After 1992 Osama began building a loose network of Islamists opposed to the Saudi royal family and American power, and using individual terrorism as their tactic. He went into exile in Sudan and then moved to Afghanistan. While the Taliban did not precisely welcome him, they did tolerate him.

The second occupation

9/11 was a humiliation for American power. US global power has always relied on a mixture of fear and consent. In the Middle East, in particular, consent has been limited and fear therefore more important. People would have to die, and in far greater numbers than in New York, to restore that fear. Within minutes of seeing the World Trade Centre burning on the television, I knew the Afghans would suffer dearly. Washington also had other motives for war. The oil corporations and the neocons in government had long wanted to take back control of Iraqi and, eventually, Iranian oil. Moreover, successful wars on Afghanistan and Iraq could establish the United States as an overwhelmingly dominant economic and political power not just in the Middle East, but across the globe.

So from 9/12, Day Two, Dick Cheney and Donald Rumsfeld were agitating to invade Iraq. The shock of 9/11 gave them their opportunity. From the Vietnam War on, ordinary Americans had been deeply reluctant to let their sons and daughters die in foreign wars. Now that reluctance was gone.[16] But an immediate jump to an Iraqi invasion was too large a step. And, of course, there was no connection between Saddam Hussein and 9/11. However, something had to be done; someone had to pay. Afghanistan was fit for purpose. There was no poorer country. The people had lived through 23 years of war and the Taliban had little popular support. Afghanistan was weak enough to make invasion possible. Because Afghans had suffered so long and so much, they would now suffer more.

The official explanation was that the US government wanted to hunt down Bin Laden. It would later become clear that this was not important—after all, they didn't get him and didn't worry much about that. But it provided an excuse Americans could believe.

The Taliban government, cornered and anxious, looked for a way out. They could not simply hand over Bin Laden and keep any legitimacy. They offered to turn him over for trial in any Muslim country. This offer was no good to Washington. For one thing, they had no evidence at that point against Bin Laden that could be produced in court. For another, Bin Laden would dominate any trial and turn it into a propaganda victory. Washington wanted him dead, not in court.

The US launched an invasion. But the American public was still not prepared for a major ground war. So the US sent in small teams of special forces, and supplied arms, money and uniforms to the Northern Alliance. The Northern Alliance grouped together the militia of one of the old Islamist parties, now based largely in Tajik areas of the north, along with the former Communist Uzbek militia of General Dostum. The US Air Force began serious bombing and a strange thing happened: the Afghans would not fight. Almost no one fought for the Taliban, including their

16: See, among many sources telling this story, Suskind, 2004.

own soldiers. The soldiers of the Northern Alliance did not fight either. Afghans had had enough war.

The Americans did not trust the Islamists in the Northern Alliance and did not want them to push on to Kabul. The Pakistani ISI and army were trying to hold back the Taliban so they could continue their own alliance with the Americans. So the bombing continued, but there was no fighting. The troops of the Northern Alliance and the Taliban looked at each other across no man's land. This lasted for weeks, and became a serious embarrassment for Washington. Then the Pakistani ISI, the Americans and the Taliban negotiated a deal. The Taliban agreed to evacuate Kabul. The Americans would get a public military victory. In return, Taliban leaders would be allowed to go home to their villages in the south or to take refuge in the Pushtun border areas of Pakistan. They would not be harassed.[17]

This agreement was honoured. All but one of the senior Taliban leaders was left unharmed. None of them ended up in Guantanamo.

The US installed Hamid Karzai as dictator. Karzai was an Afghan born Puhstun, a CIA agent, and had been an official in the Taliban government in the early days. He was an American client but not simply a puppet. His government relied on three real sources of power. One was the US army. The other was the Northern Alliance, who were willing to put up with the Americans but expected them to leave eventually. The third was a certain degree of popular support in Pushtun areas.

Then another strange thing happened, something that is very important but has been hardly remarked upon: there was no resistance to the Americans. Afghanistan was not Iraq. There was resistance in Baghdad from the first week. Indeed there had been Afghan resistance to the Russian invasion from the first week. But this time there was nothing—no shooting, no rocket-propelled grenades, no car bombs. For the next two years there was almost no resistance at all; in the third year very little. And then it began to build.

The explanation for the lack of resistance is simple. Afghans had endured 23 years of war. That meant death but also desperate insecurity, a life of all against all. There was little passionate support for the Taliban or the Islamists. People were willing to settle for almost anything not to live in perpetual fear. Afghans also thought the Americans would provide money for reconstruction and economic development. The millions who were still living in the refugee camps could finally come home. And they

---

17: There are no written sources for this deal, but it is widely known in Afghanistan.

began to come. Even in Kandahar, the strongest base of the Taliban, people were prepared to wait and see, and the longing for peace and prosperity was stronger than any hatred of foreign domination.[18]

The elections in 2004 were a clear demonstration of the willingness to give peace a chance. The Americans forbade any credible candidate from running against Karzai for president. But Afghans turned out in very large numbers to vote for him and for parliamentary representatives. The Taliban had the sense not to attack any of the voters at polling stations—people would have been furious. This did not mean people supported Karzai. It meant they supported peace and elections.

Then it all came apart.

The roots of resistance

To understand why the same Afghans who had accepted the American presence rose against them from 2004 onwards we have to begin with reconstruction.[19] It was not only the Afghans who expected American reconstruction. Almost everyone in Europe also assumed there would be substantial aid. I know, because in 2002 I was telling everyone in Britain who would listen there would be no reconstruction. No one believed me, not even anyone in the Stop the War movement. It seemed *obvious* to them, and to Afghans, that it was in Washington's interest to rebuild the country.

In fact, the US government had done nothing whatsoever to rebuild Vietnam, Laos, Cambodia or Panama. Somalia and Haiti had been permanently laid waste. As the world was to see in Iraq, the American government don't do nation building.

Part of the reason for this was simply to make a permanent example of those who would defy US power. But another reason was that the US government had turned away from social assistance at home. As we saw in 2005, they treated New Orleans like Baghdad. They could not mount the kind of social programmes abroad they would not mount at home. For instance, Saddam Hussein had run a programme to supply rations of

---

18: As can be seen by a careful reading of Chayes, 2007. Johnson and Leslie, 2004, are very good on how hard it is to live in permanent insecurity. Klaits and Gulmanadove-Klaits, 2006, is very moving, and the best way to understand the experience of ordinary Afghans over the past 20 years.

19: The account of Afghanistan under the occupation that follows is based mainly on conversations with Afghans and foreign NGO workers, and the press coverage on the British TV station Channel 4, the *International Herald Tribune*, the *Guardian*, the *Independent*, the *Financial Times*, *Dawn*, *Frontline* and *Socialist Worker*. Also particularly useful are Dorronsoro, 2005, Giustozzi, 2007, Ali, 2008, Rostami-Povey, 2007, Rico, 2007, and Rodriguez, 2007.

food sufficient to feed every Iraqi family. When the US invaded, their first instinct was to cancel this programme. It was explained to them that would mean general uprising of a starving people. So the US government has continued to feed all Iraqis regular rations. But this has been kept a complete secret from the American people, who would be outraged because so many American children go to bed hungry.

So there was very little development assistance to Afghanistan, except for feeding the two million people in Kabul. Crucially, what development assistance does arrive is then pillaged by the NGOs. The Afghan government machinery has been largely defunct since the late 1980s. The basic work of government—keeping the roads open, moving food, providing some healthcare and education—has been largely done by foreign NGOs since then. Under the Taliban the government took care of law and order, and Islam; the NGOs did the rest. Under Karzai there has been some growth in the government machine but foreign NGOs dominate.

The NGOs pillage the aid in two ways. The first comes from salaries and allowances. For instance, in Kabul the average rent for a house suitable for a foreign NGO worker—with a wall, a watchman and a defended garage—is $2,000 to $10,000 a month. The average income per person in Afghanistan is less than $30 a month. This is in a city where the housing stock was largely destroyed by war between the Islamist parties in the 1980s, and has not been rebuilt.[20] Senior NGO workers of all kinds are making far more than an Afghan cabinet minister. In an NGO office in Kabul the wage bill for one foreign worker will be larger than that for 20 Afghans working in the same office. That's not counting their car and driver. Moreover, of course, the Afghans are often highly trained, usually more experienced and they speak the language. But to justify the insane salary difference foreign NGO workers treat their Afghan colleagues as stupid.

Afghans also insist that the senior personnel in foreign NGOs are stealing money and taking bribes. Experienced development workers with radical politics say, yes, this is probably the case. But it is possible that Afghans exaggerate the corruption. After all, what they expect is American aid, and what they see is impossibly bloated NGO lifestyles. The NGOs have also been part of a wildly increased inequality in urban Afghanistan, and a culture of waste, drink, partying and desperate alienation that includes both expatriates and Afghans. There has always been prostitution in Afghanistan but

---

20: For elite housing in Kabul see Fontenot and Maiwandi, 2007.

with the NGOs has come widespread middle class prostitution. So when some American soldiers ran their vehicle into pedestrians in Kabul, killing them, and then opened fire on an angry crowd in 2006, rioting spread and the rioters attacked and burned NGO offices all across Kabul.[21]

One of the great strengths of the Taliban has been that they do not engage in bomb attacks against Afghan civilians, and on the rare occasions when these happen the Taliban issue a public statement denying involvement. Killings of foreign NGO workers, however, are not embarrassing. The NGOs are hated. People had hoped for economic development and have received nothing.

The second main cause of increasing resistance is the behaviour of the occupying troops. Johnny Rico served in the American army in Uruzgan province. His book *Blood Makes the Grass Grow Green* describes what happened in his unit, and his account fits with other more fragmentary press reports.[22] Rico's unit were young men who were trained and told to be ready for war. They were told there was an "enemy" out there and sent to patrol for them. They were also eager to see "combat" and be men, although they were appalled by real war when they encountered it. They began by patrolling, knocking down doors, treating people roughly and looking for a fight. When someone finally shot at them, they called in air strikes. When the aggrieved families and neighbours then attacked in the coming weeks, they called down more air strikes. Finally enraged civilians became "Taliban", the valley was turned over to the Special Forces who had no limits on their rules of engagement and the villages burned. Then the American forces left the valley. This pattern seems to have been repeated across the Pushtun areas in much of the south and east. In a sense, the Pushtuns became the resistance because they had been defined as the villages that needed patrolling.

The third factor feeding the resistance was insecurity. I have argued that Afghans accepted American rule in part because they were desperate for basic security. But the occupying troops perform no police duties and deliver no justice. Indeed, they are themselves an important random, unpredictable danger. Moreover, there are no government courts or functioning police in most of the country. With the American invasion, and the return of many refugees, land title is even more unclear. That means the new big landowners have to demonstrate their power, as before.

21: See Rodriguez, 2007, which is also very good on the world of the NGOs and the social degradation of middle class Kabulis.
22: Rico, 2007.

The neo-Taliban

So people are poor, frightened and angry, and since 2004 they have begun to fight back. The resistance grew first in the Pushtun areas of the south and east. As far as I can tell, these again look like local communities in revolt, although there is some regional coordination. Most of the rebels, when asked, say they owe allegiance to the Taliban, or sometimes to Hekmatyar, the leader of the biggest Islamist party in the 1980s. Both the Taliban and Hekmatyar had limited support in 2001. Now they, and especially the Taliban, have quite general support in Pushtun areas. The reason is simple: they were the only people calling for outright resistance and no cooperation with the occupation from the beginning. When villagers were forced into resistance they looked to the leaders who called for that resistance.

The Taliban have also learned, changed their strategy and displayed considerable political intelligence.[23] They do not bomb civilians. They never mention Pushtun chauvinism and constantly emphasise that all Muslims should fight together. In power they banned music and videos. Now they produce propaganda videos and cassettes of Taliban music.

Moreover, although Afghan politics were split on ethnic lines in 2001, the usual occupation strategy of divide and rule has not worked as it has in Iraq. The Northern Alliance troops and police from the north do not enter the Pushtun areas to fight for the Americans, nor do they take on the Taliban around Kabul. If the occupying forces want to fight the resistance, they do so very largely on their own. There is, for now, no fighting between ethnic groups.

From 2006 the resistance began to spread outwards from the Pushtun areas. The NGOs drew up maps showing their personnel where it was safe to travel. Early in 2006 almost the entire centre, north and west were safe. By 2008 almost all of the country was unsafe. Nuristan in the north east, not a Pushtun area, became the first fully independent province in the summer of 2008 when enraged villagers avenged an air strike in the Waigal Valley by killing 11 US soldiers and forcing an American retreat. By late August of 2008 the Taliban had control of the roads from Kabul to Kandahar in the south and Pakistan in the east. They will soon cut off the road from the north. At that point the resistance will be able to cut off food and fuel from the capital. The Americans are not capable of airlifting food and supplies for two million people for any length of time. The occupation is close to serious defeat. In 2006 a British base in Sangin in Helmand was cut off for three weeks, with helicopter pilots too afraid to resupply. The base came

---

23: For the changes in the neo-Taliban, see Giustozzi, 2007.

within a day of running out of ammunition, which would have been followed by the death of the whole unit. The Americans in Waigal lost 11 dead but many more wounded, and came close to losing everyone. The French lost ten men in one go in Sarobi, a town on the main road from Kabul to the Khyber Pass and Pakistan. In Kandahar the Taliban were able to take the main prison in the second largest city in the country and release 450 political prisoners. It is only a matter of time before a whole garrison is wiped out somewhere in the country. Imagine if Britain, Canada, France, the Netherlands or the US lost 40 or 50 soldiers in a day. There would be terrible death rained down on the local villages, but also strong political pressure at home to withdraw support.

Afghans now believe that the Americans will be defeated. They believe this because they defeated the British three times and the Russians within living memory. But they are also well aware that the butcher's bill will be severe.

One friend last month told me her whole family, who live just north of Kabul, none of them Taliban supporters or Pushtuns, knew the war was coming to them soon. Within two years, she said, it will not just be the Pushtuns. We will all fight. She and her family do not welcome this. They fear it. But they know it has to be done.

Karzai's government is being forced to turn against the Americans. Parliament is elected, and Karzai is dependent on the support of the leading figures in the Northern Alliance, in the west around Herat, and in the Pushtun south. This means the government has been forced to speak out against the bombing of civilians. Foreign news crews and UN inspectors are taken to the devastated villages, and in some cases there are now detailed and accurate counts of the dead. Karzai has had to say publicly that the US cannot bomb villages without his case by case approval. This is impossible for the American armed forces to accept, as their only tactic and only defence is massive bombing of villages. Moreover, the Northern Alliance, Dostum and his Uzbek militia around Mazar, and Ismael Khan's organisation around Herat in the west can see what way the wind is blowing. In simple political terms, it will soon be time for them to desert the American alliance.

Within Afghanistan almost all the feminists have collaborated with the occupation, or the NGOs or Karzai's government. So have most former Communists, the returned Afghan-Americans, the "modernisers" and the "secular" liberals. Many of these people supported the Russian occupation, which is why feminism and socialism disappeared for a generation. Now almost all of them support the occupation. Some former

Communists and Maoists, like Rawa (the Revolutionary Association of Women of Afghanistan), call for the Americans to leave but for all the other occupying forces to remain as the United Nations. This would change nothing, is not a serious position and amounts to choosing the occupation over the resistance.

Some socialists, secularists or feminists in the West are wary of the resistance because it is right wing and Muslim, which indeed it is. But this is to see things the wrong way round. The resistance is right wing and Muslim because the people who are left wing and secular have sided with the occupation. Now that ordinary Afghans have opted for resistance they are perforce supporting those people who lead the resistance. The tragic stupidity of the Soviet years is being repeated by people with less passion, less courage and fewer principles.

There is a way out of this vicious circle. It lies not in Afghanistan, but in Pakistan, which is being drawn into the war.

The Pakistan dimension

The government of Pakistan's military ruler Pervez Musharraf was persuaded by US pressure and the bribe of a large debt reduction to break with the Taliban and throw his weight behind the US occupation. But now the occupation is adding to deep instability in Pakistan itself. Two Pakistani provinces border Afghanistan—Baluchistan and the largely Pushtun North West Frontier Province. The people in these by and large welcomed and sympathised with the Afghan refugees in the 1980s, and they have sympathised with the Afghan resistance against the Americans this time round.

The plains areas of Pushtun Pakistan are under central government control. But millions of people live in the mountain areas along the border. These are called "tribal" areas in English and "free" areas in Pushtu. They were never conquered by the British when they held India, and the Pakistani army has until recently never tried to conquer them either. For more than a century they have been, in effect, self-governing. It is to these areas that Osama Bin Laden and many of the fleeing Taliban came in 2001 and 2002. Local militants in these areas, along with people in refugee camps, also built "local Taliban" militias after 2002, and provided safe havens and refuges for the Afghan Taliban. As resistance built in Afghanistan, the Americans put increasing pressure on the Pakistani army to attack the "local Taliban".

Then in September 2006 the Pakistani army and government signed a formal written peace agreement with the local Taliban in North Waziristan district along the border after the Pakistani army had lost 400 dead in fighting with them. The peace agreement specified that the Pakistani army would withdraw to barracks and the local Taliban would control all checkpoints on roads and border crossings to Afghanistan. All Taliban prisoners would be released, and any confiscated weapons and vehicles returned to them. The families of fighters and civilians killed by the army would be compensated and so would anyone who had lost their house to government artillery or bombs. Any foreigners (by which they meant Al Qaida) could live in Waziristan if they had the consent of the local tribal elders.

It was a nearly complete victory for the local Taliban. The Afghan Taliban now had a refuge, space for camps and an opportunity to recruit volunteers among the half a million people of the area. The agreement was hardly reported in the US, but the American military and the Bush administration were outraged. They insisted that General Musharraf had to launch a serious offensive against the Pushtun border areas. Musharraf was very reluctant to do this. Any serious offensive would involve aerial bombing and many thousands of civilian dead. No government in the world is eager to go to war with a major section of its own population, and it was by no means clear the army would fight, since 30 percent of both officers and enlisted men in the Pakistani army are Pushtuns.

To make it easier, the American government brokered a deal between Musharraf and Benazir Bhutto, under which she would return from exile to become prime minister, while Musharraf would remain president. Musharraf then launched an armed assault against an Islamist mosque and girls school in the capital, Islamabad, and unleashed the army and air force on the free border areas. Heavy bombing of villages in South Waziristan, in particular, killed large numbers. On her return Bhutto called repeatedly for an intensification of the bombings of villages, an end to any peace agreements and support for the Americans. The Islamists, she said, were the major danger facing Pakistan.

The American plans rapidly unravelled. A Pakistani army unit of over 200 men surrendered to the local Taliban in South Waziristan and were released a few days later. In effect, they had refused to fight. The second largest city in Swat, a Pushtun but not a tribal area and some distance from the border, fell to the Taliban when the Pakistani garrison retreated without a shot being fired. Then Bhutto was assassinated. Her family accused the army of complicity. It is not possible to know for sure but the more likely explanation was that she was killed by suicide bombers from Waziristan avenging the dead in the bombed villages.

All this happened at the same time as the bitter protest campaign by lawyers over Musharraf's sacking of Chief Justice Chaudhuri of the supreme court. Chaudhuri, a fair and honest judge, looked likely to rule that Musharraf's election as president was invalid. Equally seriously, Pakistani intelligence had been cooperating with the US in lifting and disappearing hundreds of suspected jihadis across Pakistan. Chaudhuri was insisting that *habeas corpus* and Magna Carta still apply in Pakistani courts, and that the disappeared had to be produced in his court. The barristers, solicitors and judges of Pakistan were outraged at Musharraf's final insult to the law and to an honest man in a soiled system. They marched, shouted and challenged the police, wearing their suits and robes. And they had enormous popular support, because they were doing what Bhutto's Pakistan People's Party and the unions should have been doing. They were standing up for another Pakistan.

The lawyers' protests, the death of Bhutto and the refusal of the army to fight came together in a perfect storm at the time of the election in February 2008. Musharraf and the Americans had to let the election go ahead. The US has now been forced to acquiesce in Musharraf's removal as president, but stability has not returned to the country. Inflation is soaring, hitting the poor particularly hard. The majority of the population wants an end to poverty and to the American alliance. In effect, they have been represented by no one. Meanwhile, the government and the local Taliban are making peace all along the border. This is a catastrophic situation for the American military. Safe areas are key to any guerrilla insurgency. The Taliban now have an enormous safe area. The American generals are arguing strongly that in order to hold Afghanistan they will have to be able to attack the Taliban in Pakistan.[24] They are already flying large numbers of unmanned drones over Pakistan, and using them to bomb Pakistani villages. In July the American forces repeatedly attacked a Pakistani army post along the border and killed all 11 soldiers at the post. The head of the Pakistani general staff went on television to say that this was a deliberate attack on the Pakistani army, which of course it was.

If American soldiers go into Pakistan in any numbers, the Pakistani military could split and there could be civil war. In that war the majority of the armed forces and a large majority of the population would be opposed to the Americans. Pakistan is not Iraq or Afghanistan. It has a population of 175 million, and almost 20 million of them live in Karachi. The resistance inside Pakistan would dwarf that in Iraq or Afghanistan. Moreover, Pakistan has the bomb, which the Americans would have to try to seize control of and which the Pakistan military might be tempted to use.

24: This discussion relies particularly on coverage in the *Herald Tribune*, but also the *Financial Times*, *Independent*, *Socialist Worker* and *Channel 4 News*.

To mention all these problems is to underline the madness of current American policy. The American military are beginning to face a stark choice. They can go for mass terror bombing of Afghan villages, but that would destroy Karzai's government and lose them all their allies. They can attack Pakistan with worse consequences. They can hold on and hope something turns up, while increasing the kill level and wasting the lives of American and European soldiers. Or they can negotiate and leave. The EU and Karzai have negotiated with the Taliban, and Karzai is still keeping lines open to the resistance. The Americans must also be talking to them through back channels. The Taliban are willing to accept a coalition government once all foreign troops leave. Indeed it is now impossible to imagine peace unless they all leave. If any stay, some Afghans will fight them and the war will resume.

A coalition government would not be a good solution. The neighbouring countries would still support their longstanding Afghan clients: Uzbekistan and Russia have Dostum, India has the Tajiks Islamists, Pakistan has the Taliban and Iran has Ishmael Khan in Herat. It would still be a bitterly poor, heavily mined country with brutal landlords. Moreover, the various forces within Afghanistan would be likely to fight, if only to test their relative power. And it would be a right wing government because all the major players are right wing.

It would still be much better than the hell that is coming to Afghanistan if the Americans, the British and the rest try to hang on. Nor should we forget that every British, American, Canadian or French soldier who goes there now is being sent to the meat grinder for no other reason than to buy time.

A negotiated settlement and withdrawal, however, would effectively mean the end of the "war on terror", marked by an American defeat. The consequences for American power around the world would be shattering. For a generation after Vietnam ordinary Americans were able to refuse to fight overseas. After Afghanistan it would be the same. That would mean the end of American global dominance.

The American strategy of simply waiting, however, is looking less and less clever. As the resistance grows, events are moving with increasing speed and the US forces are losing control of their choices. It is impossible to predict the timing. But in the first week in September this year US ground troops crossed the border and killed 20 civilians in a village in Waziristan. American military sources told the *New York Times* that this was the first of many planned incursions and that there have been many exchanges of fire across the border between American and Pakistani troops.[25] Pressures are escalating.

In this situation many on the left, and in the peace movement, in North America, Europe, India and Pakistan don't want the Americans to actually leave. They want some kind of controlled settlement that excludes the Taliban. This is a fantasy. The Taliban have walked the walk and earned their place at the table. It is also self-deception. Afghanistan is one of the few places in the world where progressives and the left have consistently lined up with brutal imperial mass murder. That is why the right wing is strong in Afghanistan.

The solution is to learn. Military coups and helicopter gunships are no road to liberation. Top-down, undemocratic dictatorship is not just wrong—it destroys the left. We need a new kind of socialism, or rather a return to the traditions of democratic, liberation socialism. And we need a peace movement that argues for peace, not for modified occupation.

None of this can be built inside Afghanistan in the near future. The country is simply too poor, too betrayed and too full of suffering. But it is possible to build democratic socialism and a peace movement in Europe. And crucially for Afghanistan, it is possible to do that in Pakistan. Most of the established political forces refuse to confront the Americans but public opinion is strong and clear. For too long most of the left in Pakistan has identified the jihadis and the Taliban as the main enemy. There is likely to be a moment of rebellion against the Americans in Pakistan in the next few months or years. When that comes, if the left is strong and passionate and enraged on the streets, that could change politics in Afghanistan too.

I hope the Afghans defeat this occupation, as they have defeated occupations before. And I wish them peace as soon as possible. They have suffered enough.

25: *International Herald Tribune*, 6 September 2008.

References

Ali, Tariq, 2008, "Afghanistan: Mirage of the Good War", *New Left Review 50* (March-April 2008), www.newleftreview.org/?page=article&view=2713

Azoy, Whitney, 1982, *Buzkashi* (University of Pennsylvania).

Anwar, Raja, 1988, *The Afghan Tragedy* (Verso).

Asad, Amirzada, and Robert Harris, 2003, *The Politics and Economics of Drug Production on the Pakistan-Afghanistan Border: Implications for a Globalized World* (Ashgate).

Barfield, Thomas, 1981, *The Central Asian Arabs of Afghanistan* (Texas University).

Bonner, Arthur, 1987 *Among the Afghans* (Duke University).

Bradsher, Henry, 1985, *Afghanistan and the Soviet Union* (Duke University).

Canfield, Robert, 1973, *Faction and Conversion in a Plural Society*, Anthropological Papers 50, University of Michigan.

Chayes, Sarah, 2007, *The Punishment of Virtue* (Protobello).

Cordovez, Diego, and Selig Harrison, 1995, *Out of Afghanistan* (Oxford University).

Crile, George, 2003, *My Enemy's Enemy* (Atlantic). Later republished as *Charley Wilson's War*.

Dorronsoro, Gilles, 2005, *Revolution Unending: Afghanistan: The Mirage of Peace* (Hurst).

Doubleday, Veronica, 1988, *Three Women of Herat* (Cape).

Emadi, Hafizullah, 1990, *State, Revolution and Superpowers in Afghanistan* (Praeger).

Fontenot, Anthony, and Ajmal Maiwandi, 2007, "Capitol of Chaos: The new Kabul of Warlords and Infidels", in Mike Davis and Daniel Monk (eds), *Evil Paradises: Dreamworlds of Neoliberalism* (The New Press).

Fry, Maxwell, 1974, *The Afghan Economy* (Brill).

Giustozzi, Antonio, 2007, *Koran, Kalashnikov and Laptop: The neo-Taliban Insurgency in Afghanistan* (Hurst).

Griffin, Michael, 1998, *Reaping the Whirlwind: The Taliban in Afghanistan* (Pluto).

Johnson, Chris, and Jolyon Leslie, 2004, *Afghanistan: The Mirage of Peace* (Zed).

Jones, Schuyler, 1974, *Men of Influence in Nuristan* (Seminar).

Kakar, M H, 1992, *Afghanistan: The Soviet Union and the Afghan Response, 1979-1982* (California University).

Khalidi, N A, 1991, "Afghanistan: Demographic Consequences of War, 1978-1987", *Central Asian Survey*, volume 10, number 3.

Klaits, Alexander, and Gulchin Gulmandova-Klaits, 2006, *Love and War in Afghanistan* (Seen Stories).

MacDonald, David, 2007, *Drugs in Afghanistan: Opium, Outlaws and Scorpion Tales* (Pluto).

Male, Beverly, 1982, *Revolutionary Afghanistan: A Reappraisal* (Croom Helm).

Maley, William (ed), 1998, *Fundamentalism Reborn? Afghanistan and the Taliban* (Hurst).

Marsden, Peter, 1998, *The Taliban: War, Religion and the New Order in Afghanistan* (Zed).

Neale, Jonathan, 1981, "The Afghan Tragedy", *International Socialism 12*, www.marxists.de/middleast/neale/afghan.htm

Neale, Jonathan, 1988, "Afghanistan: The Horse Changes Riders", *Capital and Class 35* (summer 1988), www.marxists.de/middleast/neale/horse.htm.

Neale, Jonathan, 2001, "The Long Torment of Afghanistan", *International Socialism 93* (winter 2001), http://pubs.socialistreviewindex.org.uk/isj93/neale.htm

Neale, Jonathan, 2003, "Afghanistan", in Reza Farah (ed), *Anti-Imperialism: A Guide for the Movement* (Bookmarks).

Rashid, Ahmed, 2002, *Taliban: Islam, Oil and the New Great Game in Central Asia* (Tauris).

Rico, Johnny, 2007, *Blood Makes the Grass Grow Green* (Presidio).

Rodriguez, Deborah, 2007, *The Kabul Beauty School* (Hodder).

Rostami-Povey, Elaheh, 2007, *Afghan Women: Identity and Invasion* (Zed).

Roy, Olivier, 1986, *Islam and Resistance in Afghanistan* (Cambridge University).

Rubin, Barnett, 2002, *The Fragmentation of Afghanistan* (Yale University).

Shahrani, M Nazif, 1979, *The Kirghiz and Wakhi of Afghanistan* (Washington University).

Suskind, Roy, 2004, *The Price of Loyalty* (Simon and Schuster).

Tapper, Nancy, 1991, *Bartered Brides: Politics, Gender and Marriage in a Tribal Society* (Cambridge University).

A crisis for the centre of the system[1]
Andrew Kliman

The United States is caught up in the most serious financial crisis since the Great Depression. This crisis calls into question the stability and indeed the very survival of capitalism. Unlike the savings and loan crisis 20 years ago, which was confined to a single industry, or the Asian currency crisis ten years ago, which was mostly confined to less developed and developing countries, the present crisis affects financial markets generally and emanates from the major centre of capitalism. It thus threatens to become a global crisis. And a major financial crisis cannot fail to have serious repercussions in the "real" (non-financial) economy—production, employment, trade in goods and services, and so on.

Because Marxists are famous for "predicting five out of the last three recessions", I need to point out two things before continuing. First, the term *crisis* does not mean *collapse*, nor does it mean *slump* (recession, depression, downturn). A crisis is a rupture or disruption in the network of relationships that keep the economy operating in the normal way. Whether or not it triggers a collapse or even a slump depends upon what happens next.

The US economy is not currently on the verge of collapse, and it is far too early to predict a collapse. By papering over bad debt with still more debt, policymakers have repeatedly been able to pull the national and world economies through earlier crises, and this strategy may well work again. And while the US is probably in the midst of a recession, the downturn

1:    *Editorial note: this article (a substantially revised and updated version of Kliman, 2008) was written on 23 August 2008 and therefore pre-dates the effective nationalisation of Fannie Mae and Freddie Mac by the US government.*

has been—thus far—a relatively mild and uneven one. For instance, payroll employment has fallen seven months in a row (through to July), but the total decline is less than half the decline that occurred during the first seven months of the last recession, in 2001, which itself was relatively mild.

Second, although my perspective on the crisis is perhaps not yet the majority view, it is increasingly becoming mainstream. In April, Yale University financial economist Robert J Shiller suggested that the crisis reveals "the fundamental instability of our system".[2] Just prior to the US government's announcement of a plan to rescue the giant mortgage lending firms Fannie Mae and Freddie Mac, business columnist Ambrose Evans-Pritchard wrote, "The meltdown at the[se] two federally chartered agencies amounts to a heart attack at the core of the US credit system, leaving it obvious that the Bush administration has failed to stabilise the financial system".[3] George Soros told the Reuters news agency two days later that we are in the midst of "the most serious financial crisis of our lifetime". "It is inevitable that it is affecting the real economy".[4] Alan Blinder, a Princeton University economist and former vice-chair of the US Federal Reserve, told the *New York Times*, "We haven't seen this kind of travail in the financial markets since the 1930s".[5]

Nearly six weeks after the government rescue plan for Fannie Mae and Freddie Mac was announced, Bill Seidman, former chair of the Federal Deposit Insurance Corporation, warned that these firms could still fail, which "could cause total panic in the global financial system". If the market is left alone to sort the problem out, "that could mean the end of the market and the financial institutions and banks".[6] Kenneth Rogoff, a Harvard University economist and former chief economist at the International Monetary Fund, said that "the financial crisis is at the halfway point, perhaps", and that "the worst is yet to come". He also warned that one or more of the country's biggest commercial or investment banks may fail within the next few months.[7]

2:   Robert J Shiller, "The Fed Gets A New Job Description", *New York Times*, 6 April 2008, www.nytimes.com/2008/04/06/business/06view.html
3:   Ambrose Evans-Pritchard, "Dow Dives As Paulson Rules Out Rescue Of Loan Banks", *Daily Telegraph*, 12 July 2008.
4:   "Soros Says Fannie, Freddie Crisis Won't Be The Last", Reuters, 14 July 2008.
5:   Peter S Goodman, "Uncomfortable Answers To Questions On The Economy", *New York Times*, 19 July 2008, www.nytimes.com/2008/07/19/business/economy/19econ.html
6:   John Spence, "Former FDIC Chief Urges Breakup Of Fannie, Freddie", *MarketWatch*, 21 July 2008, http://tinyurl.com/6llagc
7:   Peter Macmahon, "Worst Is Yet To Come In US Warns Rogoff", *Scotsman*, 20 August 2008, http://business.scotsman.com/economics/Worst-is-yet-to-come.4406371.jp

A new manifestation of state-capitalism

The present crisis is above all a *crisis of confidence*. To understand what this means we need to reflect on the fact that capitalism relies on credit, and the fact that the credit system is based on promises and faith. Before potential lenders will actually lend they must be promised that the monies they throw into the market in order to get a return will in fact return to them; and they must have faith (or confidence) that these promises will be honoured. So if lenders' faith in the future is shaken, the system's ability to keep going from today to tomorrow is disrupted. If their faith in the future is shaken as profoundly as it has been recently, the result is a crisis that calls into question the very ability of the financial system, and therefore also the "real" economy, to continue functioning.

The Federal Reserve, the US Treasury Department and the rest of the government are acutely aware of and afraid of this crisis of confidence. As Paul Krugman, a Princeton University economist and *New York Times* columnist, remarked in mid-March, "[government] officials—rightly— aren't willing to run the risk that losses on bad loans will cripple the financial system and take the real economy down with it".[8]

And so, with the takeover of Bear Stearns in mid-March, and what is widely recognised as the effective nationalisation of Fannie Mae and Freddie Mac in mid-July,[9] we are witnessing a new manifestation of state-capitalism. It isn't the state-capitalism of the former USSR, characterised by central "planning" and the dominance of state property; it is state-capitalism in the sense in which Raya Dunayevskaya used the term to refer to a new global stage of capitalism, characterised by permanent state intervention, that arose in the 1930s with the New Deal and similar policy regimes.[10] The purpose of the New Deal, just like the purpose of the latest government interventions, was to save the capitalist system from itself.

Because many liberal and left commentators choose to focus on the distributional implications of these interventions—who will the government rescue, rich investors and lenders or average homeowners facing foreclosure?—let me stress that I mean "save the capitalist system" in the

8:   Paul Krugman, "The B Word", *New York Times*, 17 March 2008, www.nytimes.com/2008/03/17/opinion/17krugman.html
9:   For instance, former chair of the Federal Deposit Insurance Corporation Seidman has stated, "For all practical purposes, Fannie and Freddie are nationalised". See John Spence, "Former FDIC Chief Urges Breakup Of Fannie, Freddie', *MarketWatch*, 21 July 2008, http://tinyurl.com/6llagc
10:   Dunayevskaya, 2000, p258 onwards.

literal sense. The purpose of these interventions is not to make the rich richer, or even to protect their wealth, but to save the system as such.

Consider the takeover of Bear Stearns, which was Wall Street's fifth largest firm. On 16 March the Fed attempted to sell it off to JP Morgan Chase for the fire-sale price of $2 per share, a tiny fraction of what its assets were worth on the open market and one fifth of the ultimate sale price. Bear Stearns was in serious trouble but there were other ways of dealing with it. Had it been able to borrow at the Fed's "discount window", Bear Stearns could have survived the crisis it faced, which was due to a temporary lack of cash. But the Fed waited until the following day to announce that it would now open the discount window to Wall Street firms. Alternatively, if Bear Stearns had been allowed to file for bankruptcy, it could have continued to operate, and its owners' shares of stock would not have been acquired at a fraction of their market value. Instead the Fed forced it to be sold off.

Thus the takeover was definitely not a way of bailing out Bear Stearns' owners. Nor was the Fed out to enrich the owners of JP Morgan Chase. (The Fed selected it as the new owner of Bear Stearns' assets because it was the only financial firm big enough to buy them.) Instead the Fed acted as it did in order to send a clear signal to the financial world that the US government would do whatever it could to prevent the failure of any institution that is "too big to fail", because such a failure could set off a domino effect triggering a panicky withdrawal of funds large enough to bring the financial system crashing down.

The takeover of Bear Stearns was a big deal, but the government's plan that effectively nationalises Fannie Mae and Freddie Mac is a far bigger deal. These firms own or guarantee about half of all US mortgages, and they are now making or guaranteeing about three quarters of new home loans. In late April, when the spotlight was still on the Bear Stearns takeover, I called attention to:

> what might prove to be far more important, because of its potential size and scope...a subtle government action taken three days later with respect to Fannie Mae and Freddie Mac... On 19 March the Office of Federal Housing Enterprise Oversight [OFHEO], the regulatory authority in charge of these mortgage pools, suddenly announced that they may reduce by one third the funds they hold as a cushion against losses, and that it "will consider further reductions in the future". This is the opposite of what one would normally expect. Because of the huge increase in mortgage loans that have gone bad,

Freddie Mac in particular faces large and unexpected losses. So what it needs is a *bigger*, not smaller, cushion against these losses...

By telling these mortgage pools to be less prudent, not more prudent, at a time when more prudence is called for, [OFHEO] was sending a signal that the government is there to bail them out (take over their losses) if and when they go broke. Although this signal was subtle, it was understood by "those in the know". For instance, writing on prudentbear.com, Doug Noland referred to the action as the "Nationalisation of US mortgages".[11]

Two and a half months later the moment for subtlety had come and gone. The share prices of both Fannie and Freddie plummeted by almost half during the second week of July. Until that point many observers thought that the Bear Stearns takeover had provided the financial markets with sufficient assurance that the US government was ready and willing to do whatever needed to be done to prop up the financial system. But the decline in Fannie and Freddie's share prices triggered renewed fears of the system's collapse. Wall Street executives and foreign central bankers warned the government that "any further erosion of confidence could have a cascading effect around the world".[12]

So the Treasury Department and the Fed hastily cobbled together a rescue plan over the weekend. And in a highly unusual move, Treasury Secretary Henry Paulson rushed to publicise it on Sunday (13 July), before the financial markets had an opportunity to resume activity and further damage confidence.

The rescue plan gave the Treasury unlimited authority—a "blank cheque"—to borrow whatever funds are needed to cover Fannie and Freddie's losses. The government's motivation is not to prop up these firms' share prices (after the rescue plan was announced, their share prices recovered some of the ground they had lost, but they have since fallen to new lows). Nor is the government trying to bail out the shareholders. The details of the plan have apparently not been fully worked out yet, but it seems extremely unlikely that Fannie and Freddie's shareholders will receive any money from the government. Only the institutions and investors that bought the securities they issued will be compensated, and perhaps some of them—the holders of risky subordinated debt—will also take a hit. Just as in

---

11: Kliman, 2008.
12: Stephen Labaton, "Scramble Led To Rescue Plan On Mortgages", *New York Times*, 15 July 2008, www.nytimes.com/2008/07/15/washington/15fannie.html

the Bear Stearns case, the point of the intervention is to restore confidence in the financial system by assuring lenders that, if all else fails, the US government will be there to pay back the monies that are owed to them.

The new manifestation of state-capitalism we are witnessing is essentially non-ideological in character. To be sure, some movement away from "free-market" capitalism and back to greater regulation is taking place, but this is a pragmatic matter rather than an ideological one. Given the severity of the current crisis there is an extremely broad consensus, extending even into much of the US left, that the government should do whatever is needed to prevent a collapse of the financial system. If this requires that the government assume the debts of Wall Street firms, Fannie Mae and Freddie Mac, and whatever may happen to be the next institutions that are "too big to fail", so be it. But since the government is now committed to propping up these institutions, these institutions are ultimately gambling with public money. So there is an equally broad consensus that greater regulation is necessary in order to prevent government guarantees from giving these institutions a green light to invest and lend in an even riskier fashion than they have done to date.

It is far too soon to tell how much the government will eventually have to borrow in order to cover financial sector losses. A lot depends on how deeply the housing market declines and how much the financial crisis spills over into the "real" economy. Whatever the amount proves to be in the end, it will be ultimately paid by US taxpayers in the form of interest payments on the extra funds the Treasury will borrow. This does not mean, however, that the working class will ultimately foot the bill. Under capitalism workers' after-tax earnings are ultimately governed by economic laws that higher taxes do not suspend.[13] Thus if the taxes they pay increase, their pre-tax incomes are likely to increase as well, all else being equal, and employers are likely to be the ones who bear the ultimate burden of the tax increase. But this will cut into employers' profits and thus retard investment, economic growth and job creation for some time to come—perhaps even decades if the mortgage losses turn out to be large and the government borrows for the long term. In this way and in this sense, then, working people will indeed ultimately bear the burden of the mortgage losses.

13: This does not mean that workers are all paid the value of their labour power. There is a stratification of wages, and the trajectory of wages depends on many factors. The point is rather that tax changes tend to be offset by other factors, so that standards of living remain more or less at their prior levels when all is said and done. That "who directly pays the tax" and "who bears the burden of the tax" are completely different matters (for instance, that landlords directly pay property taxes, but renters are ultimately the ones to bear the burden, in the form of higher rents) is one of the best known principles of economics.

Of course, millions of them have already been hurt more directly, by losing their homes or by losing their equity in their homes as home prices have plummeted. Millions more are likely to be hurt in the future. Delinquency rates, the proportion of those falling behind on payments, have been rising on mortgage loans of all kinds—not only subprime loans. Between April 2007 and April 2008 the delinquency rate on prime loans (the usual type) doubled, while the delinquency rate on "alt-A" loans, which stand midway between prime and subprime varieties, quadrupled.[14]

The loss of home equity is especially significant because ownership of a part or all of their homes is the main way in which working people hold what little savings they have, and because their ability to borrow depends heavily upon the equity in their homes that they can offer as collateral. Negative equity—a situation in which the homeowner's outstanding mortgage is more than his or her home is currently worth—is a particular problem. People with negative equity cannot borrow against their homes at all. But the more home prices fall, the greater the negative equity. One internet provider of housing valuations, zillow.com, recently estimated that 29 percent of homeowners who bought their homes within the past five years, and 45 percent of those who bought their homes at the 2006 peak of the housing market, are saddled with negative equity.[15]

Roots of the crisis

The financial crisis has its roots in the US housing sector bubble that formed earlier in the decade. Paradoxically, the bubble is largely attributable to the weakness of the country's economy during this decade. First stock prices plunged sharply as the "dot.com" stock market bubble burst. For instance, the S&P 500 index fell by nearly half in the three years following March 2000. Then the economy went into recession in March 2001, and it was weakened further by the 9/11 attacks later that year. In order to allay the fears of financial collapse that followed the attacks the Fed lowered short-term interest rates. Although the recession was later "officially" declared to have ended in November of 2001, employment kept falling during the middle of 2003. So the Fed kept lowering short-term lending rates. For three full years, starting in October of 2002, the real (ie inflation-adjusted) federal funds rate was actually negative (see figure 1). This allowed banks to borrow

---

14: Vikas Bajaj, "Housing Lenders Fear Bigger Wave Of Loan Defaults", *New York Times*, 4 August 2008, www.nytimes.com/2008/08/04/business/04lend.html
15: Bob Ivry, "Zillow: 29% Of Homeowners Have Negative Equity", *Arizona Daily Star*, 13 April 2008.

Figure 1: New mortgage debt as percent of after-tax personal income and real Federal Funds rate (US)

Sources: Bureau of Economic Analysis; Federal Reserve; Bureau of Labor Statistics

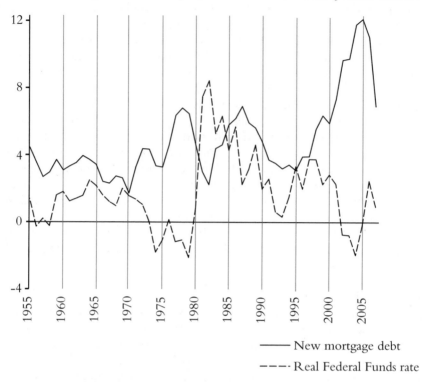

———— New mortgage debt

– – – – Real Federal Funds rate

funds from other banks, lend them out, and then pay back less than they had borrowed once inflation was taken into account.

By trying to keep the system afloat through this "cheap money, easy credit" strategy, the Fed created a new bubble. With stock prices having recently collapsed, this time the flood of money flowed at first largely into the housing market. Expressed as a percentage of after-tax income home mortgage borrowing more than doubled from 2000 to 2005, rising to levels far in excess of those seen previously. Loan funds were so ready to hand that working class people whose applications for mortgage loans would normally have been rejected were now able to obtain them. And lenders extended what became known as "liar loans", looking the other way when applicants for mortgages lied about their assets and incomes.

As Figure 1 shows, the trajectory of the mortgage borrowing to income ratio during the 2000–4 period is an almost perfect mirror image of the trajectory of the real federal funds rate. This is a clear indication of the close link between the explosion of mortgage borrowing and the easy credit conditions. And with new borrowing increasing so rapidly the ratio of outstanding mortgage debt to after-tax income, which had risen only modestly during the 1990s, jumped from 71 percent in 2000 to 103 percent in 2005 (see figure 2).[16]

Figure 2: Home mortgage debt as percent of after-tax personal income (US)
Sources: Bureau of Economic Analysis; Federal Reserve

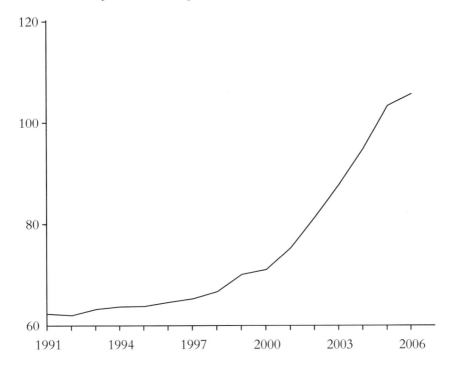

16: In principle these ratios could rise because of slower income growth, rather than because of a faster pace of mortgage borrowing, but that is not the case here. After-tax income increased by almost exactly the same average rate during the 2000–5 period as it did in the 1990s.

The additional money flooding the housing market in turn caused home prices to skyrocket. Indeed, total mortgage debt and home prices (as measured by the Case-Shiller Home Price Index) rose at almost exactly the same rates between start of 2000 and the end of 2005—100 percent and 102 percent, respectively.

Those of us who attempt, following Marx, to understand capitalism's economic crises as disturbances rooted in its system of production—value production—always face the problem that the market and production are not linked in a simple cause and effect manner. As a general rule, it is not the case that an event within the sphere of production causes an event that takes place in the market, such as an economic crisis. Instead what occurs in the sphere of production *conditions and sets limits* to what occurs in the market. And it is indisputable that, in this sense, the US housing crisis has its roots in the system of production. The increases in home prices were far in excess of the flow of value from new production that alone could guarantee repayment of the mortgages in the long run. The new value created in production is ultimately the sole source of all income—including homeowners' wages, salaries and other income—and therefore it is the sole basis upon which the repayment of mortgages ultimately rests.

But from 2000 to 2005 after-tax income (not adjusted for inflation) rose just 34.7 percent, barely one third of the increase in home prices. This is precisely why the real-estate bubble proved to be a bubble. A rise in asset prices or expansion of credit is never excessive in itself. It is excessive only *in relation to* the underlying flow of value. Non-Marxist economists and financial analysts may use different language to describe these relationships, but they do not dispute them. Indeed, it is commonplace to assess whether homes are over or under-priced by looking at whether their prices are high or low in relation to the underlying flow of income.

In retrospect, it may seem surprising that the sharp rise in home prices was not generally recognised at the time to be a bubble. But that is the case with every bubble. And some players in the mortgage market did realise that something was amiss but nonetheless sought to quickly reap lush profits and then protect themselves before the day of reckoning arrived. Moreover, there was a good reason (or what seemed at the time to be a good reason) why others failed to perceive that the boom times were unsustainable: home prices in the US had never fallen on a national level, at least not since the Great Depression.

So it was "natural" to assume that home prices would keep rising. This assumption served to allay misgivings over the fact that a lot of money was being lent out to homeowners who were less than credit-worthy, and in the form of risky subprime mortgages. Had home prices continued to go up, homeowners who had trouble making mortgage payments would have been able to get the additional funds they needed by borrowing against the increase in the value of their homes, and the crisis would have been averted.

Even if home prices had levelled off or fallen only slightly, there probably would have been no crisis. In the light of the historical record the bond-rating agencies assumed, as their *worst case* scenario, that home prices would dip by a few percent. It was because of this assumption that they gave high ratings to a huge amount of pooled and repackaged mortgage debt (mortgage backed securities) that included subprime mortgages and the like. Today these securities are called "toxic"—very few investors are willing to touch them. But if the bond-rating agencies had been right about the worst case scenario, the investors who thought that they were buying safe, investment grade securities would indeed have reaped a decent profit.

As we now know, however, the bond-raters were wrong, massively wrong, and thus there is a massive mortgage market crisis. According to the latest Case-Shiller Index figures, between the peak in July 2006 and May of this year US home prices fell by 18.4 percent. The decline is accelerating—three quarters of it has occurred since August of 2007—and eight of the 20 metropolitan areas included in the index have already experienced declines of over 25 percent.

Along with the collapse of the housing bubble came an unexpected decline in the values of a whole gamut of mortgage backed securities, which were regarded as safe investments when the worst case scenario that was envisioned was for home prices to dip slightly.

But the crisis in the housing sector is not the sole cause of the financial crisis. Another factor is that the flow of cash from mortgage payments was packaged and repackaged as various kinds of derivatives. This made it nearly impossible to identify which mortgage loans were underlying these securities. But their value depends on whether the underlying loans are still likely to be repaid or not, so potential buyers of these securities do not actually know what the sellers are offering them. Former Treasury Secretary Paul O'Neill recently compared this to ten bottles of water, one of which contains poison. If you buy one, it is very likely that you are buying safe water, but who would take the chance?[17]

17: Quoted in "The Dis-integration Of The News", economicprincipals.com, 30 March 2008, www.economicprincipals.com/issues/2008.03.30/311.html

So, although the vast majority of the outstanding mortgage loans are likely to be repaid, potential investors became unwilling to take a chance. Thus the market for mortgage backed securities became "frozen", which impeded the ability of firms throughout a wide swath of the system to get the short-term cash they need to meet their obligations. This spring the government was forced to intervene in order to get the cash circulating again. At the time these moves, together with the Bear Stearns takeover, were widely regarded as sufficient to restore confidence in the US financial system. But the fear that surrounded the decline in Fannie Mae and Freddie Mac's share prices a few months later shows that the loss of confidence is more deeply rooted than had been thought.

What's next?

Although the current recession in the US economy has thus far been relatively mild, this situation could change quickly. The credit crunch seems to have begun in earnest only since April, and one-time tax rebate cheques issued shortly thereafter have thus far served to mask its effect. A boost in export spending during the last year has also propped up the US economy, but now that recession conditions have recently spread throughout Europe, foreign demand for US made products is likely to decline.

Any new manifestation of crisis in the financial sector is sure to lengthen and deepen the recession, and the longer and deeper the recession, the greater the chances of additional financial crises. A great deal depends on how much and how long home prices keep falling. Some forecasters think they have come close to hitting bottom. But the futures market based on the Case-Shiller Index is signalling an eventual decline of 33 percent, nearly double the decline to date. And financial analyst Meredith Whitney—who has become something of a "star" since she predicted (or went public with?) Citigroup's financial difficulties well in advance of the pack—forecasts that home prices will fall by about 40 percent. She argues that a 33 percent fall would only roll back home prices to the levels of 2002–3, but that they will have to fall further, since the rate of home ownership has since declined and mortgage loans on easy terms are no longer readily available.[18]

Another factor that threatens to exacerbate the economic downturn is the bursting of what *Fortune* magazine editor Geoff Colvin

---

18:   Meredith Whitney, television interview on CNBC, 4 August 2008.

Figure 3: Household debt service (required payments on mortgage and consumer debt) and personal saving as a percent of after-tax income (US)

Sources: Bureau of Economic Analysis (NIPA data); Federal Reserve

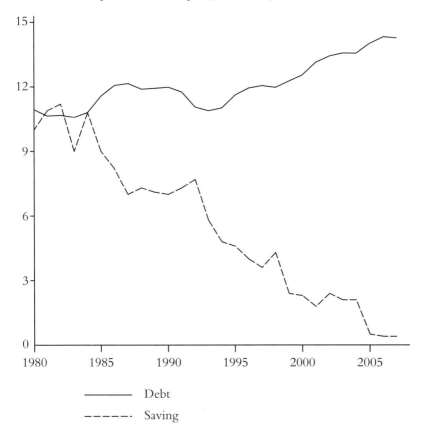

recently termed "the standard of living bubble".[19] For more than 20 years personal saving in the US has consistently fallen as a share of after-tax income. During the past three years consumers saved almost nothing (see figure 3). They have been able to save less because they have borrowed more. And until recently they often treated increases in the prices

---

19:   Geoff Colvin, "The Next Credit Crunch", *Fortune*, 20 April 2008, http://money.cnn.com/ 2008/08/18/news/economy/Colvin_next_credit_crunch.fortune/

of their homes and shares of stock as a kind of saving. But with a credit crunch under way, and home and share prices both about 20 percent below their peaks, it looks as though US consumers will finally have to live within their means and try to set aside some real money for the future. Such measures could cause consumer spending to be significantly depressed for some time to come.

The Fed and other government authorities have already had to intervene repeatedly in order to try to restore confidence in the financial system. Each time their intervention has succeeded—but only until the next eruption of the crisis of confidence. If one or more giant banks or investment houses fail, as Kenneth Rogoff has predicted, or if the financial crisis worsens in some other way, the government may not be able easily to borrow the funds it needs in order to make good on lenders' losses and thereby restore confidence. Eventually prospective lenders will question whether the US economy is strong enough for the government to meet its obligations. Or will it have to resort to paying lenders back by putting new money into circulation in excess of the new value that is created in production—in other words, to paying them back with Monopoly money? The US government can restore faith in the capitalist system only insofar as there is faith in the US government.

There are some signs that this faith is eroding. TJ Marta, a fixed income analyst at the Royal Bank of Canada's RBC Capital Markets, recently stated, "Anytime a person or a company or a country has excessive debt, they are considered a worse credit risk. Global investors remain very concerned about the US social security problem, the US shortfall in Medicare funding, the expenses for military operations and now they are hearing that the government might have to bail out the housing market. We are on the edge of a very bad crisis here".[20] Peter Schiff, head of EuroPacific Capital, a Connecticut-based brokerage that specialises in overseas investments, said that "America's 'AAA' [bond] rating has become a joke. I believe that the losses from Fannie and Freddie alone could reach $500 billion to $1 trillion. The US government will not be able to meet repayments on its debt once interest rates rise".[21]

The US government's recent state capitalist interventions are perhaps best described as the latest phase of what Marx called "the

20: "Treasurys Fall On Worries About Fannie, Freddie", available from www.fkcp.com/?p=6770 posted 12 July 2008.

21: Quoted in Ambrose Evans-Pritchard, "Dow Dives As Paulson Rules Out Rescue Of Loan Banks", *Daily Telegraph*, 12 July 2008.

abolition of the capitalist mode of production within the capitalist mode of production itself".[22] There is nothing private about the system any more except the titles to property. As the takeover of Bear Stearns and the rescue of Fannie Mae and Freddie Mac show, the government is not even intervening on behalf of private interests: it is intervening on behalf of the system itself. Such total alienation of an economic system from human interests of any sort is a clear sign that it needs to perish and make way for a higher social order.

The mainstream left in the United States no longer seriously believe this is possible, and so it has very little to say about the current crisis. For them, the only real alternatives are, on the one hand, the present system, on the other, economic chaos and disintegration. Thus their best option is to quietly become part of the new pragmatic Washington consensus. A recent editorial in *The Nation*, perhaps the biggest and most respected mainstream left publication, provides a striking example of this attitude. The editorial, entitled "For A New Economics",[23] lists problems including foreclosures, the credit crunch and job cuts. But the solutions given are "energy independence", "infrastructure programmes", investment in "job creation", and "health and retirement guarantees"—*The Nation* has nothing to say about how to get out of the crisis or how to keep it from happening again.

The current economic crisis is bringing misery to tens of millions of working people. But it is also bringing us a new opportunity to get rid of a system that is continually rocked by such crises. The financial crisis has caused so much panic in the financial world that the fundamental instability of capitalism is being acknowledged openly on the front pages and the op-ed columns of leading newspapers. We may soon be in a situation in which great numbers of people begin to search for an explanation of what has gone wrong and a different way of life. At the moment this possibility might be remote, but revolutionary socialists still need to prepare for it. We need to be prepared with a clear understanding of how capitalism works, and why it cannot be made to work for the vast majority. And we need to get serious about working out how an alternative to capitalism—one that is not just a different form of capitalism—might be a real possibility.

22: Marx, 1991, p569.
23: "For A New Economics", *The Nation*, 1/8 September 2008, www.thenation.com/doc/20080901/editors

References

Dunayevskaya, Raya, 2000, *Marxism and Freedom* (Humanity Books).

Kliman, Andrew, 2008, "Trying to Save Capitalism from Itself", 25 April 2008, http://marxisthumanismtoday.org/node/13 and www.thehobgoblin.co.uk/2008_11_AK_Economy.htm

Marx, Karl, 1991 [1894], *Capital*, volume three (Penguin). An alternative translation is available online at www.marxists.org/archive/marx/works/1894-c3/

Snapshots of union strengths and weaknesses

Chris Harman

Workers in Britain face the twin crises of recession and inflation with union organisation that has, in general, been on the retreat for nearly 30 years. A complacent attitude to the problem of rebuilding union strength and organising new groups of workers would clearly be misplaced. However, the frequently repeated claim that unions have declined to the extent that they no longer matter is also false. The strengths, as well as the weaknesses, are brought out by the latest survey published by National Statistics.[1]

Two slightly different sets of figures show the long-term decline in union strength. The first gives overall union membership since the mid-1970s as calculated by the Certification Office (figure 1). The second gives the density of union membership (the proportion of workers belonging to unions) based on the Labour Force Survey (figure 2).[2]

These figures need to be seen in a long-term perspective. Despite the decline, the proportion of workers in a union remains higher than it was just before two of the great upsurges of class struggle in the 20th century: the Great Unrest and the explosion of militancy in 1919-20. This is shown clearly by figure 3.

In fact, the only period with a sustained union density higher than today was that of the long post-war boom and the few years that followed the end of this boom.

1: Mercer and Notley, 2008.
2: On the differences, see Mercer and Notley, 2008, p47.

Figure 1: Trade union membership figures, 1975–2005/6
Source: Mercer and Notley, 2008

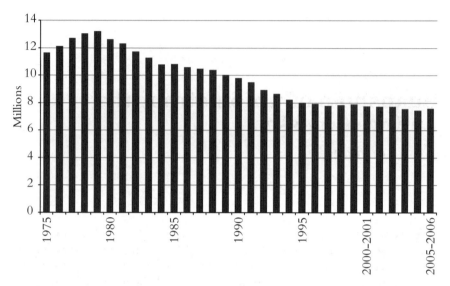

Figure 2: Trade union density, 1995–2007
Source: Mercer and Notley, 2008

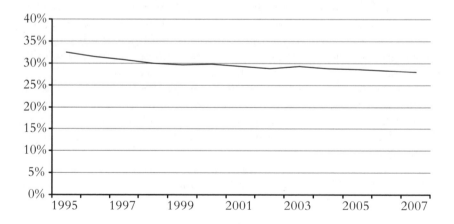

Figure 3: Proportion of workers in a union, 1900-2000
Source: Lindsay, 2003

The media makes much of the weakness of unions in the private sector, in which only about one in seven workers are unionised. Membership is certainly lower here than in the public sector (see figure 4). The media interprets this as meaning that unions in the private sector are powerless. But the figures for union density alone can underestimate the spread of membership and influence. This is shown by the relatively high proportion of workplaces covered by collective bargaining agreements and the still higher proportion (close to half) with some union members in them (figure 5).

A more detailed look at the figures, industry by industry, shows that some important parts of the private sector have high concentrations of union membership (figure 6). Over 40 percent of workers in electricity, gas and water supply, and in transport, storage and communications are unionised. Some union members are present in 75 percent and 60 percent of workplaces in these industries respectively.

The position is far worse in manufacturing, where a little over 20 percent of workers are in unions (about the same proportion, surprisingly, as in "financial intermediation"). The relatively low figure for manufacturing reflects the loss of two thirds of the jobs in the sector since the early 1970s, with the closure of such bastions of union organisation as the Sheffield steel

Figure 4: Union density by sector, 1995–2007
Source: Mercer and Notley, 2008

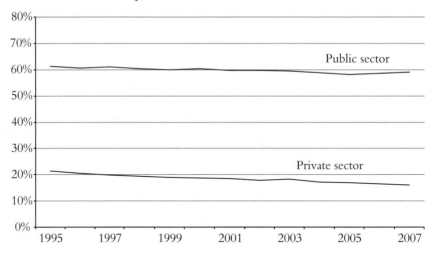

Figure 5: Union density, presence and collective agreement coverage
Source: Grainger, 2006

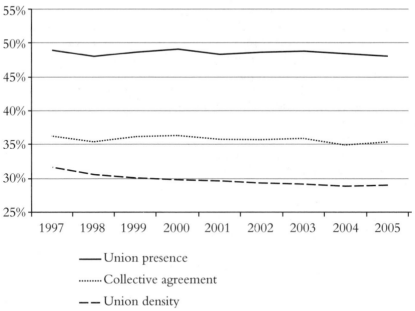

Figure 6: Union density and presence by industry, 2007
Source: Mercer and Notley, 2008

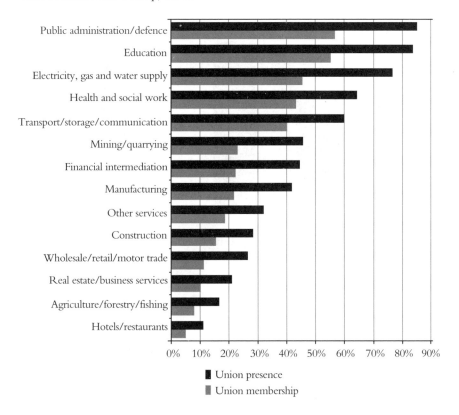

industry, Rover in Birmingham and the Ford assembly plant in Dagenham. Unionisation still exists among Britain's three million remaining manufacturing workers (including in the car industry, which has as high an output as before, but which is now largely concentrated in Japanese owned plants with few traditions of militancy). More than two in five manufacturing workplaces contain some union members, and 30 percent of "process, plant and machine operatives" are union members.[3]

Three very important interrelated factors influence the likelihood of someone being in a union. The first is age (figure 7). Middle aged

---

3: A breakdown of union density by occupation, as opposed to sector, is given in Mercer and Notley, 2008.

Figure 7: Trade union density by age

Source: Mercer and Notley, 2008

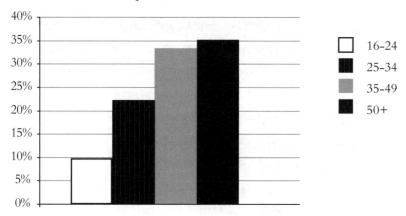

Figure 8: Trade union density by length of service

Source: Mercer and Notley, 2008

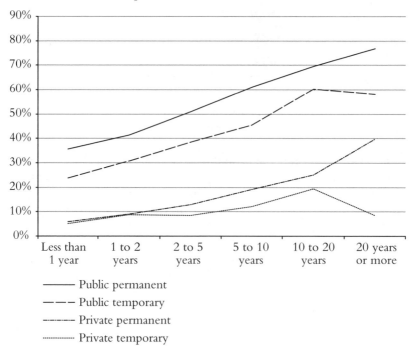

workers are one and a half times as likely to be in unions as those in their late 20s and early 30s—and more than three times as likely as young workers.

The chart giving union density for people who have been working in the same place for different periods of time shows a similar pattern (figure 8). In both the private and public sectors, workers who have been in the same job for ten years are much more likely to be union members than those with only one year's service. For those who have been in private sector jobs for 25 years, that is, since before the defeat of the miners and print workers in the mid-1980s, membership rates are comparable to those during the long boom of the 1950s and 1960s.

This trend is important. It means that traditions of unionisation still exist within the workforce and with them the potential for unions to regain their old strength. One other important set of figures confirms this—those measuring union strength by size of workplace. Table 1 gives the data for England—similar figures apply elsewhere in Britain.

Table 1: Union density by size of workplace, England, Q4 2007
Source: Mercer and Notley, 2008

Workplace size	Union density (percent)
Less than 50	16.6
50 or more	35.7

In medium and large workplaces average union membership still remains at a high level, despite the relatively low level of strikes in the past two decades compared with the two decades before them.

Dispelling myths

Recent figures for union membership also dispel another widespread myth: that the unions are a male domain (a myth summed up by some middle class feminists in the 1970s who talked of unions being the "men's movement"). Today female workers are more likely than male workers to be union members—with a union density of 29.6 percent compared to 26.4 percent for men.

Another widespread claim is also proven to be mistaken: that part-time workers form an "insecure" or "precarious" layer in the working class which cannot be organised. Most part-time workers are, in fact, permanent workers. More than two out of every five are union members. Table 2 breaks down the figures for union density.

Table 2: Union density by gender and by part-time/full-time status, UK, Q4 2007
Source: Mercer and Notley, 2008

	All workers	Gender		Status	
		Male	Female	Full-time	Part-time
Union density	28.0	26.4	29.6	30.1	21.9

Other figures show that even workers who really do suffer from temporary employment can be unionised—"precariousness" is not an absolute barrier to organisation. Some 16 percent of temporary workers are union members—34.8 percent of those in the public sector and 6.7 percent of those in the private sector. Here the figures point to both a potential for organisation and the low level of its realisation.

Unions are also far from being organisations of a supposed "white working class". Union density is at a similar level for black and white workers, and is only a few percent lower for Asian workers. The most strongly organised group are black women (figure 9).

Workers of all sorts gain significantly from union membership. Average earnings for union members are 15 percent higher than for non-union members—although the difference is greater in the public than private sector. Figure 10 gives the "wage premium"—the percentage difference in average hourly earnings for union members and non-union members.

Unevenness and possibilities
Union membership is unevenly distributed within Britain's working class today. That does not only apply to the gap between the public and private sector union presence. There is also unevenness between those employed workers for whom life under capitalism is very bad and those for whom it is slightly better—with those for whom it is worse having, on average, the lowest levels of union organisation.

National Statistics groups together different occupations into various

Figure 9: Union density by gender and race, 2007

Source: Mercer and Notley, 2008

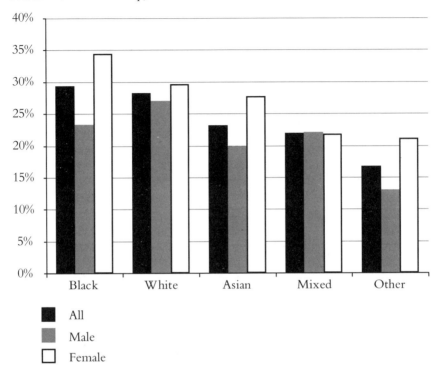

categories. Those with the highest levels of union organisation are those just below managers in its scale: the occupations it labels "professional" and "associate professional and technical occupations". These are rag bag categories, drawing together quite different occupations. So the "professionals" include all teachers as well as doctors and lawyers, while the "associate professional and technical" include nurses and similar health service grades, social workers, computer technicians, firefighters, train drivers and lower ranking police officers.

Their level of union organisation is more than twice as high as that of "elementary occupations" (another rag bag category mainly consisting of labourers, dockers, refuse collectors and waiters, but also including postal workers and printing machine minders), and between three and four times the level of those in sales and customer service (table 3).

Figure 10: Average union "wage premium", 1995–2007
Source: Mercer and Notley, 2008

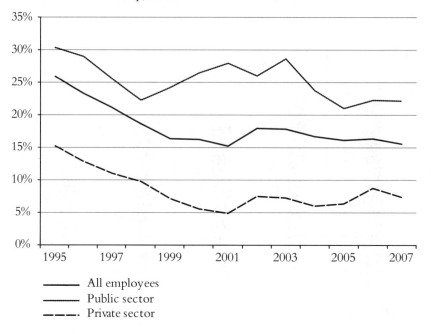

- ———— All employees
- ———— Public sector
- – – –. Private sector

Table 3: Union density by employment category, UK, Q4 2007
Source: Mercer and Notley, 2008

Category	Union density
Managers and senior officials	17.4
Professional occupations	47.1
Associate professional and technical occupations	41.5
Administrative and secretarial occupations	22.8
Skilled trade occupations	24.7
Personal service occupations	30.4
Sales and customer service occupations	12.2
Process, plant and machine operatives	29.9
Elementary occupations	20.3

The same divergence in average levels of unionisation is shown by educational qualification in table 4.

Table 4: Union density by highest qualification, UK, Q4 2007
Source: Mercer and Notley, 2008

Highest qualification	Union density
Degree or equivalent	36.0
Other higher education	40.5
A level or equivalent	25.5
GCSE grades A to C or equivalent	22.5
Other qualifications	21.6
No qualifications	20.4

These two tables indicate the concentration of union membership in white collar public sector jobs. Groups of workers who once thought of themselves as middle class have been proletarianised in recent decades. Only 40 years ago the National Union of Teachers rejected affiliation to the TUC in a ballot. Teachers held their first strike 39 years ago. The change in attitude by such groups of workers should blow apart New Labour's claim that the way to win support from "middle England" is to reject union demands.

However, the figures also point to the weakness of the unions when it comes to organising the traditional manual working class (which still makes up almost half of the workforce) and the growing numbers in low level, white collar employment in the private sector.

The same weakness is reflected in the low union membership among those earning less than £250 a week: 17.5 percent, compared to 41.9 percent for those earning between £500 and £999 a week.

There is nothing new in the concentration of unions within the sections of the working class that suffer a little less than most—even if it seems strange to those of us who are old enough to remember teachers wearing mortar boards and civil servants bowler hats. Skilled rather than unskilled workers have usually managed to hold their union organisation together through periods of defeat or demoralisation. They have been under less pressure, with more time and energy to devote to union matters.

But there has always been a danger that the more skilled also hold on to "labour aristocrat" attitudes that treat with disdain the mass of semi-skilled and unskilled workers. The danger today is that union activism can be concentrated in areas such as education, the health service, local government or the civil service—cut off from the majority of workers. Sometimes activism is even focused on those who have been drawn into playing a semi-managerial role (union membership among of female managers runs at 37.4 percent, higher than membership for non-managerial or non-supervisory roles).

The dynamics of union growth

This briefing gives snapshots of a dynamic process. Unions do not simply recruit and hold on to members. There is a continual turnover of members, with new, usually younger, people getting jobs and others, usually older, leaving them. There are also transformations in the structure of employment and of the potentially unionisable workforce with every change in the structure of capitalism—and with each economic crisis (we are now entering the fifth in 35 years). Finally, the very instability and unpredictability of the system leads to sudden changes in the willingness of workers to challenge their bosses and cause union organisation to break through in new sectors of industry. It was such upsurges in militancy that explained the sudden spells of union growth after 1889, 1912, 1919 and the late 1960s. Today, whenever strikes take place, the result is a rush of workers to join unions.

It was not, in any of the upsurges in the past, established union leaderships that led to new sectors being organised. Unions are bureaucratic organisations, with career structures for officials that encourage them to prefer certainties of established routines to the risks of struggle, or even to the effort involved in recruiting new union members—with occasional very important exceptions. So upsurges of militant struggle generally *preceded* the growth of unions. Likewise the defeats, such as those of the general strike in 1926 and of the miners in 1985, precipitated big declines.

The struggles always had a strong spontaneous element. Nevertheless, socialist activists played an important role at each stage of the upsurges— Tom Mann, John Burns, Will Thorne and Eleanor Marx in the late 1880s; the syndicalists (again including Tom Mann) during the Great Unrest of 1912-4; the shop stewards movement during the First World War; and those involved in the rank and file groupings in various unions and industries in the late 1960s and early 1970s.

No one can say with certainty how various sections of the working

Figure 11: Working days lost due to labour disputes, 1901–2001
Source: Lindsay, 2003

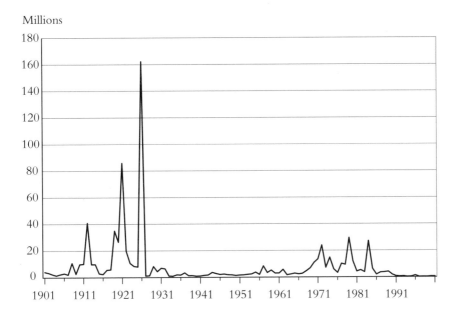

class in Britain will react to the combination of recession and inflation, which is cutting real living standards of those with jobs for the first time for a generation, alongside deep disillusion with the Labour government.

The long decline in union organisation means many sectors are still suffering the hangover from the defeats of the 1980s and successive waves of restructuring. But the figures presented here show that a large proportion of workers are still committed to the ideals of trade unionism, even in workplaces and sectors where unions barely exist. The possibility of an explosion of anger remains, as shown by big recent votes for industrial action in the public sector and flashes of militancy in the private sector. The job of revolutionary socialists is to try to do something few union officials will—to give direction to the anger, draw in new groups of workers, rebuild organisation and infuse the unions with a different politics to that of the Labour Party.

References

Grainger, Heidi, 2006, *Trade Union Membership 2005*, Department for Business, Enterprise and Regulationary Reform (National Statistics), www.berr.gov.uk/files/file25737.pdf.

Lindsay, Craig, 2003, "A Century of Labour Market Change: 1900 to 2000", *Labour Market Trends*, volume III, number 3 (National Statistics), www.statistics.gov.uk/downloads/theme_labour/LMT_March03_revised.pdf

Mercer, Sally, and Richard Notley, 2008, *Trade Union Membership 2007*, Department for Business, Enterprise and Regulationary Reform (National Statistics), http://stats.berr.gov.uk/UKSA/tu/tum2008.pdf

Where is the radical left going?

Alex Callinicos

The past decade has seen the emergence of a new left, particularly in Europe. Fragile and uneven though this process has been, it represents a real attempt to develop a progressive alternative to neoliberalism, war and indeed capitalism itself, giving a political voice to the new movements of resistance that have developed since the Seattle protests of November 1999. The convergence of these movements and the radical left, and the political horizons this seemed to open up were perhaps most visible at the first European Social Forum (ESF) at Florence in November 2002. This took place between the mass protests against the G8 summit in Genoa in July 2001 and the giant global demonstrations against the invasion of Iraq on 15 February 2003. At the largest and most euphoric "seminar" 10,000 people packed into a hall to hear leading representatives of the radical left—most notably Fausto Bertinotti, general secretary of the Partito della Rifondazione Comunista (PRC) and Olivier Besancenot, chief spokesman of the Ligue Communiste Révolutionnaire (LCR)—discuss the relationship between social movements and political parties.[1]

Diverging paths

That heady moment seems very distant now. In the past couple of years the fortunes of the radical left have diverged sharply. The most important case on the negative side was provided by the PRC itself. The party of Genoa and

---

1: For an assessment at an earlier stage of the radical left's development, see Callinicos, 2004.

Florence moved from 2004 onwards sharply to the right, denouncing the resistance to the Anglo-American occupation of Iraq as fascist and joining the centre-left coalition government of Romano Prodi that held office briefly in 2006-8. PRC deputies and senators voted for Prodi's neoliberal economic programme, and for the participation of Italian troops in the occupation of Afghanistan and in the United Nations "peacekeeping" mission to Lebanon.[2] In April 2007 the PRC leadership expelled a far-left senator, Franco Turigliatto, for voting against government foreign policy. Despite the PRC's participation in a new "Rainbow" formation with other elements on the left of the governing coalition, it was punished in the general elections of April 2008 for its association with a disastrous government. Amid a crushing victory for the right under Silvio Berlusconi, the Rainbow won only 3.1 percent of the vote, compared to 5.8 percent for the PRC alone two years earlier, and lost all its parliamentary seats. Bertinotti, unceremoniously deprived of the presidency of the Chamber of Deputies to which he had been elevated under Prodi, announced his retirement from politics.

The radical left also suffered reverses elsewhere. In Britain first the Scottish Socialist Party and then Respect split: when the rival fragments ran against each other, both sides predictably suffered electoral eclipse.[3] In the Danish general election of November 2007 the Red-Green Alliance lost two of the six seats it had previously held. The setbacks were not confined to Europe. In South Korea the Democratic Labour Party, formed in 2000 and closely linked to the Korean Confederation of Trade Unions, suffered a right wing breakaway after the 2007 presidential elections. In Australia the Democratic Socialist Perspective, the far-left organisation that had been the driving force behind the Socialist Alliance electoral regroupment, also experienced a split in May 2008, an issue in which was the failure of the alliance to make a breakthrough. In Brazil the Party of Socialism and Liberty (PSol), formed in 2004 after the ruling Workers Party expelled five far-left parliamentarians, has been weakened by the willingness of Heloísa Helena, its candidate in the 2006 presidential elections, to collaborate with the right over issues such as political corruption and abortion.

Fortunately, there are more positive experiences. The most exciting of these has been the initiative taken by the LCR to launch a New Anti-Capitalist Party (Nouveau Parti Anticapitaliste, NPA). This followed Besancenot's emergence during and after the French presidential elections of April-May 2007 as the most credible and popular voice of opposition to Nicolas Sarkozy's

---

2:    Trudell, 2007.
3:    See Gonzalez, 2006, and Harman, 2008a.

attempt to drive France rightwards. Around 800 delegates representing some 300 initiative committees for the NPA met in Paris on 28 and 29 June 2008.[4] On one estimate, the committees organised around 10,000 activists—going, therefore, well beyond the ranks of the LCR, which has a membership of about 3,500. In an opinion poll conducted in July 2008, 62 percent rated Besancenot positively and 7 to 8 percent intended to vote for his party.[5]

In Germany Die Linke, officially constituted as a party in June 2007 and the result of a convergence between dissident social democrats in western Germany and the Party of Democratic Socialism (PDS), the heir of the old East German ruling party, continues to make electoral inroads into the base of the German Social Democratic Party (SPD). By the time of its second congress in May 2008 Die Linke claimed around 75,000 members. In Greece the radical left coalition Synaspismos has soared in the opinion polls as a result of the crisis of both the centre-right government and the Blairite opposition Pan-Hellenic Socialist Movement (Pasok).

And even in Italy, the country that has seen the most catastrophic collapse of the radical left, the trend is not uniformly negative. In reaction to electoral eclipse the PRC national congress, when it met in July 2008, moved left. Bertinotti and his allies were defeated by a coalition of left wing currents led by Paolo Ferrero. The delegates, elected by meetings attended by 40,000 members, voted for a document calling for "a shift to the left" and declaring an end to "organic collaboration [with the centre-left Democratic Party] in governing the country". It continued:

> It is important to recover the idea that the opposition is not merely a collocation in the political spectrum but must be a phase of reconstruction, of taking root, of social relations, of cultural and political battles. In the crisis of capitalistic globalisation, the alternative has to be built through social and political struggle against the Berlusconi government, the projects of Confindustria [the employers' organisation] and fundamentalist outlooks. Within this perspective, it is indispensable to strengthen the alternative left through the collaboration between the diverse anti-capitalist, communist and leftist movements; aggregating the collective and individual realities which are found outside of political parties in diverse social, cultural and labour strata.[6]

4: Hayes, 2008.
5: Zappi, 2008.
6: Rifondazione, 2008.

The primacy of politics

Nevertheless, the sense of participating in a general forward movement that prevailed a few years ago has been replaced by a marked divergence. What has caused this shift? To answer this question we need to understand the driving forces behind the rise of the radical left, particularly in Europe. Two main objective coordinates were involved. First, the emergence of mass resistance to neoliberalism and war, starting with the French public sector strikes of 1995 but gaining momentum after the 1999 Seattle protests. Second, the experience of "social liberalism" as social democratic governments, brought to office all over Europe in the second half of the 1990s by popular opposition to neoliberalism, proceeded to implement neoliberal policies, and in some cases—New Labour under Tony Blair in Britain and the Red-Green coalition headed by Gerhard Schröder in Germany—to go further than their conservative predecessors had dared.[7]

The rightward shift of mainstream social democracy opened up a space to its left. Furthermore, the revival of resistance created a pressure to fill this space. Various political formations took on the role of trying to fill it. They were of very diverse origins and histories—some already established, such as the PRC and the LCR, others very new, for example, the SSP and the Portuguese Left Bloc, yet others only formed in response to the new situation, such as Respect and Die Linke. Generally they did not attempt to fill the space on the left on the basis of an explicitly revolutionary programme. Hence the name that came to be attached to them—"radical left", which implied a break with the mainstream centre-left but not a commitment to socialist revolution.

In some cases this reflected a tactical decision by far-left organisations to attract allies and a broader audience. But as often it was a consequence of the fact that many of the leaders of the new formations were themselves reformists, often seeking to restore a more "authentic" social democracy that, as they saw it, had been corrupted by the likes of Blair and Schröder. Thus George Galloway, who helped to found Respect in 2004 after being expelled from the Labour Party for opposing the Iraq War, said of Blair, "If he breaks the Labour Party, the need for a labour party will not have gone away. Some of us will be prepared to rebuild a labour party from the wreckage".[8]

The emergence of this radical left marked an extremely important and positive development. It represented an opportunity to remake the left

---

7: See the analysis of the early stages of this process in Callinicos, 1999.
8: Galloway, 2003.

on a much more principled basis than had prevailed in the heyday of the social democratic and Stalinist parties. From the perspective of the new movements of resistance, it marked an important strategic shift, towards intervention in the political field.[9] But this, while a step forward, generated its own problems. In the first place, politics has its own logic, which subjects to its hazards and contingencies all those who try to grapple with it. This is most obvious in the case of the constraints imposed by electoral systems, which in most bourgeois democracies work severely to the disadvantage of the small parties of the radical left.

Second, the various radical left formations were confronted with the question of how to continue in an environment that was somewhat less favourable to that of the forward momentum of the initial period. The initial period was bounded roughly by the years 1998, when left opposition to social liberalism first became visible, and 2005, when Respect made its greatest advance with Galloway's election as MP for Bethnal Green & Bow and the European Constitution was defeated in the French and Dutch referendums. But after this period the radical left was forced to come to terms with one in which the mass opposition to the war in Iraq was receding, while the anti-capitalist movement had undergone a significant decline due to its failure to address important problems effectively.[10]

The response of the radical left formations was, of course, conditioned by the politics prevailing in them. This proved in the case of two key figures—Bertinotti and Galloway—to be a reformism that began to shift rightwards. Bertinotti's reaction to the decline of the social forums that had spread throughout Italy after Genoa, and driven the mobilisations for Florence and the anti-war protests, was to turn back towards the centre-left with the disastrous consequences already noted. The retreat was imperfectly concealed behind a cloud of radical rhetoric exploiting the vagueness and ambiguity of the autonomist Marxism that continues heavily to influence the Italian movement.

In the case of Galloway and the circle around him the decline of the anti-war movement from the peak it achieved in 2003 combined with pessimism about the capacity of organised workers to mount effective resistance to the attacks mounted by New Labour and the bosses. The conclusion was that the way forward for Respect lay in sustaining alliances with local Muslim notables who could deliver votes. But this reasoning—and

9: Kouvélakis, 2005.
10: Callinicos and Nineham, 2007.

the split that it produced in Respect—was overlain by a growing recon-
ciliation between Galloway himself and New Labour. This was reflected
first in his support for Ken Livingstone's unsuccessful re-election campaign
for Mayor of London in May 2008 and then in his rallying to the aid of
Gordon Brown's beleaguered government during the Glasgow East parliamentary by-election that July, when a Blairite candidate was defeated by a
massive swing to the Scottish National Party.[11]

Elsewhere the politics has played out better, so far. The
majority in the LCR leadership seized the initiative amid general disarray on the French left reflected, for example, in the crisis in the main
anti-globalisation coalition, Attac. They ran Besancenot in the first round
of the French presidential elections in April 2007 and then, capitalising on
his relative success (winning 4.08 percent of the vote despite the general
rout of the left), launched the NPA.[12] Die Linke is a much more solidly
reformist formation than anything envisaged by the LCR. It is, however,
defined by the struggle between two tendencies—a right wing, powerful both numerically and in the apparatus, constituted largely by the
ex-leadership of the PDS, and a more left reformist current dominated
by the ex-SPD trade union officials clustered around the figure of Oskar
Lafontaine. From a historical perspective, the latter group is extremely
significant, since it represents a fracture in the most powerful social democratic party in the world.

Lafontaine is a former party chairman and chancellor candidate
for the SPD, and was briefly its finance minister in 1998-9, till he was
driven from office by a big business campaign. He is pursuing a project
of reconstituting German social democracy on a more left wing basis. In
his speech at Die Linke's national congress in May 2008 he denounced
the SPD leader Friedrich Ebert for betraying the German Revolution of
November 1918, invoked Karl Liebknecht and Rosa Luxemburg, and
quoted not only Karl Marx and Frederick Engels but the Marxist philosophers Walter Benjamin, Theodor Adorno and Max Horkheimer—a
rather unusual list of authorities for any social democratic politician to
cite. More concretely, Lafontaine pledged Die Linke to opposition to
war and to Nato, condemned the massive repression of wages suffered
by German workers in recent years, and called for the strict regulation of
financial markets.[13]

11:    See for example Galloway, July 2008.
12:    On the crisis in Attac, see Wintrebert, 2007.
13:    Lafontaine, 2008.

What kind of party?

The recent advances of Die Linke and the LCR show that the objective coordinates responsible for the initial rise of the radical left remain. But the experiences of the PRC and Respect highlight the political dangers faced by these formations. How can these dangers best be addressed? The response of the LCR is particularly interesting. It is influenced by the negative examples of centre-left governments, not only in Italy, but in France itself and in Brazil. Lionel Jospin's plural left government (1997-2002) corralled together the Socialist, Communist and Green parties to implement a social-liberal programme that involved the privatisation of €36.4 billion worth of state enterprises, more than its six predecessor governments combined.[14]

The experience of the Workers Party in Brazil since the victory of its leader, Lula, in the 2002 presidential election is an especially galling one for the LCR. Democrazia Socialista (DS), then the Brazilian section of the Fourth International, decided to participate in Lula's government, despite his continuing a more rigorous version of the neoliberal economic policies pursued by the previous president, Fernando Henrique Cardoso. The resulting controversy led the DS eventually to break with the Fourth International, in which the LCR is very much the dominant force.

Determination to avoid any repetition of a situation where the radical left could be integrated into a social-liberal coalition government shaped the response of the LCR majority towards the attempt to make the collectives that had driven the No campaign against the European Constitution in 2005 the launch pad for a unitary "anti-liberal" candidate in the 2007 presidential campaign.[15] The LCR leadership took the line that the very broad spectrum of forces involved in the No collectives—ranging from the left wing of the Socialist Party and the Communist Party through various anti-globalisation coalitions to the Ligue itself—was politically incoherent. More specifically, and crucially, the reformist currents involved would not rule out participation in a centre-left government, raising the spectre of another plural left coalition. The LCR's scepticism about the project of a unitary "anti-liberal" candidate led to a negative and sometimes ultimatist attitude towards the collectives, which caused its isolation in the period

14: Phillip Gordon, "Liberté! Fraternité! Anxiety", *Financial Times*, 19 January 2002.
15: The LCR has an institutionalised regime of rival political tendencies that for many years has pitted the majority of the leadership against a right wing faction led by Christian Piquet. The right are in now in disarray, partly because they supported the now discredited unitary candidacy approach, and partly because the NPA initiative has united the rest of the Ligue behind the old majority.

before the efforts to find a candidate collapsed in early 2007. But the Ligue was at least partially vindicated by the behaviour of José Bové, who, after running in the first round on behalf of the rump of the collectives, associated himself with Ségolène Royal, the Socialist Party right winger defeated by Sarkozy in the run-off.

It is to ward off this kind of danger that the LCR insists that the new party must be anti-capitalist and not simply opposed to neoliberalism ("anti-liberal" is the term used in France):

> The question of power profoundly divides the so-called anti-liberal left. Every party must pose to itself the question of power, and we can't make ourselves an exception to this rule. The question is to know in which framework, for whose benefit. For us, the question is to move from a situation where a minority decides and imposes its choices, its profits, and its privileges, to a situation where the greatest number take over the political and economic levers for managing society. We don't desire power for ourselves but as an instrument of a movement from below...a powerful social movement, a May 1968 that goes to the end, that begins to control the direction of the economy.
>
> The institutions are essential elements for maintaining social order and capitalist property. We don't want to build a party of management but a party of rupture. That's why independence from the Socialist Party is a key question. Liberal capitalism and anti-capitalism can't cohabit in the same government. Our perspective is thus not to unite the left as it exists today, or some of its fragments, but to build a social and political movement of the majority for a rupture with capitalism. Then the question of power will be posed![16]

So what precisely is this anti-capitalist party? It is, the same LCR text says, "a party for the revolutionary transformation of society", yet not a revolutionary party in the specific sense in which it has been understood in the classical Marxist tradition.[17] In that tradition, socialist revolution is assumed to take a particular form, particularly as a result of the experiences of the Russian Revolution of October 1917 and the early years of the Communist International (1919-24). It involves mass strikes, the development of dual power counterposing institutions

---

16: LCR, 2008.
17: See, on the LCR's conception of the NPA, Sabado, 2008.

of workers' democracy to the capitalist state, an armed insurrection to resolve this crisis by establishing the dominance of the workers' councils, and, running through all this, the emergence of a mass revolutionary party with majority support in the working class. This broad conception of the revolutionary process is common to both the Fourth International and the International Socialist Tendency, to which the Socialist Workers Party belongs.[18]

On the LCR's view, the NPA should not commit itself to this specific understanding of revolution, but simply to the necessity of "a rupture with capitalism". If this notion may seem vague, its political significance lies in what it rules out. Specifically, the Ligue correctly argues, it is necessary to oppose capitalism as a system, not simply neoliberalism as a set of policies. Failing to draw this distinction can lead to participation in centre-left governments in the hope (usually the illusion) that they will produce a more benign mix of policies.[19]

There is much to commend the LCR's conception of the NPA. Not only are they correct in insisting on the difference between anti-(neo)liberalism and anti-capitalism, but it is also right not to make explicit commitment to the revolutionary Marxist tradition the basis of the new party. This is for long-term strategic reasons. The political experience of the 20th century shows very clearly that in the advanced capitalist countries it is impossible to build a mass revolutionary party without breaking the hold of social democracy over the organised working class. In the era of the Russian Revolution it was possible for many European communist parties to begin to do this by splitting social democratic parties and winning substantial numbers of previously reformist workers directly to the revolutionary programme of the Communist International. October 1917 exercised an enormous attractive power on everyone around the world who wanted to fight the bosses and imperialism.

Alas, thanks to the experience of Stalinism, the opposite is true today. Social liberalism is repelling many working class people today, but, in the first instance, what they seek is a more genuine version of the reformism that their traditional parties once promised them. Therefore, if the formations of the radical left are to be habitable to these refugees from social

---

18: There is a detailed discussion of the Fourth International's version in Mandel, 1979, chapter I, while the SWP's is restated in Harman, 2007. Henceforth, by "revolutionaries" I mean, not the adherents of a specific current, say the International Socialist Tendency or the Fourth International, but those who continue to support this conception of the revolutionary process.

19: See, for example, Harman, 2008b.

democracy, their programmes must not foreclose the debate between reform and revolution by simply incorporating the distinctive strategic conceptions developed by revolutionary Marxists.[20]

All the same, navigating between the Scylla of opportunism and the Charybdis of sectarianism is never easy. On the one hand, drawing the dividing line between anti-liberalism and anti-capitalism isn't necessarily straightforward. Given that, as the LCR would put it, anti-capitalism has "incomplete strategic delimitations"—ie it leaves open how the "rupture with capitalism" would be achieved—there is plenty of room for debate about what concrete steps are necessary. There are perfectly respectable left-reformist strategies for achieving a break with capitalism that presumably would have a right to a hearing in these debates. But—and here is where the complication arises—these strategies merge in with proposals that seek to target neoliberalism rather than capitalism itself. For example, on its own, the Tobin Tax on international financial transactions that is advocated by Die Linke and Attac is not an anti-capitalist measure. But it is perfectly possible to imagine how a real struggle for the Tobin Tax could develop into a confrontation with capital itself, and some of those who advocate it may well welcome such a prospect. The last serious wave of left reformism in the 1970s, associated with Tony Benn in Britain and Jean-Pierre Chevènement in France, sought, not to expropriate capital, but to use the state to harness it to socialist objectives.[21]

On the other hand, while the LCR are entirely right to oppose as a matter of principle participation in a centre-left government, they can't assume that everyone attracted to the NPA will share this attitude. On the contrary, many of them may want to see Besancenot in government. In an August 2008 poll 18 percent said the Socialist Party should come to an understanding with him.[22] In Germany Lafontaine's project of a Red-Red government on his terms, ie of a coalition with the SPD in which Die Linke sets the agenda, will make a lot of sense to many of those rebelling against social liberalism. They are mistaken about this—in all probability such a government would, like the British Labour governments of the early post-war period or François Mitterrand's presidency in 1981-3, crumble under the pressures imposed on it by capital.

It is important that revolutionaries warn against the dangers posed

---

20: For an exchange on these issues, see Bensaïd and others, 2003, especially pp15-19, and Callinicos, 2003.
21: For example, Holland, 1976.
22: Zappi. 2008.

by the radical left participating in centre-left governments. But they should not make the fact that these formations, if they are successful, will confront the problem of participation a reason for not building them now. This is, in effect, the line taken by the German section of the Committee for a Workers' International,[23] who sought to split the west German precursor of Die Linke because of the PDS's participation in social liberal coalitions in Berlin and elsewhere.

The role of revolutionaries

The underlying problem at work here is that it is the breach in reformism that has given the radical left its opening. How then does it try to draw in people from a reformist background while avoiding the betrayals of reformism—betrayals recapitulated in a highly concentrated way by Bertinotti's trajectory? The LCR's solution to the problem seems to be to install a kind of programmatic security lock—commitment to anti-capitalism and opposition to centre-left governments. But this is unlikely to work: the more successful the NPA, the more it is likely to come under reformist pressures and temptations.

One very important question in addressing this problem concerns the role played by organised revolutionary socialists within the formations of the radical left. One widely discussed answer has been provided by the model offered by the Scottish Socialist Party (SSP). Here existing far left organisations dissolved themselves to form a unitary socialist party. Different political currents were permitted to form organised platforms, though not to conduct open political propaganda. But the SSP had a programme with "incomplete strategic delimitations" and so was avowedly open to those with reformist politics (though the sectarian and dismissive attitude it took towards those from a Labourist background tended to inhibit this in practice). Defenders of the SSP model argued that the party would not capitulate to reformist influences thanks to the "leadership of revolutionaries". But this begged the question of how this leadership was secured. In practice this was less by the influence of revolutionary ideas on the largely passive membership of the SSP than by highly effective factional organising by the leaders of the platform that had founded the party, the International Socialist Movement (ISM). This allowed the party to cohere so long as the ISM leadership stuck together, but when they fell out in the autumn of 2006 the result was the disintegration of the SSP itself.[24]

23: To which the Socialist Party in England and Wales belongs.
24: On the SSP model, see the following exchange: Rees, 2002, and Smith, 2003.

These problems were reinforced by the tendency for the parliamentary wing to predominate after the SSP's capture of six seats in the Scottish Parliament in May 2003. As Mike Gonzalez puts it:

> The election result led...to...an over-emphasis on parliamentary activity at the expense of grassroots activity. Parliaments can be a useful propaganda platform in the building of socialist organisation—as Tommy Sheridan had shown so emphatically when he was the sole member between 1999 and 2003. With six members in the parliament the party became entitled to a number of full-time research and case workers, and the commitment to the MSPs remitting half their parliamentary salary to the party added to the party's resources. But it also reinforced the party's bureaucratic character, and focused its attention on a parliamentary role which could not but be limited and constrained.[25]

The development of an overblown apparatus centred on the Holyrood Parliament reinforced the tendency to factionalism within the dominant ISM. This experience offers an important negative example for other attempts to build radical left parties. Thus the organisational strength and political cohesion of the Ligue mean that it could very easily continue to dominate the NPA, and indeed the suspicion that it will has been expressed even by some of those attracted by the project.[26] It is clear that this isn't the intention of the LCR leadership, hence their insistence on the openness of the new party. It would indeed be a disastrous mistake for revolutionary socialists to seek to dominate the NPA and its counterparts elsewhere thanks to their organisational weight. Any such attempt would severely hold back the development of the radical left. But this does not solve the problem of the struggle between left and right that is unavoidable in any dynamically developing political formation.

When it first became involved in the process of left regroupment at the beginning of the present decade, the SWP came up with its own conception of the nature of the new radical left formations. This was articulated by John Rees when he argued, "The Socialist Alliance [the precursor to Respect] is thus best seen as a united front of a particular kind applied to the electoral field. It seeks to unite left reformist activists and

---

25: Gonzalez, 2006, pp69-70.
26: See, for example, the open letter by various notable anti-liberal intellectuals—Autain and others, 2008.

revolutionaries in a common campaign around a minimum programme".[27] Though an innovation, this extension of the united front tactic isn't completely unprecedented. In May 1922 the Communist International declared that "the problem of the United Political Front of Labor in the United States is the problem of the Labor Party", a policy that led its American section, the Workers Party (WP), to participate in 1923-4 in the Federated Farmer-Labor Party founded by John Fitzpatrick, leader of the Chicago Federation of Labor.[28]

The conception of a united front of a particular kind informed our approach to Respect. By contrast, those on the far left in the minority that followed Galloway in splitting from Respect (mainly the English Fourth International section, the International Socialist Group and a few ex-SWP members) tended to support the SSP model and to criticise the SWP for not dissolving itself into Respect. It is extremely fortunate that we refused to liquidate the SWP, since in that case the crisis in Respect would have led, not just to the temporary electoral eclipse of the radical left in Britain, but to a far deeper fragmentation and weakening of the organised socialist left.

The idea that the NPA should be conceived as a united front of a particular kind has recently been criticised by one of the project's main architects, François Sabado:

> There isn't a linear continuity between united front and party, just as "politics" isn't a simple continuation of the social. There are elements of continuity but also of discontinuity, of specificities, linked precisely to political struggle... It is from this point of view that it is incorrect to consider the new party as a kind of united front. There is then a tendency to underestimate the necessary delimitations, to consider the NPA as merely an alliance or a unitary framework—even of a particular kind—and therefore to underestimate its own construction as a framework or a mediation for building the revolutionary leaderships of tomorrow. There is the risk that if we consider the NPA as a

---

27: Rees, 2001, p32. See also Callinicos, 2002, and Jaffard, 2008.
28: Quoted Draper, 1985, p375. An up-to-date account of the Farmer-Labor Party, which succumbed to a combination of factionalism within the WP and Fitzpatrick and other trade union lefts getting cold feet about working with Communists, will be found in Palmer, 2007, chapters 7 and 8. Trotsky's acerbic criticisms of the episode focus on American Communists' support for Senator Robert LaFollette, who ran as the anti-Communist Progressive Party candidate in the 1924 presidential election, refusing Farmer-Labor endorsement, and the attempt by John Pepper, the dominant figure in the WP, to justify the policy on the basis of a populism that dissolved the differences between workers and small farmers: see Trotsky, 1970, pp119-122, 219-220.

kind of united front of making it wage only united front battles. For example, we don't make the unity of action of the entire workers' and social movement conditional on an agreement on the question of the government; but is this a reason for the NPA to relativise a struggle over the question of government? No, we don't think so. The NPA makes the question of government—refusal to participate in governments of class-collaboration—a delimitation of its political fight. That shows, self-evidently on this issue, that the NPA isn't a kind of united front. Our aim to construct it as a confluence of experiences and activists doesn't mean that we must give up seeing this party as one of the decisive links of a global political alternative and of an accumulation of class struggle and even revolutionary cadres for future crises.[29]

Sabado is right in two important respects. First, as he indicates in the last sentence, successfully building the radical left today is a step towards, not away from, the construction of mass revolutionary parties. Second, he is also right that the fact that radical left formations intervene in the political field shapes their character. Even if their organisational structure is that of a coalition, as that of Respect was, they need to define their global political identity by means of a programme, and function in many ways like a conventional political party, particularly when engaging in electoral activity.

But what the formula of a united front of a particular kind captures is the political heterogeneity characteristic of the contemporary radical left. Sometimes this reflects the specific origins of a particular formation—thus one of the most successful, the Left Bloc in Portugal, was founded in 1999 as a coalition of the far left, notably the ex-Maoist União Democrática Popular (UDP) and the Partido Socialista Revolucionário (PSR), the Portuguese section of the Fourth International. The successful development of the Bloc has led to the adoption of a more unitary party structure, but, if anything its internal heterogeneity has increased as the Bloc has attracted dissident elements from the strongly Stalinist Communist Party, many of whom share the same politics as the Bertinotti wing of the PRC.

This indicates that the politically diverse nature of the contemporary radical left is more than a matter of the specific history of individual formations. The particular form taken by the crisis of social democracy today has created the conditions for a convergence among elements from the reformist and revolutionary lefts in opposition to social liberalism. The fact that this political convergence is only partial, and in particular doesn't abolish the choice between reform and revolution, demands organisational structures

---

29: Sabado, 2008.

that, if not explicitly those of a coalition, give the different currents space to breathe and to coexist. But it also helps to explain the programmatic basis that Sabado seeks to give the NPA, which is essentially against social liberalism rather than against reformism altogether. Anyone who thinks this is a distinction without a difference should compare the Communist International's famous "21 conditions" for membership with Sabado's much more modest ban on participating in centre-left governments.

It is very important, as I have already noted, not to take fright at the political ambiguities inherent in the contemporary radical left. Any revolutionary worth his or her salt should throw themselves enthusiastically into building these formations. But this does not alter the fact that these ambiguities can lead to a repetition of the kind of disasters to have befallen the PRC and Respect. More positively, if the NPA is really to see what Sabado calls "an accumulation of class struggle and even revolutionary cadres for future crises", then this is not going to happen automatically. It will require a considerable effort to train the new activists won to the NPA and its like in the revolutionary Marxist tradition. But who is going to undertake this task? Some political education can occur within the framework of the party itself. But this can only be within well defined limits; otherwise the revolutionaries in the NPA can justifiably be accused of violating the political openness of the party and seeking to exploit its structures to put over their own distinctive politics.

A related issue concerns debate within radical left formations. Both the relatively open nature of their programmes and the uncertainties and surprises of which the neoliberal era is full mean that vigorous debate is even more important than usual to clarify their tasks. But where the formations are, either formally or in practice, coalitions, a vigorous debate can threaten to upset the delicate equilibrium between the different currents. The result can be a tendency to avoid serious arguments, at least outside the relatively closed arena of the leadership bodies. The dilemmas involved are quite real. When serious differences over strategy began to develop between Galloway and the SWP after the council elections of May 2006, the SWP leadership sought to contain the dispute by limiting it to the areas most affected in east London and Birmingham. This response made sense as a way of trying to prevent the development of a crisis that would destabilise Respect, but when the crisis came anyway with Galloway's attack on the SWP in August 2007, the result was that most of the membership of both Respect and the SWP were taken by surprise.

No simple formula can avoid this kind of difficult tactical problem. But it is possible to define a general approach. It is right to build the radical left on a broad and open basis, but within the resulting formations revolutionary socialists should organise and fight for their own politics. Both parts of this sentence deserve their proper emphasis. It is a mistake to try to define the boundaries of radical left parties too narrowly. Sinistra Critica, a far left tendency within the PRC dominated by Italian supporters of the Fourth International, broke with the PRC at the end of 2007 and ran its own candidates in the parliamentary elections. As a result, when in July 2008 Bertinotti and his supporters were defeated at the PRC congress by a coalition of more left wing currents, Sinistra Critica was no longer part of the argument. It is to be hoped that it can shift to re-establish an organised connection with the tens of thousands of activists who had hitherto looked towards the PRC.

But, while building on a broad and open basis, revolutionary socialists should maintain their own political and organisational identity. The precise form this may take will naturally vary—sometimes an independent organisation participating in a coalition, as the SWP did within the Socialist Alliance and Respect, sometimes a current in a larger organisation. A revolutionary socialist identity within the broader radical left is necessary not for reasons of narrow sectarian loyalty but because the theory and politics of revolutionary Marxism matter. They matter because they provide an understanding of the logic of capitalism as a system and because they recapitulate the accumulated revolutionary experiences of the past two centuries. Of course, the relevance of such a tradition to the present is not something that can be taken for granted. On the contrary, it has to be shown in practice, and this always involves a process of selection, interpretation and creative development of the tradition. But, because of the importance of practice, revolutionaries must retain the capacity to take their own initiatives. In other words, they should maintain their identity within the broader radical left not as a theoretical debating club but, whatever the circumstances, as an interventionist organisation.

Prospects

Of course, the presence of organised revolutionaries can be a source of tension within a radical left formation. They can be targeted and denounced by the right within the party. This can be a particular issue if the revolutionaries have a relatively substantial weight, as the SWP did within Respect and as the LCR will in the NPA. The far-left elements who broke away with Galloway have sought to justify their actions by accusing the SWP of seeking to dominate Respect. This was the opposite of our intention. We would have been very happy to have been a relatively smaller force within a much larger radical left coalition. The problem was that, despite the enormous political upheaval surrounding Britain's participation in the invasion of Iraq, Galloway was the only leading Labour figure who was prepared to break with the party over the issue. This meant there was a structural instability built into Respect from the start. The coalition was dominated by two forces—Galloway and the SWP. This was fine so long as they worked together relatively harmoniously. But a conflict between a revolutionary organisation and a reformist politician was all too likely to develop sooner or later, and, once it happened, there were no other forces powerful enough to contain it.

This structural imbalance is a consequence of the particular form taken by the decline of social democracy today. I wrote soon after the formation of Respect in 2004:

> The Labour Party is like a huge iceberg that is gradually shrinking thanks to global warming. The membership, social roots, and voting base are in pretty continuous decline. Tony Blair won a huge parliamentary majority in the 2001 general election with fewer votes than those with which Neil Kinnock lost the 1992 election. But the iceberg itself, though shrinking, remains pretty cohesive. Labourism hangs together thanks to the enduring strength of the trade unions, which remain the core of its social base, the capacity of the leadership to buy off the activists through a mixture of rhetoric, patronage and very limited social reforms, and the hope against hope of MPs, party activists, and trade union officials that somehow things really will get better. Decline takes place gradually, through a process of attrition, a series of individual decisions through which demoralised activists drop out and disillusioned voters stay at home.[30]

This picture continues broadly to fit the accelerating decline of New Labour under Gordon Brown, as it does much of the rest of European social democracy. The social base of reformism shrinks, not thanks to organisational splits, but through a gradual wearing away. This does not alter the fact that there is a space that the radical left can fill, but it will probably take the form of quite a long-term process of electoral interventions and other campaigns that gradually attract voters and activists. And the erosion of the old reformist social base gives the extreme right an opportunity to appeal to working class people who feel disenfranchised and unrepresented, as is shown very starkly by the ugly racist

---

30: Callinicos, 2004, p4.

forces unleashed by the victory of Berlusconi and his allies in the Italian general election of April 2008.

The general form taken by the crisis of social democracy underlines the importance of the case of Die Linke, where a real crack has taken place in the SPD monolith. This is partly a reflection of the sheer accumulated strength of German social democracy. Perry Anderson wrote of the SPD soon after its election victory in September 1998, "It is a very different party from New Labour. Twice the size, with 700,000 individual members, its culture remains noticeably working class. The atmosphere of an SPD rally in any big industrial town is closer to Labour meetings of the 1960s or 1970s than to anything in Britain today".[31] This made the shock of the Schröder government all the greater: after being relatively shielded from the worst of neoliberalism in the 1980s and 1990s, the German working class suffered, particularly in the Red–Green coalition's second term (2002-5), a sharp attack, with the Hartz IV dismantling of unemployment benefits and an employers' offensive that succeeded in forcing real wages down and productivity up.

This is the context that has allowed Die Linke to make such spectacular advances and Lafontaine to mount a serious attempt to revive left reformism. It is one reason why it would be unwise to claim that reformism singing its swan song, as the LCR sometimes implies, as, for example, when it declares, "Social democracy is completing its mutation. After having explained that socialism can be built step by step within the framework of the institutions of the capitalist state, it henceforth accepts its conversion to capitalism, to neoliberal policies".[32] This seems to posit a unilinear trend for social democratic parties to transform themselves into straightforwardly capitalist parties like the Democrats in the United States. As such, it is mistaken.

Reformism cannot be identified simply with specific organisations but arises from workers' tendency, as long as they lack confidence in their ability to overturn capitalism, to limit their struggles to winning improvements within the framework of the existing system. This tendency finds political expression despite the development of social liberalism. Die Linke is one example; another is the skill with which Alec Salmond, leader of the Scottish National Party, has, as first minister of Scotland, succeeded, while remaining within the limits set by the neoliberal economic policy regime, in projecting his government as pursuing a more authentic social democratic programme than New Labour is any longer capable of.

31: Anderson, 1999.
32: LCR, 2008.

Understanding this is important for immediate political reasons. The attractive power of reformist politics means there is no programmatic or organisational magic bullet that can exclude its influence from the new formations of the radical left. It is precisely for this reason that revolutionaries need to maintain their identity within these formations. The radical left has to be open to reformists if it is to fulfil its potential, but the examples of Bertinotti and Galloway should serve as a reminder that left reformists can move right as well as left.[33] This is important to bear in mind in the case of Die Linke. Lafontaine has been a bulwark of the left, but, should he decide the time has come to cut a deal with the SPD, he is quite capable of turning on it brutally. But revolutionaries preserving their political and organisational autonomy should not be seen as a form of sectarian defensiveness. On the contrary, this autonomy should give us the confidence boldly to build the radical left on the broadest and most dynamic basis—but preserving an instrument that will be needed to wage the political battles that any real success will bring.

In Britain the electoral projects of the radical left have succumbed to a process of mutually assured destruction in the Scottish and London elections that will make them difficult to resurrect in the short term. Nevertheless, this setback has taken place against the background of an accelerating crisis of New Labour. One feature of this crisis is that, with a general election in prospect by mid-2010 at the latest, the trade union bureaucracy, while rallying round the government, is doing so with a visible lack of enthusiasm. The process of attrition that is diminishing Labourism's social base is gradually wearing away its links with the organised working class. This is likely to lead, before long, to new initiatives aimed at creating a political alternative to New Labour. While bearing in mind the lessons of past attempts, revolutionaries need to be attentive to these opportunities.

33: It is also important to note, however, that they had previously moved left. Some of those who sided with Galloway in the split in Respect criticised the SWP for breaking with him after having previously worked amicably with him. This is, for example, one of Mark Steel's main beefs in *What's Going On?* (2008). The difference is simple: in the early 2000s both Bertinotti and Galloway moved left in response to the rising movements and the SWP was able to work well with both of them. When these movements began to decline, both Bertinotti and Galloway move rightwards, with the results reviewed in this article. Confronted with this development, the SWP defended itself against Galloway's attempt to subordinate us within Respect. This doesn't mean it was wrong to have worked with him or with Bertinotti earlier, but it does underline the importance of revolutionaries maintaining their political and organisational independence.

References

Anderson, Perry, 1999, "The German Question", *London Review of Books*, 7 January 1999.

Autain, Clémentine, and others, 2008, "Adresse Aux Initiateurs Du NPA", *Le Monde*, 30 May 2008.

Bensaïd Daniel, and others, 2003, "A Letter from LCR Comrades", *IST International Discussion Bulletin 2* (January 2003), www.istendency.net/pdf/international_2_2003.pdf

Callinicos, Alex, 1999, "Reformism and Class Polarisation in Europe", *International Socialism 85* (winter 1999), http://pubs.socialistreviewindex.org.uk/isj85/callinicos.htm

Callinicos, Alex, 2002, "Unity in Diversity", *Socialist Review 262* (April 2002), http://pubs.socialistreviewindex.org.uk/sr262/callinicos.htm

Callinicos, Alex, 2003, "A Letter to LCR comrades", *IST International Discussion Bulletin 2* (January 2003), www.istendency.net/pdf/international_3_2003.pdf

Callinicos, Alex, 2004, "The European Radical Left Tested Electorally", *IST International Discussion Bulletin 5* (July 2004), www.istendency.net/pdf/bulletin_5_2004.pdf

Callinicos, Alex, and Chris Nineham, 2007, "At an Impasse? Anti-Capitalism and the Social Forums Today", *International Socialism 115* (summer 2007), www.isj.org.uk/?id=337

Draper, Theodore, 1985, *The Roots of American Communism* (Ivan Dee).

Galloway, George, 2003, "Avalanche Heading For Blair Turmoil In Labour", *Socialist Worker*, 1 March 2003.

Galloway, George, 2008, "Nationalism Never Helped This Country", *Daily Record*, 7 July 2008.

Gonzalez, Mike, 2006, "The Split in the Scottish Socialist Party", *International Socialism 112* (autumn 2006), www.isj.org.uk/?id=247

Harman, Chris, 2007, *Revolution in the 21st Century* (Bookmarks).

Harman, Chris, 2008a, "The Crisis in Respect", *International Socialism 117* (winter 2008), www.isj.org.uk/?id=396

Harman, Chris, 2008b, "Theorising Neoliberalism", *International Socialism 117* (winter 2008), www.isj.org.uk/?id=399

Hayes, Ingrid, 2008, "Le Nouveau Parti, c'est Parti!", www.lcr-rouge.org/spip.php?article2020

Holland, Stuart, 1976, *The Socialist Challenge* (Quartet).

Jaffard, Sylvestre, 2008, "Le Nouveau Parti comme Cadre de Front Unique", *Que faire? 7*, (January/March 2008), http:// quefaire.lautre.net/articles/07npafrontunique.html

Kouvélakis, Stathis, 2005, "France: The Triumph of the Political", *International Socialism 108* (autumn 2005), www.isj.org.uk/?id=134

Lafontaine, Oskar, 2008, "Great and Severe Tasks Lie Ahead of Us", Speech at Die Linke congress, Cottbus, 24 May 2008, http://tinyurl.com/5nxuaq

LCR, 2008, "Pour un Anticapitalisme et un Socialisme du XXIe Siècle", contribution to meeting of 28 and 29 June 2008, www.lcr-rouge.org/spip.php?article1685

Mandel, Ernest, 1979, *Revolutionary Marxism Today* (New Left Books).

Palmer, Bryan, 2007, *James P Cannon and the Origins of the American Revolutionary Left 1890-1928* (University of Illinois).

Rees, John, 2001, "Anti-Capitalism, Reformism and Socialism", International Socialism 90 (spring 2001), http://pubs.socialistreviewindex.org.uk/isj90/rees.htm

Rees, John, 2002, "The Broad Party, the Revolutionary Party and the United Front", *International Socialism 97* (winter 2002), http://pubs.socialistreviewindex.org.uk/isj97/rees.htm

Rifondazione, 2008, "Let's Start Again: A Shift to the Left", political document approved by the majority (342 out of 646 in favour) of the congress, 27 July 2008, http://home.rifondazione.it/xisttest/index.php?option=com_content&task=view&id=2905

Sabado, François, 2008, "Nouveau Parti Anticapitaliste et Front Unique", *Que faire? 8* (May/ June 2008), http://quefaire.lautre.net/articles/08sabado.html

Smith, Murray, 2003, "The Broad Party, the Revolutionary Party and the United Front: A Reply to John Rees", *International Socialism 100* (autumn 2003), http://pubs.socialistreviewindex.org.uk/ isj100/smith.htm

Steel, Mark, 2008, *What's Going On?* (Simon & Schuster).

Trotsky, Leon, 1970, *The Third International after Lenin* (Pathfinder).

Trudell, Megan, 2007, "Rifondazione Votes for War", *International Socialism 113* (winter 2007), www.isj.org.uk/?id=284

Wintrebert, Raphaël, 2007, *Attac, la Politique Autrement?* (Découverte).

Zappi, Sylvia, 2008, "Olivier Besancenot Intensifie Son Offensive Sociale", *Le Monde*, 23 August 2008.

Decyphering The Internationale: the Eugène Pottier code

Donny Gluckstein

The Internationale has long been the anthem of the workers' movement throughout the world. Its power to move people has survived the repression of fascism, the cruel parody that was Stalinism and free market capitalism. Those who sing it need know nothing about it, and be familiar with only the first verse and the chorus, yet feel a strong sense of international unity. Why has it proved both so durable and inspirational?

The verses were written on 30 June 1871[1] in the immediate aftermath of the brutal crushing of the Paris Commune, when the author, Eugène Pottier, was hiding in fear of his life. His lyrics (the music came later)[2] were intended to impart the historical experience of an important workers' struggle to a worldwide audience. At the same time they inevitably reflect Pottier's views. He was a follower of Proudhonism, an ideology popular in France until it was destroyed along with the Commune. It is a measure of Pottier's achievement, however, that The Internationale can function simultaneously as history, political argument and a rallying statement.

Pottier was born in Paris in 1816, a year after Napoleon's defeat at Waterloo and the consequent restoration of the Bourbon monarchy. The city had been the cradle of the 1789 French Revolution and of the unprecedented social turbulence that followed. During Pottier's lifetime it was

---

1: Bourgin and Henriot, 1945, p202.
2: The tune was added by Pierre Degeyter in 1888, a year after Pottier's death.

the epicentre of world political life, the "capital of the 19th century".[3] Although the bourgeoisie were now in the saddle and the country was industrialising rapidly, the aspirations for liberty, equality and fraternity that had been unleashed by the storming of the Bastille could not be quelled by a foreign-imposed ruler. The genie was out of the bottle. French capitalists interpreted the motto of 1789—Liberty, equality, fraternity—as meaning freedom for market forces to operate, equality as a level playing field for those keen to exploit the workers and fraternity as all classes uniting behind the French flag. But for people such as Pottier it meant the promise of a society in which poor people, like himself, had justice.

Pottier held a number of jobs, none of them well paid. He left school at the age of 13 to work with his father making packing cases, later becoming a shop worker, usher and eventually a textile printer.[4] But from early on his passion was poetry and politics. At the age of 14 he witnessed the insurrection of 1830 that cost the lives of 1,800 revolutionaries. At that time he wrote his first song—"Vive la liberté!"[5] In 1848 he was on the barricades once more, participating in the establishment of the Second Republic. Pottier was outraged when a relative of Napoleon, Louis Bonaparte, made himself emperor in 1851. In response he wrote a poem entitled "Who Will Revenge This?"[6]

The answer came in 1870 when the Parisian masses rose up and overthrew the emperor, following this with the creation of the Commune in March 1871. Pottier already had established a reputation as the workers' poet. It earned him a seat on the Communal Council representing the 2nd *arrondissement*. He came top of the poll with a 93 percent share of the vote[7] and served on the Public Services Commission of the Commune. After 72 days the French government, then based at Versailles, sent in the army to massacre the communards in what became known as "Bloody Week". Pottier sought asylum first in Britain and later in the US. He eventually returned to Paris and died there in 1887. Even in his coffin Pottier remained controversial. Ten thousand people, including many leading former communards, turned up at his funeral, but the cortege was attacked by police who attempted to seize the red flag carried by mourners.[8]

The power of Pottier's Internationale lies in the fact that he was able

---

3:   Walter Benjamin, quoted in Andrew Benjamin, 1989, p1.
4:   Musuex, 1896, p5.
5:   Musuex, 1896, p6.
6:   Musuex, 1896, p6.
7:   Bourgin and Henriot, 1945, p305.
8:   Museux, 1896, p152.

to encapsulate his personal experience of a specific event and yet express it in universal terms. This can be seen from the first lines:

Arise ye starvelings from your slumbers
Arise ye criminals of want.

Under capitalism the working class everywhere suffers poverty while those who protest are often criminalised. In Paris this phenomenon took the sharpest of forms—mass hunger and civil war. In 1870 Louis Bonaparte launched an attack on Prussia which failed disastrously. The emperor himself was captured and food supplies to the capital city, containing the second largest concentration of people in the world, were cut off for months. While the few wealthy citizens who had not fled continued to live in luxury the rest were reduced to eating cats, dogs and rats to survive. Yet far from hunger cowing working class Parisians it radicalised them. They still rejected the humiliating peace treaty the reactionary new government signed. For this snub they would indeed be treated as criminals. When the Commune was finally defeated many thousands were massacred, but even more, some 50,000, were put on trial.[9] Pottier himself was condemned to death in his absence.

The first verse continues:

For reason in revolt now slumbers
And at last ends the age of cant.
So away with all your superstitions
Servile masses arise, arise,
We'll change forthwith the old conditions
And spurn the dust to win the prize.

These references to "reason" and "supersitition" arose from the role played by the Catholic church which had always supported reaction and authority in France. Ever since the Enlightenment in the 18th century battle had been joined between the church, which insisted that the existing order had been divinely ordained and could not be changed by human beings, and those who said that all institutions could and should be judged by reason and abolished if found wanting.

Adolphe Thiers, who as head of the French government was the architect of Bloody Week, insisted that religion was necessary because it could:

9:   See Lissagaray, 1976, p320.

propagate that good philosophy which teaches that man is here to suffer, and not that philosophy which says the contrary—be happy... If you think that here below you are entitled to a little bit of happiness, and if you do not find it in your actual situation, you will strike at rich people fearlessly for having kept you away from your happiness.[10]

After 1871, in revenge for the perceived humiliation of the church at the hands of the Commune, the enormous basilica of the Sacré-Coeur was built on the hill of Montmartre. Visible from every corner of the city it was Paris's most striking landmark until the construction of the Eiffel Tower.

Pottier's call to reason therefore reflected the motivation behind many of the Commune's policies. Education was taken out of the hands of priests and nuns. Marriage became a civil affair with divorce easier to obtain. While daytime religious ceremonies continued in Parisian churches, in the evenings they became great meeting halls where the mass of the population could debate and democratically control power.

The second verse reads as follows:

No more divided by reaction
On tyrants only we will make war
The soldiers too will take strike action
They will break ranks and fight no more
And if those cannibals keep trying
To sacrifice us to their greed
They soon shall hear the bullets flying
We will shoot the generals on our own side.

This is an exact description of the outbreak of the Commune itself. On 18 March 1871, shortly after the end of the Franco-Prussian War, the French government sent its army to seize the cannons of the Parisian citizen militia. However, confronted by masses of women protesters the soldiers decided to mutiny rather than follow orders. When General Lecomte insisted that his troops fire on the people he was seized and executed by his own men. Verses three and four show the influence of Proudhonism on Pottier:

10:   Quoted in Gluckstein, 2006, p37.

No saviour from on high delivers
No faith have we in prince or peer
Our own right hand the chains must sever
Chains of hatred, greed or fear.
E'er the chiefs will out with their booty
And give all a happier lot
Each at the forge must do their duty
And we will strike while the iron is hot.

Laws cheat and the state oppresses
Their taxes drain the people more
The rich themselves escape such stresses
So now what rights have the poor?
We've enough of languishing in misery
Equality's why we fight
No more rights without any duties
And no duties without our rights

Here Proudhonist thinking on power and the state is laid out. While various rival political currents were present in Paris, the Proudhonists dominated the organised workers' movement and controlled the French section of the International Workingmen's Association (IWMA, or First International). In the March 1871 Communal Council elections they captured one third of the seats. Their version of anarchism owed much of its attraction to the fact that under the *Ancien Régime* and the Napoleonic Empires the French state had been a model of centralised bureaucracy and physical repression in the service of the ruling elite. Proudhon (1809-1865) concluded that freedom was impossible while a state structure existed. He therefore called on workers to ignore politics and the state, and focus their efforts on grassroots self-activity.

When, in 1864, the IWMA was founded and Marx was tasked with formulating its platform he acknowledged the positive part of the Proudhonist argument. The "General Rules" begin with these words: "That the emancipation of the working classes must be conquered by the working classes themselves".[11] Pottier's rejection of any "saviour from on high" expresses this sentiment perfectly.

However, Proudhonism had serious weaknesses. Whether or not workers choose to ignore it the capitalist state plays an active role

---

11: IWMA, 1864.

in maintaining the system. Furthermore, the theory took no note of the unevenness in consciousness that exists in the working class. As a result Proudhonists did not recognise the need for the more advanced and conscious sections of the working class to provide leadership in the struggle against capitalism and its state. Marx disagreed with the anarchist attitude to politics and therefore supplemented his initial statement on workers' self-emancipation with the following: "To conquer political power has, therefore, become the great duty of the working classes".[12]

In the Commune arguments about the state and issue of leadership culminated in bitter disputes. Opponents of Proudhonism warned that it was not enough to establish a model of democracy and liberation for others to emulate. The French state was, after all, preparing to attack Paris and drown the Commune in blood. They proposed countermeasures, which involved forming a Committee of Public Safety armed with extensive powers, to take a leadership role in combatting the government forces massing at Versailles. Pottier showed that the experience of struggle had taken him beyond the strictures of Proudhonism and he voted for the new body, though with misgivings: "The situation demands energy and unity of action. So despite its title, I vote for 'the Committee'".[13]

> Those mining bosses and the rail kings
> It's they, the real monsters
> Throughout their lives they do just nothing
> But rob the poor workers
> Whilst in their bank vaults they hoard
> All our labour does create
> By demanding that it is restored
> We now ask for a just fate.

Here Pottier reflected the current state of French industrialisation which was built on railway expansion generally and mining in the north east, the most economically developed area of France. The reference to banking is pure Proudhon, however. His approach to economics was summed up in the famous aphorism, "Property is theft." Where Marx located the exploitation of workers at the core of the capitalist production process, for Proudhon poverty and riches were explained by the taking of bank interest, dividends and "unearned increments".

12: IWMA, 1864.
13: Bourgin and Henriot, 1945, p34.

If workers could obtain interest free loans they could organise cooperative industrial production which would link together in local communes. Proudhon believed this could successfully compete against the capitalists, whereupon the current economic system would collapse and a new society would emerge. He himself made several abortive attempts to set up a People's Bank and get the process started. There is no space here to discuss the flaws in this vision, only to note its presence in The Internationale.

Women played an enormous role within the Commune, both in defence of the cannons on 18 March and during its short life. Examples include the actions of people such as Louise Michel, the Women's Union, the mass assemblies and the fighting of Bloody Week. Although line two of the last verse only hints at this, in the context of prevailing nineteenth century attitudes any reference to women being part of the struggle, rather than bystanders, was noteworthy:

We peasants, artisans and others
Enrolled as daughters, sons of toil
Let's claim the earth for workers
Drive the indolent from the soil

Pottier's verses end by affirming that despite the terrible suffering inflicted by the Versailles army the struggle would revive:

On our flesh long has fed the raven
We're too long vultures' prey
But now farewell the spirit craven
The dawn brings a brighter day.

The dawn that Pottier foresaw would not appear for many years, because repression of the communards was so savage and thorough. But his hope for a brighter future was not misplaced. Paris itself experienced an insurrectionary situation in 1944, and the biggest general strike in history during May 1968. To defiantly predict such possibilities from the depths of the abyss into which the communards were thrown required deep commitment and courage.

We now turn to the chorus:

So comrades come rally
And the last fight let us face

This first section is straightforward. The battles of 1871 had indeed been the "last fight" for many tens of thousands of communards. In Bloody Week some 30,000 working class women and men were slaughtered in cold blood. Furthermore, it is the notion of a final all-out struggle with capitalism that marks out The Internationale as a revolutionary song. In taking this stance Pottier again showed that the experience of the Commune had carried him beyond Proudhon's gradualism and disregard for the question of the state.

It is worthwhile comparing his words to the British Labour Party's (now defunct) anthem, The Red Flag. Although one would be hard put to discover any bloodsoaked banners in the history of the Labour Party, that song has suitably dramatic references:

> The people's flag is deepest red,
> It shrouded oft our martyrs dead

The position of the apostrophe in "people's" is interesting. Had it been placed after the "s" it would have implied solidarity across borders. In fact the song was written by an Irishman in 1889, no doubt reflecting his people's long national struggle against British imperialism. They had had many martyrs, but The Red Flag's historical provenance means it lacks the internationalism or proletarian roots of the communard's work. And despite the emotive language The Red Flag's lyrics are non-committal as regards the question of reform or revolution, whereas Pottier's call to final struggle is unequivocal.

The concluding part of The Internationale's chorus is the most enigmatic section of all. What do the words "The Internationale unites the human race" actually mean? Things become even more mysterious if an exact rendering of the original French words is considered: "Groupons nous, et demain; l'Internationale sera le genre humain"; literally "Let us group together, and tomorrow the International will be the human race".

The International referred to here is clearly the IWMA, and it is this body's composition and character that holds the clue to the meaning of the lines. Although the First International had adherents from many lands its core was provided by four countries—Germany, Italy, Britain and France—with radically different movements.

In Germany support came from socialist organisations which would merge to form the Social Democratic Party (SPD). In Italy the followers of Mazzini formed the IWMA. Organised in small conspiratorial groupings they were dedicated to stoking up popular revolts. Britain's contingent was composed of trade union affiliates whose officials mostly gave political allegiance to the Liberal Party. Their motivation in linking up with the International was economic rather than political: the IWMA could provide solidarity to workers on strike and, in particular, prevent the shipping in of foreign scab labour.

Unlike the Germans, the French section of the IWMA rejected the idea that its local branches constituted the base of a socialist party (since it eschewed political leadership). It dismissed Mazzini who was not only "an opponent of socialism", but whose "sole aim...was to secure a united bourgeois republic".[14] As we have seen, Proudhonists ignored state issues. Equally, British trade unionism was not seen as a model to follow because the French aim was far more ambitious than limited reforms or improvements in pay and conditions. For Pottier and his comrades the First International was already the germ of a new society based on comradeship.

These differences conditioned what it meant to be a member of the IWMA. In Britain and Germany the masses of working class people became part of the organisation through their leading institutional organ (party committees or union executives). In Italy only a tiny dedicated minority was involved. In France members did not join a party or a union; they joined the IWMA directly and in so doing believed they were engaging in self-emancipation and self-activity from below. In their terms they had begun the process of superseding capitalism.

It is interesting, therefore, that the immediacy of the relationship between the IWMA and its members posited in Pottier's chorus was altered in translation. Eleanor Marx, who first put Pottier's lyrics into English, changed his phrase "The Internationale...*will be* the human race" to "The Internationale...*unites* the human race". This latter form was more suitable for British supporters of the IWMA. Franz Mehring's German version departed even further from the original: "Die Internationale erkämpft das Menschenrecht"—"The International fights for human rights".

Pottier's words also show the exceptional emphasis the French section placed on internationalism. For Germany and Italy the decade up to 1871 was one of unification out of disparate small states. Mehring explains that in both countries "the national struggles naturally forced the idea of internationalism into the background".[15] British trade unions were, as their name implied, organised into separate bodies along craft lines and their

---

14: Mehring, 1936, p408.
15: Mehring, 1936, p317.

main emphasis was on the benefits of solidarity across borders rather than abolishing borders themselves.

Pottier and his comrades hoped *every* worker in *every* country would become part of the First International. They believed that through this self-governing communes would develop and the state would disappear along with the divisions caused by the existence of different governments. So the meaning of the chorus is literal. If the masses grouped together in the International this organisation would come to embody the human race.

The Paris Commune did indeed display remarkable internation-alism. Many of the key figures in the Commune had originated abroad. Alongside Louise Michel and Jean Varlin stood people like Leo Frankl, a Hungarian Jew who headed the important Labour Commission charged with advancing workers' economic rights. Elizabeth Dmitriova, a Russian, led the Women's Union. The most prominent generals leading the Parisian workers' militia—the National Guard—included Cluseret (an American citizen), Dombrowski and Wroblewski (Poles). Before 1871 French workers had seen the national anthem, the Marseillaise, as their hymn. Afterwards it would be The Internationale. The experience of struggle and of the Commune had changed mass consciousness.

Understanding Proudhonism or the Commune helps to decode Pottier's Internationale, but this does not convey its full meaning. If this song had been merely a Proudhonist tract it would suffered the fate of Proudhonism itself. That ideology along with the Commune's other currents—Blanquism and neo-Jacobinism—reflected an early stage of development. None provided the answers needed by the workers of Paris in their confrontation with the French ruling class, its state and army. Consequently these movements faded away after 1871, curiosities relegated to the museum of ideology. Equally, though a history of 1871 in verse might be interesting it would not have an enduring impact.

The secret of the poem is that Pottier was able to use his imme-diate experience and ideological framework and yet transcend them to weave a universal message in which the internationalist heart and soul of the Parisian workers in their titanic fight comes through. No knowledge of the Commune's exciting new vision of women's liberation, education, art, justice and workers' control is needed to sense what the struggle for socialism can mean, or that workers share a common interest the world over.

As a result of this masterful act of creation Pottier's verse has sustained a life of its own long after his death. Its substance has been added to by the people who have sung it and the struggles they engaged in. It was sung by mutinous sailors on the Battleship Potemkin during

Russia's 1905 revolution; by workers in Madrid during 1936 who vowed *¡No pasarán!*—Franco's fascists would not pass; and by the protesters in Tiananmen Square in 1989.

Perhaps the most poignant rendering was on May Day 1943 during the Warsaw Ghetto uprising when the Nazis were about to liquidate the last remnants of resistance. One of the few survivors wrote:

> The Internationale was sung. The entire world, we knew, was celebrating May Day on that day and everywhere forceful, meaningful words were being spoken. But never yet had The Internationale been sung in conditions so different, so tragic, in a place where an entire nation had been and was still perishing. The words and the song echoed from the charred ruins and were, at that particular time, an indication that Socialist youth was still fighting in the Ghetto, and that even in the face of death they were not abandoning their ideals.[16]

Reciting Pottier's verse today therefore links us to a long and proud tradition. Now, at a time of imperialist wars abroad, the stoking up of racism on the domestic front and a global crisis of capitalism The Internationale continues to play a role in inspiring an alternative vision.

16: [16] M Edelman, The Ghetto Fights, London 1990, p. 83

References

Benjamin, Andrew (ed), 1989, *The Problems of Modernity* (Routledge).

Bourgin, George, and Gabriel Henriot, 1945, *Procès-Verbaux de la Commune de 1871*, volume 2, (Paris).

Edelman, Marek, 1990, *The Ghetto Fights* (Bookmarks).

Gluckstein, Donny, 2006, *The Paris Commune* (Bookmarks).

IWMA, 1864, "General Rules". Available online at www.marxists.org/history/international/iwma/documents/1864/rules.htm

Lissagaray, Prosper Olivier, 1976, *History of the Paris Commune* (New Park).

Mehring, Franz, 1936, *Karl Marx: The Story of his Life* (Allen Unwin), www.marxists.org/archive/mehring/1918/marx/

Musuex, Ernest, 1896, *Eugène Pottier et son Oeuvre* (Paris).

Marxism and ethics[1]
Paul Blackledge

In place of the old bourgeois society, with its classes and class antagonisms, we shall have an association, in which the free development of each is the condition for the free development of all.[2]

There is a widespread myth that Marx either rejected ethics altogether or that his comments on ethics and morality are at best incoherent.[3] These claims have a superficial plausibility. For instance, he could argue that the emergence of a contradiction between capitalists and workers "shattered the basis for all morality, whether the morality of asceticism or of enjoyment",[4] yet he used moral language to condemn the "vampire-like" nature of capitalism and the "hired prizefighters" who attempted to justify it, while heaping moral praise on the honesty of the British Factory Inspectors.[5]

Such apparently contradictory statements have been seized upon to suggest not only that Marx's criticisms of morality are incoherent but also that his use of a fairly standard moral vocabulary in *Capital* undermines the

1:   Thanks to Colin Barker, Joseph Choonara, Neil Davidson, Kristyn Gorton, Chris Harman, Rob Jackson, Rick Kuhn and Jonathan Maunder for comments on a draft of this paper. My understanding of Marx's ethics is greatly indebted to the early Marxist writings of Alasdair MacIntyre—see Blackledge and Davidson, 2008. See also Harman, 1996.
2:   Marx and Engels, 1973, p87.
3:   See, for instance, Critchley, 2007, p93, and Cohen, 2000, pp101-103.
4:   Marx and Engels, 1987b, p419.
5:   Marx, 1976, pp416, 97, 406.

scientific pretensions of this work. As we shall see, these criticisms miss their mark.

It is true that Marx did aim to escape the "impotence"[6] of the moralistic forms of anti-capitalism he encountered in the 1840s. But this did not involve an outright rejection of ethics.[7] His criticisms of morality should be understood as a more limited rejection of the modern liberal assumption, perhaps best expressed by Immanuel Kant, that moral behaviour involves the suppression of natural desires that are seen as selfish and individualistic.[8]

The starting point for Marx's alternative ethics is the collective struggles of workers against their exploitation. He argued that these struggles expose the limitations of freedom in a capitalist society while simultaneously engendering virtues of solidarity that point beyond the limits of liberal conceptions of morality.

It is from this perspective that he revealed the historical and political biases that are assumed by modern moral theory while pointing beyond it to a justifiable ethical critique of capitalism, and from which we are able to differentiate between what Leon Trotsky called "their morals and ours".[9]

Ethics before Marx

The novelty of modern post-Kantian moral theory becomes apparent if we compare it with the classical Greek conception of ethics. Greek ethics, especially as developed by Aristotle,[10] was unlike modern moral philosophy in that it did not suppose that to be good entailed acting in opposition to our desires. Aristotle held to a naturalistic ethics that related the idea of good to fulfilling human needs and desires.[11] The good for man is *eudaimonia*.[12] This is usually translated as happiness, wellbeing, self-realisation or flourishing, and Aristole relates it to our human nature or essence. In his model the virtues are those qualities which would enable individuals to flourish within

---

6:   Marx, favourably quoting the utopian socialist Charles Fourier in *The Holy Family*—Marx and Engels, 1987a, p201.

7:   Brenkert, 1983, p17.

8:   Wood, 2005, pp132-134, 149. For the distinction between ethics and morality see Williams, 2006, p6.

9:   Trotsky, 1973. While considerations of space preclude a discussion of Trotsky's pamphlet here, I discuss it in the context of the ideas of Georg Lukács, Lenin, Henryk Grossman and Evgeny Pashukanis in Blackledge, 2008. For MacIntyre's reply see MacIntyre, 2008. Interested readers might also wish to consult Blackledge, forthcoming.

10: Marx described Aristotle as the "greatest thinker of antiquity". Marx, 1976, p532.

11: MacIntyre, 1985, pp122, 135.

12: Aristotle 1976, p63.

a community.[13] And because Aristotle recognised that humans are only able to flourish within communities—he defines us as "political animals"—he made a direct link between ethics and politics. The question of how we are to flourish led directly to questions of what form of social and political community would best allow us to flourish. Consequently, as against those who would suggest an unbridgeable gulf between ethics and politics, Aristotle declared the subject matter of his book on ethics to be politics: "The science that studies the supreme Good for man is politics".[14]

While the specificities of Aristotle's account of what it is to flourish were distorted by his "class-bound conservatism",[15] there is nothing intrinsically elitist about his system.[16] It does, however, presuppose a pre-Darwinian model of human nature that is at odds both with modern liberal conceptions of individual egoism and with Marx's historical humanism.

At the centre of liberal political theory is the egoistic individual. While this model of our individuality is often assumed to be obviously true, the biological fact of our individuality should not be confused with the ideology of individualism. To see why this is so it is instructive to recognise that the first intellectuals to put the figure of the individual at the centre of their works were Machiavelli and Luther, both writing in the early 1500s,[17] and the first systematic attempt to conceptualise individualism was articulated more than another century later by Thomas Hobbes in *Leviathan* (1651).

According to Hobbes the central fact of human nature is a desire for self-preservation. From this physiological starting point he concludes that in a situation of material scarcity individuals would tend to come into conflict with each other over resources and this would result in a "war of all against all".[18] He argues that in this context concepts such as good and bad relate to the need for self-preservation. Consequently, if by killing you I acquire the resources necessary to live, then while this would be bad for you it would be good for me. Accordingly, the might of the individual becomes the basis for what is right.

Since the 17th century, moral theory has attempted to escape the relativistic consequence of Hobbes's thought while continuing to accept something like his model of competitive individualism.

Marx points to a fundamental problem with this approach. The

13: MacIntyre, 1985, p148.
14: Aristotle, 1976, p64; MacIntyre, 1966, p57.
15: MacIntyre, 1966, p68.
16: Knight, 2007, p14 onwards; see also Nederman, 2008.
17: MacIntyre, 1966, p121.
18: Hobbes, 1998. See especially chapter 13.

further one looks back into history, he writes, "the more does the individual…appear as dependent, as belonging to a greater whole". Through pre-history and on through pre-capitalist modes of production the individual's sense of self was mediated through family and clan units. Conversely, it is only with the rise of capitalism that social relations between people "confront the individual as mere means towards his private purposes, as external necessity".[19] The "private interests" assumed to be natural by Hobbes, and following him modern moral theory, are a product of history. They are "already a socially determined interest, which can be achieved only within the conditions laid down by society and with the means provided by society".[20] Whereas in pre-capitalist societies individuals conceive themselves through mutual relations involving obligations; in modern capitalist society individuals appear "unconstrained by any social bonds".[21]

Engels points out that in the medieval period, despite the fact that the bulk of peasant production and appropriation was carried out individually, local bonds of solidarity among feudal Europe's peasantry were underpinned by those forms of communal land which the peasantry needed in order to survive and which helped them resist lordly power.[22] By contrast the emergence and eventual dominance of capitalist market relations involve production becoming *socialised* while appropriation remains individualised.[23] This generates a contradictory relationship. Socialised production means that humans depend for their very existence upon a massive web of connections through each other, whereas individual appropriation implies that these individuals confront each other merely as competitors. Modern moral theory arose against the background of this contradiction. So, whereas pre-modern thinkers had assumed that people are social animals and thus that individuals cannot be understood except as part of society, modern moral theory is confronted by the reality of society but can only conceive it negatively as a series of Hobbesian competitors.

Social contract theory, utilitarianism, Kantianism and even modern virtue ethics can all be understood as attempts to provide an answer to the problem of how to formulate a common good in a world of egoistic individuals. While Marx's criticisms of morality involve a rejection of these approaches, his criticism of Kant does not involve a crude materialist rejection of the concept of human freedom. Rather he follows Kant in putting

---

19:   Marx, 1973a, p84.
20:   Marx, 1973a, p156.
21:   MacIntyre, 1966, pp121-128.
22:   Engels, 1972, pp123, 216. See also Anderson, 1974, p148.
23:   Engels, 1947, pp. 327-328.

human freedom at the centre of his social theory, while arguing that Kant fails to understand real human freedom.

Roughly speaking, Kant argued that morality involves the use of reason to overcome our natural competitiveness so as to allow us to come together in mutual respect. The moral law for him, as for the Protestant tradition in which he was raised, acts as an impediment to our selfish and sinful desires. He could not accept Aristotle's naturalistic approach to ethics since he believed our selfish nature prevents our needs from underpinning a moral order. It is this that underlies the modern claim that there is no necessary connection between statements of fact and value judgements—or between "is and ought" as it is often put. The 18th century philosopher David Hume had asked how, if it all, it was possible to move from describing a situation to judging it.[24] Kant answered that there was an unbridgeable gulf between these two terms: there could be no non-moral reasons for a moral act.

Kant's aim was to provide good reasons for acting in line with an unconditional moral requirement he called the "categorical imperative". One of its formulations was to "act in such a way that you always treat humanity, whether in your own person or in the person of any other, never simply as a means, but always at the same time as an end".[25] Such arguments had a powerful appeal to generations of radicals. Writing in 1925, the "Austro-Marxist" Max Adler argued that "Kant's ethic represents a philosophical expression of the human aims of socialism",[26] and a revolutionary of the stature of Karl Liebknecht embraced Kant's ideas. However, so too have much more conservative figures, and Kant himself accepted a number of what we would consider to be "very extreme (even repellent) positions on certain ethical issues".[27] Indeed, precisely because he sought to provide existing moral opinion with theoretical rigour his thought has been labelled as "an essentially conservative view".[28]

This ambiguity points to an important problem with his approach: it fails to provide a concrete guide to action. The later German philosopher Hegel pointed to the abstract nature of Kant's morality, which he characterised at one point by its "sublime hollowness and uniquely consistent

---

24: The classic statement of this argument comes in the final paragraph of book III, part I, section i of Hume, 1965. See also MacIntyre, 1966, pp171-174 and MacIntyre, 1971a.

25: Kant, 1948, p91.

26: Adler, 1978, p63.

27: Wood, 2005, p130.

28: MacIntyre, 1966, p191.

vacuity".[29] More generally, he argued that Kant's moral standpoint, far from being the perspective of pure reason, in fact reflected "the ethical life of the bourgeois or private individual".[30]

The Marxist philosopher Lucien Goldmann, commenting on Hegel's claim, suggests a more general weakness with modern moral theories. He argues that "it is not Kant's ethic which is an empty form but that of actual man in bourgeois individualist society". By assuming bourgeois individualism Kant is compelled to conclude that the universal moral community posited by the categorical imperative can only exist at a formal rather than at a real level. For him, our very nature causes our needs and desires to be those of atomised, competitive individuals, and so he could conceive of no social basis for acting as he believed we should, except by way of some duty which pulls against those needs and desires.[31] Other bourgeois moral theories, by assuming an egoistic model of human nature, are just as incapable of envisaging a way of overcoming the gap between our individual needs and desires on the one hand, and the reality that we live in a social world on the other.

Consequently, such theorists tend to view morality and community as top-down impositions on people. And whereas conservatives embrace this authoritarianism, anarchists and liberals either reject or seek to ameliorate it. Alternatively, utilitarianism, the dominant voice of moral theory in the English speaking world over the last couple of centuries, attempts to deal with the problem by denying its existence. Instead the utilitarians argue that individual selfishness leads to a general increase in wealth, which in turn makes us all happier. Whatever its radical roots, this approach has been used to justify all manner of inhuman acts in the name of their future consequences,[32] and by conflating happiness with increased wealth it is blind to the way that modern societies generate so much unhappiness.[33]

The fact that utilitarianism is simultaneously so inadequate as a moral theory and so popular among apologists for the status quo reflects a deeper problem with modern moral theory. Because we live in a fragmented world of competing interests reason itself becomes fragmented into so many competing arguments for different visions of what is right. So modern moral philosophers can agree, for example, that the world is an incredibly socially

---

29: Lukács, 1975, p287; Taylor, 1975, p371; Hegel, 1952, pp89-90.
30: Wood, 1990, p132.
31: Goldmann, 1971, p174.
32: See, for instance, Bentham, 1990, pp9-10. For a critique of utilitarianism see MacIntyre, 1964.
33: Ferguson, 2008; See also Frank, 1999, and Wilkinson, 2005.

unequal place, but disagree as to whether or not this is a desirable situation. For instance, contemporary political philosophy is dominated by a debate between libertarians such as Robert Nozick who excuse social inequalities by defending private property rights and egalitarians such as John Rawls who justify such inequalities only in so far as they "benefit the least advantaged".[34] In a classic commentary on such debates Alasdair MacIntyre suggested that the variety of arguments deployed to rationally justify each modern approach to the question of how we ought to live are best understood as varieties of "emotivism"—the belief that the phrase "this is good" can essentially be translated as "I approve of it".[35] This explains both the intractability of these debates, and the fact that moral and political philosophy tends to be a graveyard for political practice. By suggesting that there is no way of agreeing about the kind of world we should live in, these debates undermine any positive model of a better world and therefore tend to act as a tacit apology for the status quo.[36]

One attempt to escape this predicament involves a return to classical (Greek) virtue ethics.[37] Instead of focusing on the intentions of actors or the consequences of actions, virtue ethicists insist that the key ethical question should be, "What kind of person ought I be?" Unfortunately, while these writers hark back to classical discussions of ethics, Aristotle's model of human nature is not only inadequate once we accept Darwin's proof that humans are a product of natural evolution, but it is also at odds with liberal conceptions of our natural state as one of conflict. Developing a virtue ethics that goes beyond the limits of liberalism by drawing together individual and social conceptions of the good requires that we indicate some social and historically specific practices through which non-egoistic forms of human relations might emerge. It was Hegel who first pointed towards a solution to this dilemma by suggesting a historical model of human nature.

Both modern and classical conceptions of ethics share one common theme. They tend to treat the very different social contexts in which they were formulated as unchanging features of nature.[38] Hegel's great contribution to moral theory started from a historical comparison of these two contexts: asking how and why we (or more precisely Germans at the turn of the 19th century) are different from ancient Greeks. By doing this he

---

34: Callinicos, 2000, pp36-87.
35: MacIntyre, 1985, p12.
36: Reiman, 1991, p147.
37: For a readable introduction to virtue ethics see Slote, 1997.
38: MacIntyre, 1985, p159.

began a process, later completed by Marx, of synthesising and overcoming the limitations of both Kantian morality and Aristotelian ethics.

Just as Aristotle sought to base his ethics on a model of human essence, Hegel insisted that ethics must start from a model of "what human beings *are*". It is only when they are so grounded that it is possible to say "that some modes of life are suited to our nature, whereas others are not".[39] He followed Aristotle in assuming that the goal of life is self-realisation, but he broke with him by arguing that it is only by way of freedom that this is possible. Whereas Aristotle insisted that happiness is the end of life, Hegel believed with Kant that the end of life was freedom.[40] But unlike Kant, who counterposed freedom to necessity, he insisted that to act freely was to act in accordance with necessity.[41] He thus criticised "Kant for seeing dichotomies in the self between freedom and nature...where he ought to have seen freedom as actualising nature".[42] Moreover, he believed that moral laws, far from being universal in some transhistoric sense, are in fact only intelligible "in the context of a particular community", and can be universalised only to the extent that "communities grow and consolidate into an international community".[43]

Hegel thus provided a social content to the concept of freedom by relating it to the movement of "a living social whole".[44] In so doing, he simultaneously worked a dramatic change on Aristotle's concept of happiness. For if human nature evolves with the cultural evolution of communities then so too does the meaning of self-realisation. His ethics is therefore best understood as a form of "dialectical or historicised naturalism".[45] It was this historical understanding of human nature that provided Marx with the basis from which he went beyond existing materialist (Hobbesian) and idealist (Kantian) models of agency.

There is something appealing about both materialist and idealist models of human behaviour. It seems intuitively right to suppose that underlying the complex web of our actions is a desire to meet our natural needs, but it also true that on many occasions we choose to act so as to either suppress or order our desires. If the materialists reduce us to little more than machines built for the satisfaction of our natural desires, the

---

39: Wood, 1990, pp32, 17.
40: Wood, 1990, pp33, 20.
41: Hegel, 1956, p26; Lukács, 1975, p354; Engels, 1947, p140.
42: Wood, 1990, p70.
43: Solomon, 1983, pp480-481.
44: Lukács, 1975, p153.
45: Wood, 1990, p33.

idealists suggest that we should repress our natural desires when we make decisions about the ways we ought to act. These two approaches therefore look less like alternatives than they do opposite variations on the same mistake: both analyse our actions in a way that makes them "unintelligible as a form of *human* action".[46] Marx aimed to overcome this opposition between materialism and idealism in his theory of history. In effect he took Hegel's attempt to synthesise causal, materialist models of behaviour with purposeful, idealist accounts of action and, by divesting the result of its religious colouration, provide a framework through which our actions could be understood as free *human* actions.[47] It was from this perspective that Marx disassociated his theory of history from both crude materialism and idealism (moralism):

> The chief defect of all hitherto-existing materialism...is that the thing, reality, sensuousness, is conceived only in the form of the object, or of contemplation, but not as sensuous human activity, practice, not subjectively. Hence, in contradiction to materialism, the active side was developed abstractly by idealism—which, of course, does not know real, sensuous activity as such.[48]

Against both materialism and idealism Marx outlined a historical model of agency which underpinned both the scientific and moral aspects of his anti-capitalism. Thus his ethics escape the nihilistic limits of modern moral discourse without totally dismissing moral language.

Marxism and the moral standpoint

There is an important difference between social and natural "facts". Physical laws operate irrespective of whether or not people are there to experience them, whereas social systems are reproduced through human practice and so are dependent for their reproduction on conscious human action. The law of gravity is a fact, and my thoughts about it are irrelevant to how it operates on me; the law of value, by contrast, can be transformed by human action. However, to any isolated individual in the modern world social laws appear to be as objective as natural laws. The capitalist system seems to carry on regardless of our individual actions, such that while we are free to act howsoever we please, our freedom seems to have little impact beyond our personal relations. We are free to do anything except change the world.

46: MacIntyre, 1998, p42.
47: Lukács, 1975, p345.
48: Marx, 1975a, p422.

The situation is somewhat different when we engage in collective struggles. The sheer scale of the 2003 global demonstrations against the war in Iraq gave rise to a feeling that the "facts" of imperialism could be challenged. Even more profoundly, when workers are involved in heightened periods of class struggle not only are they able to recognise their power to reorder the world, but in so doing they can begin to recognise that social "facts" are not as stable as they appear to atomised individuals.

Such actions create the possibility that workers might begin to see that the alienated world, which normally appears as a power over them, is actually a product of their labours and that it is within their powers to change it. If the social world appears as a pre-given brute fact when we engage with it as atomised individuals, when we act together, and especially when workers act together, its true nature as a product of our labour can become apparent. Marx argued that this is precisely what happened in 1844 when the Silesian weavers rose against their bourgeois masters, and it was in the light of this movement that he became a "Marxist".[49] Typically modern moral theory fails to recognise the importance of this kind of practice because it assumes that egoism is a fact of nature.

A consequence of this assumption is brought out in Marx's critique of Max Stirner's anarchism. In *The Ego and His Own* (1844) Stirner set out to deny the "truth" of concepts such as nation, state, god, humanity, etc, which had up to that point, he claimed, ruled over individuals through the mechanism of moral ideology. He dismissed any movement, including communism, which sought to overcome egoism as but a new version of authoritarian moralism.[50] In a devastating critique of this argument Marx argued that Stirner was unable to conceptualise community except as a moral imposition upon individuals because he believed that modern egoism was a universal fact of human nature.[51] This assumption informed Stirner's belief that the concept of workers' solidarity was "quite incomprehensible". By contrast, Marx showed that because egoistic and more social forms of individualism had emerged in the modern world, morality, as it was understood by Stirner, was an essential authoritarian characteristic only of bourgeois communities. Alternatively, Marx argued, because solidarity had become a real need for workers, there was no need to impose the idea of community on them. This is why, in stark contrast to modern

---

49: See Marx, 1975b, p415; Blackburn, 1977, pp27-30.
50: Arthur, 1970, pp. 25, 28-29. See also McLellan, 1969, p119.
51: Marx and Engels, 1987b, p211.

liberal criticisms of the implicit authoritarianism of his ideas,[52] he claimed that "communists do not preach morality".[53]

Marx insists that it is a mistake to reduce all modern forms of individualism to the egoistic type. Collective revolts against capital expose the limitations of the liberal concept of freedom while expressing the deep, shared and growing need for solidarity that could provide a concrete content to a new form of social individuality. It is from this perspective that he concretises the abstract idea of freedom by asking "Whose freedom?"[54]

As against the standard textbook caricature of his ideas as crudely materialist, Marx does not deny the concept of human freedom. Rather he exposes liberalism's treatment of the unfreedoms of capitalist society as ordained by nature. Indeed, the concept of human freedom is a major theme of both his early and his mature work. Thus in the *Grundrisse* he defined freedom as a process through which "social individuals" come to realise themselves through their labours.[55] Similarly, in *Capital* he argued:

> Freedom…can consist only in this, that socialised man, the associated producers, govern the human metabolism with nature in a rational way, bringing it under their common control instead of being dominated by it as a blind power.[56]

In fact "the central theme of Marx's moral theory is how to realise human freedom".[57] Concretely, he points to the way that the meaning of freedom evolves over time through a process of collective struggles that are best understood against the background of the development of humanity's productive forces.[58] This should in no way be read as evidence that Marx reduced freedom to economic growth, for he insists that "although an individual cannot become free in isolation from others, nonetheless it is only individuals who are free".[59]

Marx's ethical judgements therefore relate to real historical struggles for freedom. Specifically, workers' struggles against exploitation not only

---

52: Berlin, 1997.
53: Marx and Engels, 1987b, p247.
54: Marx, quoted in Draper, 1977, p273.
55: Gould, 1978, pp101-128; Gilbert, 1981, p98; Sayers, 1998, pp36-59; Marx and Engels, 1987b, pp218, 225; Marx, 1976, p283; Wood, 1981, p17.
56: Marx, 1981, p959.
57: Mészáros, 1975, p162.
58: Marx and Engels, 1987b, pp74 onwards; Marx, 1981, p959.
59: Gould, 1978, p108.

provide him with a basis from which he condemns modern society,[60] but also expose the limitations of freedom within it. From the "legal standpoint" commodity exchange presupposes nothing more than "the worker's power to dispose freely of his own capacities, and the money owner or commodity owner's power to dispose freely of the values that belong to him". Nonetheless, despite their formal freedoms workers have no control over the means of production. They feel a "silent compulsion" to work for capitalists,[61] and factory work itself "confiscates every atom of freedom" from them.[62] This is a consequence of the very structure of capitalist production, where Marx recognised a mutual connection between the anarchic relations between units of capital and the despotic relationship between capitalists and workers within the factory.[63]

This relationship provides the backdrop to the "dialectical inversion" that Marx argues occurs at the point of production between, on the one hand, the equal exchange of commodities and, on the other hand, the appropriation of value from the worker by the capitalist. Far from being a confusing and unnecessary addition to an otherwise powerful argument,[64] this claim comes after around 400 pages in my Penguin edition of *Capital* in which Marx excavates in great detail the process whereby the capitalists "consume" labour power.[65] Moreover, it is built upon what he claims was one of "the best points" in his book: "*the twofold character of labour, according to whether it is expressed in use value or exchange value*".[66] It is through the process of the production of absolute and relative surplus value that capitalists attempt to profit from their investment in labour power by forcing workers to work as hard, and for as long, as is possible. Moreover, the ensuing struggle at the point of production—the "protracted more or less concealed civil war between capitalist class and the working class"—is the very basis for both Marx's politics and his ethics.[67]

This ethics is not to be confused with abstract morality. There is no standpoint from which we might agree on the "fair distribution of the

---

60: Sayers, 1998, p124. See also Husami, 1980, p49.
61: Marx, 1976, pp729, 899.
62: Marx, 1976, p548.
63: Barker, Colin, 1991, p207. Marx's references to the "despotism in the manufacturing division of labour" and the "organised despotism of the factory system" can be found in Marx, 1976, p477 and Marx, 1994, p29.
64: A claim made in Geras, 1989.
65: Marx, 1976, chapters 7-17; the comment on consumption is to be found on p291.
66: Marx, 1987a, p407.
67: Marx, 1976, p412.

proceeds of labour". "Does not the bourgeoisie", he wrote, "claim that the present-day distribution is 'just'? And given the present mode of production is it not, in fact, the only 'just' system of distribution?"[68] To attempt to persuade the bourgeoisie of the injustices of the capitalist system would be to miss the point. What appears unjust from the perspective of workers' struggles appears perfectly fair from the capitalist's perspective. This is why the class struggle within bourgeois society manifests itself as a conflict of "right against right", and that between "equal rights, force decides".[69]

Importantly, Marx claims that the truth of the process of exploitation is obscured so long as it is seen from the point of view of atomised individuals, to become fully apparent only when examined from the point of view of workers' struggles which hold the key to grasping the totality of the capitalist system:

> To be sure, the matter looks quite different if we consider capitalist production in the uninterrupted flow of its renewal, and if, in place of the individual capitalist and the individual worker, we view them in their totality, as the capitalist class and the working class confronting each other. But in so doing we should be applying standards entirely foreign to commodity production.[70]

This claim provides the all-important point of contact between Marx's scientific, explanatory account of the dynamics of the capitalist mode of production and his normative critique of capitalism. As against the bourgeois separation of "is" and "ought", these two aspects of Marx's social theory are best understood as two sides of the same coin: the labour theory of value underpins Marxism both as a social science and as a normative critique. Moreover, this argument provides the key to understanding Marx's condemnation of morality. He dismisses those moral attitudes which pretend to offer some mechanism through which a universal good might be promoted in a world in which social divisions undermine such a project, and he does this from the point of view of a class based morality which, he believes, is in its purpose genuinely universal in a historical sense.[71]

Marxism, therefore, both presupposes and reaffirms the sort of social practice—collective working class struggles—which not only reveals the facts of exploitation but also points to a potential alternative mode of production.

68: Marx, 1974, p344.
69: Marx, 1976, p344.
70: Marx, 1976, p732.
71: Engels, 1947, p118; Marx, Karl, 1975c, p255.

As Terry Eagleton argues, "In the critical consciousness of any oppressed group or class, the understanding and the transforming of reality, 'fact' and 'value', are not separable processes but aspects of the same phenomenon".[72]

It is from this perspective that Marx criticises, among other ideas, Proudhon's concept of "eternal justice", an idea that informs more recent campaigns for "fair trade". He argues that Proudhon's attempt, in *What is Property?*, to "turn political economy's premises...against its conclusions"[73] reflects his inability to look beneath the surface appearance of equal exchange in a system of generalised commodity production to the underlying appropriation of value from workers. "We may well", wrote Marx, "feel astonished at the cleverness of Proudhon who would abolish capitalist property—by enforcing the eternal laws of property which are themselves based on commodity production!"[74] Marx's criticism of Proudhon's concept of "eternal justice" is simply a rejection of Proudhon's confused moralism, rather than a rejection of moral discourse *per se*.

Marx first explored the superficiality of political economy in his *Economic and Philosophical Manuscripts* (1844). Here he argued that, while Adam Smith and David Ricardo, the fathers of modern economics, show that capitalism is dehumanising, they do not prove that it is natural. Smith's and Ricardo's variations on the labour theory of value entail that capital "is nothing but accumulated labour", yet they justify a situation in which the worker, "far from being in a position to buy everything, must sell himself and his humanity". Marx explains that capital itself is no neutral arbiter set up to mediate the exchange of commodities in the marketplace. On the contrary, it is a social relationship through which labour is controlled: "Capital is, therefore, the power to command labour, and its products. The capitalist possesses this power not on account of his personal or human properties but insofar as he is an owner of capital." Given Smith's claim that capital is nothing but "a certain quantity of labour stocked and stored up",[75] it follows that as the store of labour expands so does the power of the capitalist over the worker. Consequently, "the misery of the worker is in inverse proportion to the power and volume of his production".[76] This is quite the most perverse of situations. Increasing social wealth goes hand in hand with decreasing autonomy!

While the direct costs of this mode of production are felt most

72: Eagleton, 1990, p225.
73: McNally, 1993, pp141-143; see also Proudhon, 1994.
74: Marx, 1976, p734.
75: Marx, 1975d, p295.
76: Marx, 1975d, p322.

acutely by the working class, the capitalists are by no means immune to the power of capital. The market imposes its logic upon them just as much as it does upon the workers. While "the capitalist, by means of capital, exercises his power to command labour…capital, in its turn, is able to rule the capitalist himself".[77] Capital acts as an ever expanding power over everyone within the capitalist system. This, broadly speaking, is the meaning of Marx's concept of alienation. Whereas it is our nature to work together to meet our needs, under capitalism we lose control over what and how we produce, and consequently lose sight of the fact that producing together is our essence. Indeed, rather than realising ourselves through production, that which we produce comes to stand opposed to us "as *something alien, as a power independent* of the producer".[78] It is because of this that capitalist relations of production warp our very nature.

Alienation therefore is "the obverse of self-realisation".[79] Moreover, the ends of production are alienated from workers and capitalists alike, and the act of producing becomes for both groups a mere means to maintain their existence. Thus the division between means and ends proves to have social roots.

Therefore, just as facts and values are separated in the modern world, alienation means that whereas life had once been lived as a totality it was now split into various contradictory spheres of existence—the moral, the economic and so forth—each with its own distinct standards. Marx illustrates this situation with an example taken from contemporary French society. When French working class women felt compelled to prostitute themselves so that the family might eat, they experienced the contradictory pressures of moral and economic pressures. If the former taught them to respect their humanity, by the standards of the latter they were mere commodities to be sold to the highest bidder in the marketplace.[80]

Although both main classes in capitalist society are affected by alienation, they experience this in different ways:

> The propertied class and the class of the proletariat present the same human self-estrangement. But the former class feels at ease and strengthened in this self-estrangement; it recognises estrangement as *its own power* and has in it the *semblance* of a human existence. The class of the proletariat feels annihilated

77: Marx, 1975d, p295.
78: Marx, 1975d, pp322-334; Marx, 1975e, pp266-269.
79: Norman, 1983, p174. See also Miller, 1989, p178; Miller, 1984, pp76 onwards; Wood, 1981, p126.
80: Marx, 1975d, p362.

in estrangement; it sees in it its own powerlessness and the reality of an inhuman existence.[81]

It is this differential experience of alienation that underpins the modern form of class struggle. On this issue, Marx was keen to point out that, while socialist writers ascribe both a revolutionary and an emancipatory role to the proletariat, this should not be understood as implying that they believed workers to be "gods". Conversely, neither did they fall into the trap of dismissing the emancipatory potential of the working class. Marx argued that it was capitalism's inhumanity that compelled workers to rebel against their situation and to grasp towards those forms of association through which they could make concrete that which for Kant was merely an abstract proposition: the goal of treating others not as means to their ends but as an end in themselves.[82] This was no abstract deduction on Marx's part, but rather was an empirical observation of existing tendencies.

It was thus from the standpoint of the struggles of the working class that the split between facts and values on the one hand, and means and ends on the other was put into a historical context, and the conception of individual rights challenged from the point of view of workers' collective struggles.[83]

Virtues, working class struggle and the party

Recently it has been argued that Marx failed to justify the ethical significance of working class practice, and therefore wrapped himself in a contradiction from which he was unable to escape.[84] According to this argument, Marx's theory of alienation simultaneously seems to imply that "knowledge of human nature gives the standard for political change" but that our alienation from this nature prevents workers developing such a knowledge.[85] Thus, whereas Marx's eleventh thesis on Feuerbach famously proposes a break with philosophy—"the philosophers have only interpreted the world in various ways, the point is to change it"—this is an impossible dream because alienated human life cannot provide a window to some supposed real humanity.[86]

Such claims about a dichotomy within Marx's thought between human nature as it could be under socialism and as it is under capitalism miss the point. For Marx, our nature evolves in a context of humanity's

---

81:   Marx and Engels, 1987a, p36.
82:   Goldmann, 1971, pp199, 211.
83:   Marx, 1975f, p231.
84:   Brudney, 1998, p197.
85:   Brudney, 1998, pp4, 224-226.
86:   Brudney, 1998, p361.

developing productive powers and the struggle for control over those powers. He argues against any romantic notion of a natural human solidarity, claiming that "individuals cannot gain mastery over their own social interconnections before they have created them". If "in earlier stages of development the single individual seems to have developed more fully", this was only because these individuals had not yet fully worked out their mutual "relationships". Bourgeois thought tends to confront the horrors of bourgeois society with an impotent, romantic alternative, but it is "ridiculous to yearn for a return to that original fullness".[87] The problem Marx addresses is not whether workers have the capacity to recreate some pristine humanity out of their alienated existence. Rather he criticises the existing social order from the point of view of real struggles against it, judging that workers' struggles point towards a fuller realisation of human freedom. This is why, as Hal Draper points out, rather than use the abstract word "socialism" to describe their goal, Marx and Engels more usually wrote of "workers' power".[88]

Workers feel their alienation as dehumanisation against which they tend to struggle for self-realisation. Moreover, it is through such collective struggles that they tend to change as the need for solidarity engenders a more socialistic attitude. So in 1853 Marx wrote that "the continual conflicts between masters and men are...the indispensable means of holding up the spirit of the labouring classes, of combining them into one great association against the encroachment of the ruling class, and of preventing them from becoming apathetic, thoughtless, more or less well-fed instruments of production".[89] Six years earlier he had pointed out how the struggle to form associations (trade unions), became inexplicable to classical political economy once workers began to turn over to the associations, for the sake of association, "a good part of their wages". "The domination of capital has created for this mass a common situation, common interests." Consequently, whereas political economy was able only to understand atomised individualism, Marx showed how a new social rationality emerged within the working class.[90] Marx thus suggests not only that workers feel compelled to struggle against the power of capital, but that in so doing they begin to create modes of existence, which also offer a virtuous alternative to the egoism characteristic not only of capitalist society generally, but also of working class life within that society.

87: Marx, 1973a, pp161-162.
88: Draper, 1978, p24.
89: Marx, 1987b, p43.
90: Marx, from the "The Poverty of Philosophy", quoted in Lapides, 1987, p34.

When communist workmen gather together, their immediate aim is instruction, propaganda, etc. But at the same time, they acquire a new need—the need for society—and what appears as a means has become an end. This practical development can be most strikingly observed in the gatherings of French socialist workers. Smoking, eating, and drinking, etc, are no longer means of creating links between people. Company, association, conversation, which in turn has society as its goal, is enough for them. The brotherhood of man is not a hollow phrase, it is a reality, and the nobility of man shines forth upon us from their work worn figures.[91]

By forming and being active within trade unions and working class political parties, workers create institutions through which they change themselves. Working together in such institutions becomes a day to day practice that both presupposes the need for solidarity and engenders a spirit of solidarity within the working class. The virtues or character traits that are thus promoted stand in direct opposition to the competitive individualism of the capitalist marketplace.

These struggles provide the basis for Marx's involvement in the "creation of an independent organisation of the workers' party".[92] Because he insisted that socialism can only come from below, he realised that it will necessarily emerge out of sectional and fragmented struggles which create differences between more and less advanced workers, and consequently results in the emergence of socialist leaders.[93] As John Molyneux has argued, Marx's conception of the revolutionary party "absolutely ruled out" both the "conspiratorial" idea of the party of as a small elite acting for the working class and the "authoritarian view" of the party handing orders down to the class from above. Against both of these models, Marx firmly established "the concept of leadership won on the basis of performance in the class struggle".[94] Whereas socialist and anarchist sectarians prescribed a set course, deduced from doctrine, to the workers' movement, Marx looked "among the genuine elements of the class movement for the real basis of his agitation".[95] In his political practice both in the 1840s and in the period of the First International he was concerned centrally with the need to foster the struggles of the working class as a class, while simultaneously challenging those forces, for instance anti-Irish racism in England,

91: Marx, 1975d, p365.
92: Marx, 1973b, p324.
93: Lih, 2006, p556.
94: Molyneux, 1986, p17.
95: Marx, 1987c, pp111-112.

which grew out of and acted to reinforce and extend divisions within the proletariat.[96]

Among subsequent generations of Marxists perhaps Georg Lukács and Antonio Gramsci most powerfully extended these ideas in their commentaries on Lenin's contribution to Marxism. In his *Lenin* Lukács argued that the workers' councils or soviets, which had emerged spontaneously in periods of heightened class struggle since the Russian Revolution of 1905, were "already essentially the weapons of the proletariat organising itself as a class" against the old state and the bourgeoisie.[97] Moreover, they acted as a potential bridge between the "is" of existing society and the "ought" of socialism. As opposed to the institutions of bourgeois democracy which relate to voters as "abstract individuals", these structures organise workers as "concrete human beings who occupy specific positions within social production". So, whereas bourgeois parliaments tend towards "disorganising" the working class, soviets represent an organic attempt by the proletariat to "counteract this process".[98] These spontaneous institutions of workers' struggle provided, he claimed, a potential ethical basis from which to criticise the alienation of capitalist society. Thus, while "class consciousness is the 'ethics' of the proletariat" which is concretely expressed through "the party",[99] this ethical standpoint is itself rooted in the spontaneous institutions of workers' struggle.

A similar argument was developed by Gramsci. In an allusion to a phrase from Marx's preface to the *Contribution to the Critique of Political Economy* he wrote that "the scientific base for a morality of historical materialism is to be looked for, in my opinion, in the affirmation that 'society does not pose for itself tasks the conditions for whose resolution do not already exist'. Where these conditions exist 'the solution of the tasks becomes "duty", "will" becomes free'".[100] More generally he took up the notion of "ethico-political history" developed by the idealist philosopher Benedetto Croce in an attempt to place individual agency at the centre of the historical process. Gramsci argued that authentic Marxism "does not exclude ethico-political history", and that Lenin's revolutionary practice lay in asserting the fundamental importance of this moment, the moment of hegemony, to the historical process.[101]

Concretely, in the midst of the struggles of the Turin factory workers

---

96: Collins and Abramsky, 1965, pp39, 45; Harris, 1990, pp44-45; Gilbert, 1981.
97: Lukács, 1970, p63.
98: Lukács, 1970, pp65-66.
99: Lukács, 1971, pp41-42.
100: Gramsci, 1971, pp409-410.
101: Gramsci, 1995, pp329; 345-346; 357; 360.

in 1919 and 1920 the group around Gramsci's newspaper *L'Ordine Nuovo* sought to provide an answer to the question of how "the dictatorship of the proletariat" might move from being an abstract slogan to a concrete end of action.[102] In answer to the question, "How are the immense social forces unleashed by the war to be harnessed?" Gramsci answered that "the socialist state exists potentially in the institutions of social life characteristic of the exploited working class".[103] In thus rooting revolutionary politics within the real movement of workers, Gramsci's Marxism began to realise an ethics that went beyond the contradictions of bourgeois thought.[104]

From this perspective the moral dimension of politics is neither an abstract imperative imposed upon individuals in the name of some supposedly disembodied reason, nor a distraction from an otherwise automatic process of the growth of working class socialist consciousness. Rather socialist morality is the flipside of the scientific critique of political economy As Michael Löwy argues:

> At bottom what we have here is not even an interpretation "linked with" or "accompanied by" a practice but a total human activity, practical-critical activity in which theory is already revolutionary praxis, and practice is loaded with theoretical significance.[105]

Collective working class struggles both reveal and provide a basis for the condemnation of exploitation and alienation while simultaneously acting as the concrete form of solidarity that is both the means to and end of socialism. Whereas modern moral philosophy is a reflection of our alienated existence under capitalism, Marxism, both as an explanatory account of the dynamics of capitalism and as a condemnation of this system, is rooted in these collective struggles of workers against alienation. Practice does not and cannot therefore follow theory in the way that modern moral theory would have us suppose, for it is universally true that we can theorise only from specific standpoints. As Alasdair MacIntyre argued when he was still a Marxist, "One cannot first understand the world and only then act on it.

102: Gramsci, 1977, p68.
103: Gramsci, 1977, p65.
104: Some people have claimed that Gramsci's embrace of Leninism undermined the powerful ethical dimensions of his earlier Marxism (see, for instance, Boggs, 1976, p86), but his stress on the need for the party did not mean he had forgotten the strengths of the *Ordine Nuovo* period. See the section of *International Socialism 114* devoted to Gramsci, with articles by Megan Trudell, Chris Bambery, Chris Harman and Adrian Budd.
105: Löwy, 2003, p109.

How one understands the world will depend in part on the decision implicit in one's already taken actions. The wager of action is unavoidable".[106]

Conclusion

Terry Eagleton suggests that "Marx does indeed possess an 'absolute' moral criterion: the unquestionable virtue of the rich, all-round expansion of capacities for each individual. It is from this standpoint that any social formation is to be assessed".[107] To flourish in this way requires both that our basic needs are first met, and that new needs are also met. Marx's famous needs principle—from each according to abilities, to each according to need[108]—is therefore best understood as referring to historically evolving needs which are articulated at specific junctures through debates, first within the various historical movements of the oppressed and finally under socialism.[109] And because Marx recognises that we are social individuals, he implies a model of discrimination between various powers: "We should foster only those powers which allow an individual to realise herself through and in terms of the similar free self-realisation of others. It is this, above all, which distinguishes socialism from liberalism".[110] Furthermore, Marx shows that liberalism, far from representing the disinterested power of reason, in fact acts to legitimise modern capitalist social relations by treating them as natural facts.[111] And if liberalism emerged in the 17th century as a reflection of the "interests of the new commercial middle classes",[112] in so far as it continues to naturalise modern social relations it continues to reflect similar interests today.

Socialism, by contrast, is not a moral doctrine in the modern sense of this term because it neither pretends to be disinterested nor is it to be imposed upon otherwise egoistic individuals from above. Marx argued that although socialism is rooted in the particular interests of the working class its success is ultimately in the universal interest. And in stark contrast to the liberal conflation of individual rights with property rights, Marx argues that because capitalist relations of production lead to "the domination of material relations over individuals and the suppression of individuality", modern individuals are set the "definite task" of

---

106: MacIntyre, 1971b, p84.
107: Eagleton, 1990, pp223, 226; see also Marx, 1973a, pp487-488.
108: Marx, 1974, p347.
109: Sayers, 1998, pp125-129; Geras, 1989, p264.
110: Eagleton, 1990, p224.
111: Reiman, 1991, p147.
112: Ramsay, 1997, p7.

overthrowing this mode of production and replacing it with a communist reorganisation of society.[113]

One of the roles of intellectuals in this movement against alienation is to make explicit that which is implicit in those struggles. "We do not say to the world: cease your struggles, they are foolish; we will give you the true slogan of struggle. We merely show the world what it is really fighting for, and consciousness is something that it has to acquire even if it does not want to".[114] Marx's socialism is therefore, in Engels' words, "nothing but the reflex, in thought" of the social conflicts endemic to capitalism.[115] Nevertheless, Marx was well aware that although revolutions are inevitable their success is not, and his social theory consequently involves a call to action. In the modern world this entails both engagement with, and fanning the flames of, those collective struggles against the dehumanising and alienating effects of capitalism through which our need for solidarity both emerges and is realised. This perspective is ethical in the sense that Marx completed Hegel's attempt to synthesise Kant's concept of freedom with the Aristotelian aim of fostering those forms of life that allow us to "excel at being human".[116]

Marx's ethics thus act as a pivot between his theories of history, economics and politics. If the collective struggles of workers reveal the true essence of capitalism as an exploitative mode of production, they also show that the world in which we live is not a ready made thing but is rather a product of human agency[117] that can be remade by the "new fangled" working class.[118] And if the workers' need for solidarity grows as a response to the collective experience of exploitation, this kind of solidarity also acts as the basis for a real alternative to capitalist competition.[119]

113: Marx and Engels, 1987b, p438.
114: Marx, 1975g, p144.
115: Engels, 1947, p325.
116: Eagleton, 2003, p142; see also Eagleton, 2007.
117: On this, see Lukács's claim that from the standpoint of workers' struggles we are able to recognise "the problem of the present as a historical problem". Lukács, 1971, pp157-158.
118: This phrase is taken from Marx, 1973c, p300.
119: Goldmann, 1968, p18.

References

Adler, Max, 1978, "The Relation of Marxism to Classical German Philosophy", in Tom Bottomore and Patrick Goode (eds), *Austro-Marxism* (Oxford University).

Anderson, Perry, 1974, *Passages from Antiquity to Feudalism* (Verso).

Aristotle, 1976, *Ethics* (Penguin). An alternative translation is available at http://etext.library. adelaide.edu.au/a/aristotle/nicomachean/

Arthur, Chris, 1970, "Introduction", in Marx, Karl, *The German Ideology: Student Edition*, (Lawrence and Wishart).

Barker, Colin, 1991, "A Note on the Theory of the Capitalist State", in Simon Clarke (ed), *The State Debate* (Macmillan).

Bentham, Jeremy, 1990 [1781], "Of the Principle of Utility", in Jonathan Glover (ed), *Utilitarianism and its Critics* (Macmillan). Also available at www.utilitarianism.com/jeremy-bentham/

Berlin, Isaiah, 1997, "Two Concepts of Liberty", in *The Proper Study of Mankind* (Pimlico).

Blackburn, Robin, 1977, "Marxism: Theory of Proletarian Revolution", in Robin Blackburn (ed), *Revolution and Class Struggle* (Fontana).

Blackledge, Paul, 2008, "Alasdair MacIntyre's Contribution to Marxism: A Road not Taken", *Analyse and Kritik*, volume 30, number 1.

Blackledge, Paul, forthcoming, "Alasdair MacIntyre: Social Practices, Marxism and Ethical Anti-Capitalism", *Political Studies*.

Blackledge, Paul, and Neil Davidson (eds), 2008, *Alasdair MacIntyre's Engagement with Marxism: Essays and Articles 1953-1974* (Brill).

Boggs, Carl, 1976, *Gramsci's Marxism* (Pluto).

Brenkert, George, 1983, *Marx's Ethics of Freedom* (Routledge).

Brudney, Daniel, 1998, *Marx's Attempt to Leave Philosophy* (Harvard University).

Callinicos, Alex, 2000, *Equality* (Polity).

Critchley, Simon, 2007, *Infinitely Demanding* (Verso).

Cohen, GA, 2000, *If You're an Egalitarian, How Come You're So Rich?* (Harvard University).

Collins, Henry, and Chimon Abramsky, 1965, *Karl Marx and the British Labour Movement* (Macmillan).

Draper, Hal, 1977, *Karl Marx's Theory of Revolution*, volume one (Monthly Review).

Draper, Hal, 1978, *Karl Marx's Theory of Revolution*, volume two (Monthly Review).

Eagleton, Terry, 1990, *The Ideology of the Aesthetic* (Blackwell).

Eagleton, Terry, 2003, *After Theory* (Penguin).

Eagleton, Terry, 2007, *The Meaning of Life* (Oxford University).

Engels, Frederick, 1947 [1877], *Anti-Dühring* (Progress), www.marxists.org/archive/marx/ works/1877/anti-duhring/

Engels, Frederick, 1972 [1884], *The Origin of the Family, Private Property, and the State* (Lawrence and Wishart). An alternative translation is available at www.marxists.org/archive/marx/ works/1884/origin-family/

Ferguson, Iain, 2008, "Neoliberalism, Happiness and Wellbeing", *International Socialism* 117 (winter 2008), www.isj.org.uk/?id=400

Frank, Robert 1999, *Luxury Fever* (Free Press).

Geras, Norman, 1989, "The Controversy about Marx and Justice", in Alex Callinicos (ed), 1989, *Marxist Theory* (Oxford University). Originally published in *New Left Review 150* (March-April 1985).

Gilbert, Alan, 1981, *Marx's Politics* (Martin Robertson).

Goldmann, Lucien, 1968, "Is there a Marxist Sociology?", *International Socialism 34*, first series, www.marxists.org/history/etol/newspape/isj/1968/no034/goldmann.htm

Goldmann, Lucien, 1971, *Immanuel Kant* (New Left Books).

Gould, Carol, 1978, *Marx's Social Ontology* (MIT).

Gramsci, Antonio, 1971, *Selections from the Prison Notebooks* (Lawrence and Wishart).

Gramsci, Antonio, 1977, *Selections from Political Writings 1910-1920* (Lawrence and Wishart).

Gramsci, Antonio, 1995, *Further Selections from the Prison Notebooks* (University of Minnesota).

Harman, Chris, 1996, "Where's the Moral", *Socialist Review 203* (December 1996), http://pubs.socialistreviewindex.org.uk/sr203/harman.htm

Harris, Nigel, 1990, *National Liberation* (Penguin).

Hegel, Georg, 1952 [1821], *Philosophy of Right* (Oxford University). An alternative translation is available at www.marxists.org/reference/archive/hegel/works/pr/

Hegel, Georg, 1956, *The Philosophy of History* (Dover), www.marxists.org/reference/archive/hegel/works/hi/lectures.htm

Hobbes, Thomas, 1998 [1651], *Leviathan* (Oxford University), available at http://oregonstate.edu/instruct/phl302/texts/hobbes/leviathan-contents.html

Hume, David, 1965 [1739], *A Treatise of Human Nature*, in Alasdair MacIntyre (ed), *Hume's Ethical Writings* (Macmillan). Also available at http://ebooks.adelaide.edu.au/h/hume/david/h92t/

Husami, Ziyad, 1980, "Marx on Distributive Justice", in Cohen, Marshall et al (eds), *Marx, Justice and History* (Princeton University).

Kant, Immanuel, 1948 [1785], *Groundwork of the Metaphysics of Morals* (Routledge). An alternative translation is available at http://ebooks.adelaide.edu.au/k/kant/immanuel/k16prm/

Knight, Kelvin, 2007, *Aristotelian Philosophy* (Polity).

Lapides, Kenneth, 1987, *Marx and Engels on the Trade Unions* (International Publishers).

Lih, Lars, 2006, *Lenin Rediscovered* (Brill).

Löwy, Michael, 2003, *The Theory of Revolution in the Young Marx* (Brill).

Lukács, Georg, 1970 [1924], *Lenin: A Study in the Unity of his Thought* (New Left Books), www.marxists.org/archive/lukacs/works/1924/lenin/

Lukács, Georg, 1971, *History and Class Consciousness* (Merlin), www.marxists.org/archive/lukacs/works/history/

Lukács, Georg, 1975 [1938], *The Young Hegel* (Merlin), www.marxists.org/archive/lukacs/works/youngheg/

MacIntyre, Alasdair, 1964, "Against Utilitarianism", in THB Hollins (ed), *Aims in Education*, (Manchester University).

MacIntyre, Alasdair, 1966, *A Short History of Ethics* (Routledge).

MacIntyre, Alasdair, 1971a [1964], "Hume on 'is' and 'ought'", in *Against the Self Images of the Age* (Duckworth).

MacIntyre, Alasdair, 1971b [1964], "Pascal and Marx", in *Against the Self Images of the Age* (Duckworth).

MacIntyre, Alasdair, 1985, *After Virtue* (Duckworth).

MacIntyre, Alasdair, 1998 [1958], "Notes from the Moral Wilderness", in Kelvin Knight (ed), *The MacIntyre Reader* (Polity), also available at www.amielandmelburn.org.uk/collections/nr/07_90.pdf and www.amielandmelburn.org.uk/collections/nr/08_89.pdf

MacIntyre, Alasdair, 2008, "What More Needs to be Said? A Beginning, although only a Beginning, at Saying it", *Analyse and Kritik*, volume 30, number 1.

Marx, Karl, 1973a [1857], *Grundrisse* (Penguin), www.marxists.org/archive/marx/works/1857/grundrisse/

Marx, Karl, 1973b [1850], *Address of the Central Committee to the Communist League (March 1850)*, in *The Revolutions of 1848* (Penguin). An alternative translation is available at www.marxists.org/archive/marx/works/1847/communist-league/1850-ad1.htm

Marx, Karl, 1973c [1856], "Speech at the Anniversary of the *People's Paper*", in Karl Marx, *Surveys from Exile* (Penguin). Also available at www.marxists.org/archive/marx/works/1856/04/14.htm

Marx, Karl, 1974 [1875], *Critique of the Gotha Programme*, in Karl Marx, *The First International and After* (Penguin). An alternative translation is available at www.marxists.org/archive/marx/works/1875/gotha/

Marx, Karl, 1975a [1845], *Theses on Feuerbach*, in *Early Writings* (Penguin). An alternative translation is available at www.marxists.org/archive/marx/works/1845/theses/theses.htm

Marx, Karl, 1975b [1844], *Critical Notes on the "King of Prussia and Social Reform"*, in *Early Writings*: (Penguin). An alternative translation is available at www.marxists.org/archive/marx/works/1844/08/07.htm

Marx, Karl, 1975c [1844], *Critique of Hegel's Philosophy of Right: Introduction*, in *Early Writings* (Penguin). An alternative translation is available at www.marxists.org/archive/marx/works/1843/critique-hpr/intro.htm

Marx, Karl, 1975d [1844], *The Economic and Philosophical Manuscripts*, in *Early Writings* (Penguin). An alternative translation is available at www.marxists.org/archive/marx/works/1844/manuscripts/preface.htm

Marx, Karl, 1975e, *Excerpts from James Mill's Elements of Political Economy*, in *Early Writings* (Penguin). An alternative translation is available at www.marxists.org/archive/marx/works/1844/james-mill/

Marx, Karl, 1975f [1843], *On the Jewish Question*, in *Early Writings* (Penguin). An alternative translation is available at www.marxists.org/archive/marx/works/1844/jewish-question/

Marx, Karl, 1975g [1843], *Letters from the Deutsch-Französische Jarbücher*, in Marx and Engels, *Collected Works*, volume three.

Marx, Karl, 1976 [1867], *Capital*, volume one (Penguin). An alternative translation is available at www.marxists.org/archive/marx/works/1867-c1/

Marx, Karl, 1981 [1894], *Capital*, volume three (Penguin). An alternative translation is available at www.marxists.org/archive/marx/works/1894-c3/

Marx, Karl, 1987a [1867], "Letter to Engels", 24 August 1867, in Marx and Engels, *Collected Works*, volume 42. An alternative translation is available at www.marxists.org/archive/marx/works/1867/letters/67_08_24.htm

Marx, Karl, 1987b [1853], "The Value of Strikes", in Kenneth Lapides, *Marx and Engels on the Trade Unions* (International Publishers). Also available from www.marxists.org/archive/marx/works/subject/trade-unions/

Marx, Karl, 1987c [1868], "Letter to Schweitzer", in Kenneth Lapides, *Marx and Engels on the Trade Unions* (International Publishers). An alternative translation is available at www.marxists.org/archive/marx/works/1868/letters/68_10_13.htm

Marx, Karl, 1994, *Economic Manuscripts of 1861-1863*, in *Collected Works*, volume 34 (Lawrence and Wishart).

Marx, Karl, and Frederick Engels, 1973 [1848], *Manifesto of the Communist Party*, in Karl Marx, *The Revolutions of 1848* (Penguin). An alternative translation is available at www.anu.edu.au/polsci/marx/classics/manifesto.html

Marx, Karl, and Frederick Engels, 1987a [1845], *The Holy Family*, in Marx and Engels, *Collected Works*, volume four (Lawrence and Wishart). Also available at www.marxists.org/archive/marx/works/1845/holy-family/

Marx, Karl, and Frederick Engels, 1987b [1845], *The German Ideology*, in Marx and Engels, *Collected Works*, volume five (Lawrence and Wishart). Also available at www.marxists.org/archive/marx/works/1845/german-ideology/

McLellan, David, 1969, *The Young Hegelians and Karl Marx* (Macmillan).

McNally, David, 1993, *Against the Market* (Verso).

Mészáros, István 1975, *Marx's Theory of Alienation* (Merlin).

Miller, Richard, 1984, *Analyzing Marx* (Princeton University).

Miller, Richard, 1989, "Marx and Aristotle", in Alex Callinicos (ed), 1989, *Marxist Theory* (Oxford University).

Molyneux, John, 1986, *Marxism and the Party* (Bookmarks).

Nederman, Cary, 2008, "Men at Work", *Analyse and Kritik*, volume 30, number 1.

Norman, Richard, 1983, *The Moral Philosophers* (Oxford University).

Proudhon, Pierre, 1994 [1840], *What is Property?* (Cambridge University). An alternative translation is available at www.marxists.org/reference/subject/economics/proudhon/property/

Ramsay, Maureen, 1997, *What's Wrong with Liberalism?* (Leicester University).

Reiman, Jeffrey, 1991, "Moral Philosophy", in Terrell Carver (ed), *The Cambridge Companion to Marx* (Cambridge University).

Sayers, Sean, 1998, *Marxism and Human Nature* (Routledge).

Slote, Michael, 1997, "Virtue Ethics", in Marcia Baron and others, *Three Methods in Ethics* (Blackwell).

Solomon, Robert, 1983, *In the Spirit of Hegel* (Oxford University).

Taylor, Charles, 1975, *Hegel* (Cambridge University).

Trotsky, Leon, 1973 [1938], *Their Morals and Ours* (Pathfinder), www.marxists.org/archive/trotsky/1938/morals/morals.htm

Wilkinson, Richard, 2005, *The Impact of Inequality* (Routledge).

Williams, Bernard, 2006, *Ethics and the Limits of Philosophy* (Routledge).

Wood, Allen, 1981, *Karl Marx* (Routledge).

Wood, Allen, 1990, *Hegel's Ethical Thought* (Cambridge University).

Wood, Allen, 2005, *Kant* (Blackwell).

A fiftieth birthday for Marxist theory

Ian Birchall

September 1958 saw the first issue of a journal called *International Socialism*. It was in duplicated form and undoubtedly had a very limited circulation, being produced and distributed by the tiny Socialist Review Group which counted its members in tens rather than hundreds. Even in the small world of 1950s British Marxism it was marginal in comparison to the Communist Party's monumentally tedious *Marxism Today*,[1] to the *New Reasoner* and *Universities and Left Review*, which in 1960 would merge to form *New Left Review*, and, on the Trotskyist fringe, to the Socialist Labour League's *Labour Review,* which in the late 1950s was a lively journal with such contributors as Peter Fryer, Brian Pearce and Alasdair MacIntyre.[2]

But for the far left it was a time of new opportunities. The ferment of debate provoked by the Hungarian Revolution of 1956 continued. At Easter 1958 the first Aldermaston march for unilateral nuclear disarmament had taken place. In the summer and autumn there was a minor wave of industrial struggle involving bus crews, dockers and building workers. There were also threats: over the Channel in France the Fourth Republic had collapsed and been replaced by a more authoritarian regime under General de Gaulle. The presentation of the new journal was, in a modest and highly realistic manner, optimistic:

1:   This was drably orthodox in its Stalinism, quite unlike the Eurocommunist *Marxism Today* of the 1980s, which impaled itself on its own trendiness.

2:   See www.marxists.org/history/etol/newspape/lr/ for *Labour Review*.

The decline in Western capitalism—however protracted—is steadily undermining the stranglehold of reformism, its servant, over the working class. Stalinism—the ideological expression of the state capitalist world—is losing its potency as an alternative. Once again the international working class is looking to its own resources for strength and inspiration.

The two main articles were by the main theoreticians of the group Tony Cliff and Mike Kidron. Cliff's article, "Changes in Stalinist Russia", examined changes in industrial management in the Khrushchev period and the attempts to deal with lagging labour productivity.[3] Despite developments since Joseph Stalin's death Russia remained a repressive, irrational society. Kidron's "The Economic Background of the Recent Strikes" took up two themes that would be developed in his later contributions to the journal: the decline in Britain's imperial role and the significance of the arms budget.[4]

In a sense the launch of the journal was a false start. In 1959 what purported to be a double issue of the journal was in fact a small book by Cliff on *Rosa Luxemburg*.[5] Then, in the autumn of 1960, the journal was relaunched as a quarterly. This time its editorial board was not limited to the Socialist Review Group but included supporters of the Fourth International (including two who were to become followers of Juan Posadas[6]) and others who would become members of the Solidarity grouping.[7] As so often this effort at left unity collapsed, and from 1963 the journal was simply the organ of the International Socialism group (as the Socialist Review Group was now known).[8] It appeared quarterly and then monthly until 1977 when it was replaced by a new quarterly series in book format which has continued to the present.

Fifty years for a theoretical journal is a substantial achievement.[9] There are close on 1,000 articles plus editorials, reviews and letters. Obviously the quality is uneven. There are mediocre, boring and obscure

---

3: www.marxists.org/archive/cliff/works/1958/xx/changes.htm
4: www.marxists.org/archive/kidron/works/1958/xx/strikes.htm
5: www.marxists.org/archive/cliff/works/1959/rosalux/
6: Posadas advocated a pre-emptive nuclear strike by Russia against the West.
7: Solidarity was a "libertarian" (ie anti-Leninist) group, inspired by the French organisation Socialisme ou Barbarie, which opposed activity in the Labour Party and focused on workplace struggle.
8: See my obituary of Mike Kidron, Birchall 2003a, and my account of Kidron's editorship, Birchall, 2003b.
9: References to articles from the two series are indicated by IS1/ and IS2/ plus the issue number. Wherever there is an online version available at the time of writing I have given a URL.

articles, and polemics that seemed terribly important at the time but are now of little interest. There are also some historical curiosities of particular interest to students of renegacy. These include youthful efforts by Christopher Hitchens,[10] actually more intelligent and better written than his current output, and some industrial commentaries by Roger Rosewell,[11] later unofficial spokesperson for Dame Shirley Porter and more recently author of a tome on medieval wall paintings. There are also some dubious predictions such as Duncan Hallas's claim in 1977 that "it may well be the case that Callaghan's is the *last* majority Labour government".[12]

However, overall a collection of the two series provides a rich store of political analysis and commentary. In comparison with its main rival, *New Left Review*, which for long periods produced relatively little that was directly relevant to contemporary struggle,[13] *International Socialism* was always geared to practice, to an interpretation of the current world in the perspective of changing it.

But if the journal has always been a party journal, geared to the priorities of the organisation, it has been alive to the various debates on the British and international left. It has published contributions from all parts of the spectrum of the left on both directly political and broader cultural questions. Thus the journal has carried pieces by Tariq Ali and others on the Fourth International (IS2/6), Robin Blackburn on Cuba (IS2/9), John Saville on the Marshall Plan and the Cold War (IS2/46), Dan Atkinson and Larry Elliot on Keynes and the economic crisis,[14] John Berger on mass demonstrations[15] and Picasso (IS2/40), Terry Eagleton on Shakespeare (IS2/49) and Steven Rose on animal rights (IS2/54).

From the international left there have been contributions from Jean-Jacques Marie on Gaullism (IS1/3), Ellen Wood on alternatives to reformism (IS2/35), Ernest Mandel on the analysis of Russian society (IS2/49, IS2/56),

---

10: In 1972 Hitchens was joint reviews editor of the journal. See IS1/50 www.marxists.org/history/etol/newspape/isj/1972/no050/hitchens.htm and IS1/51 www.marxists.org/history/etol/newspape/isj/1972/no051/hitchens.htm

11: IS1/50 www.marxists.org/history/etol/newspape/isj/1972/no050/rosewall.htm and IS1/57 www.marxists.org/history/etol/newspape/isj/1973/no057/rosewall.htm

12: IS1/94 www.marxists.org/archive/hallas/works/1977/01/prospects.htm

13: See Birchall, 1980.

14: IS2/82 http://pubs.socialistreviewindex.org.uk/isj82/elliot.htm

15: IS1/34 www.marxists.org/history/etol/newspape/isj/1968/no034/berger.htm

and Susan George,[16] Walden Bello[17] and Boris Kagarlitsky[18] on perspectives for the anti-capitalist movement.

Until recently comrades who wished to consult material from back issues had to hunt it down in libraries or beg, steal or borrow it from older comrades who had kept files. Now, thanks to the wonders of modern technology,[19] a great many articles from the past 50 years are available at the click of a mouse. In particular comrades can consult three valuable websites.

The Encyclopaedia of Trotskyism Online has a complete index of the first series of *International Socialism* with the full text of many articles and reviews.[20] It is worth checking this site regularly as new material is being added all the time. The Socialist Review and International Socialism Journal Index has an index arranged by subject covering the first 108 issues of the second series with the full text of articles from issue 61 onwards.[21] And the International Socialism website has the full text of all issues from 100 onwards together with a small archive of items from earlier issues.[22] Again it is worth checking for updates.[23]

What follows is intended simply as a guide to a small selection of articles that comrades may find of interest. It will be no more than a brief survey of *International Socialism* over the past 50 years. This is not a greatest hits compilation. The decision of what to include has been largely subjective. My sincere apologies to comrades whose late night labours and cherished brainchildren do not get a name-check. I hope it will encourage readers to explore the resources available and make their own discoveries. If I have devoted more space to the earlier period, it is because it is probably less familiar to most readers.

16:   IS2/91 http://pubs.socialistreviewindex.org.uk/isj91/george.htm

17:   IS2/90 http://pubs.socialistreviewindex.org.uk/isj90/bello.htm and IS2/91 http://pubs.socialistreviewindex.org.uk/isj91/bello.htm

18:   IS2/89 http://pubs.socialistreviewindex.org.uk/isj89/kagarlitsky.htm and IS2/92 http://pubs.socialistreviewindex.org.uk/isj92/kagarlitsky.htm

19:   As any Marxist knows, "wonders" always derive from human labour. Einde O'Callaghan, Bob Cox, Edward Crawford and several other comrades are to be warmly thanked for their efforts in making this material available.

20:   1958-68: www.marxists.org/history/etol/newspape/isj/index.html 1969-74: www.marxists.org/history/etol/newspape/isj/index2.html and 1974-78: www.marxists.org/history/etol/newspape/isj/index3.html

21:   www.socialistreviewindex.org.uk

22:   www.isj.org.uk

23:   It is also worth checking the collections on the Marxist Internet Archive (www.marxists.org) for Cliff, Kidron, Hallas, Jim Higgins, Peter Sedgwick, David Widgery and Paul Foot. These archives contain articles from *International Socialism* and from other publications.

In many ways the years before 1968 were the golden age of the journal. Doubtless that claim contains an element of nostalgia on my part (as anyone from my age group will tell you, music and sex were better in those days too). But it was also a question of the journal's role in relation to the organisation. Membership was very small—well under 100 in 1960, just over 400 by the start of 1968. Comrades were active in campaigns—nuclear disarmament and anti-apartheid, then in the mid-1960s tenants' movements and some industrial struggles—but the organisation was far too small to intervene in its own name. In the early 1960s most activity took place in the sectarian hothouse of the Labour Party Young Socialists.

As a result the struggle for ideas was vital, and the fact that in 1962 the Socialist Review Group was renamed the International Socialism group was a clear indication of just how central the role of the journal was. The Marxism of the journal in those years was confident and flexible. Confident because unlike those who saw Russia as socialist or even a "degenerated workers' state" we had nothing to make contorted apologies for. Confident too because first Harold Macmillan's Tories and then Harold Wilson's Labour government showed themselves utterly inept at solving the problems of British society. Meanwhile a rising level of industrial struggle showed that the class struggle was far from dead, as it had been pronounced by Labour politicians. Marxism was clearly relevant to the world we lived in.

But because the Marxism of *International Socialism* was confident it was also adaptable. Tony Cliff was quite happy to describe his work as "revisionist".[24] Some of the central tenets of orthodox Trotskyism were called into question. Mike Kidron showed that Lenin's *Imperialism: the Highest Stage of Capitalism* was "supremely good theory in its day" but in a radically changed world "no more the complete manual".[25] Cliff showed that the theory of permanent revolution needed updating in the light of the Chinese and Cuban revolutions.[26]

The work of Cliff and Kidron provided the theoretical core of the journal. Cliff had spent most of the 1950s developing the theory of state capitalism with books on Russia, China and the Eastern European satellites. Now he was pursuing the implications of this into a more general attempt to develop and revise Marxism for the modern epoch. In "Trotsky on Substitutionism" he discussed what form of organisation was appropriate

---

24: See his "Marxism and the Collectivisation of Agriculture", IS1/19 www.marxists.org/archive/cliff/works/1964/xx/

25: IS1/9 www.marxists.org/archive/kidron/works/1962/xx/imperial.htm

26: IS1/12 www.marxists.org/archive/cliff/works/1963/xx/permrev.htm

for revolutionary socialists in the modern period.[27] In so doing he was polemicising against both the ultra-Bolshevism of the Socialist Labour League and the anti-Leninists of the Solidarity current. In "The Labour Party in Perspective" he made some important observations on the nature of class consciousness, though his conclusion was that Marxists would continue working within the Labour Party for the foreseeable future.[28] There was also a savage polemic entitled "The End of the Road" against Isaac Deutscher,[29] who had just published the final volume of his biographical trilogy on Trotsky. Cliff claimed that "under Deutscher's pen, Stalinism is the legitimate child of the revolution". The article should be read alongside Peter Sedgwick's "Tragedy of the Tragedian"[30] which recalls Deutscher's very real merits, neglected by Cliff in his polemical zeal.

Meanwhile Mike Kidron was developing his work on the "permanent arms economy"—an explanation of the very real but impermanent boom in post-war capitalism.[31] Kidron's work was an important corrective to the Third Worldism widespread on the left. Amid the relative tranquillity of British society many were tempted to believe that the real action was in Algeria, Vietnam and Cuba. In "International Capitalism" Kidron sternly reminded them that the main struggle was at home:

> To believe nowadays that the short route to revolution in London, New York or Paris lies through Calcutta, Havana or Algiers, is to pass the buck to where it has no currency. To act on this belief is to rob the revolutionary socialist movement of the few dollars it still possesses.[32]

Cliff and Kidron had gathered around themselves a talented team of writers. For a few years Alasdair MacIntyre, later a world renowned philosopher, was a regular contributor to the journal.[33] One of his more controversial offerings was "Prediction and Politics"[34] which argued that the overthrow of capitalism depended on a "long-term mass change in

---

27: IS1/2 www.marxists.org/archive/cliff/works/1960/xx/trotsub.htm
28: After 15 years in Britain this was Cliff's first article on the British labour movement. IS1/9 www.marxists.org/archive/cliff/works/1962/xx/labour.htm
29: IS1/15 www.marxists.org/archive/cliff/works/1963/xx/deutscher.htm
30: IS1/31 www.marxists.org/archive/sedgwick/1967/xx/deutscher.htm
31: IS1/28 www.marxists.org/archive/kidron/works/1967/xx/permarms.htm
32: IS1/20 www.marxists.org/archive/kidron/works/1965/xx/intercap.htm
33: A collection of MacIntyre's Marxist writings has recently been published. See Blackledge and Davidson, 2008.
34: IS1/13 www.marxists.org/history/etol/newspape/isj/1963/no013/macintyre.htm

consciousness; and there are no conditions which can make such a change either inevitable or impossible". Cliff and Kidron, feeling that this made too many concessions to voluntarism, insisted on reprinting Hal Draper's "The 'Inevitability of Socialism'" which argued for "strict determinism" and "the historic inevitability of man's ascent to humanity".[35] Belief in the inevitability of socialism is not much of a problem today as the spectre of barbarism looms ever larger, but the debate is well worth reading to see two powerful minds exploring the logic of Marxism.

Peter Sedgwick was a remarkable and original writer who had the rare gift of being very funny and profoundly serious at the same time. He will be remembered among other things for his translations of Victor Serge.[36] His essay on "Victor Serge and Socialism" introduced a writer who was virtually unknown to the British left.[37] Serge was a dissident even among dissidents and Sedgwick's fascination with Serge reflected his own unease at accepting any orthodoxy.[38] Sedgwick also contributed an article on "The Two New Lefts", a perceptive critique of the strengths and weaknesses of the post-1956 British left.[39] A complement to this was Sedgwick's "Pseud Left Review", a caustic scatological parody of the convoluted style which characterised Perry Anderson's *New Left Review*: "Nowhere has the archaic insularity and parochialism of the British intelligentsia been more suffocating than in its failure to render a totalising synthesis of the means of excretion in our society".[40] It was an important reminder to *International Socialism* contributors to keep their writing concrete and accessible.

Labour historian Ray Challinor's "Zigzag: The Communist Party and the Bomb" (IS1/3) provided useful ammunition for comrades in the nuclear disarmament movement faced with a Communist Party which was enjoying a brief revival. Jim Higgins's "Ten Years for the Locust" gave a pioneering account of British Trotskyism during and after the Second World War ("a history of failure but…also a history of struggle and high endeavour") providing valuable background to current disputes in the Young Socialists.[41]

By the mid-1960s some of the new generation recruited as students

---

35: IS1/15 www.marxists.org/archive/draper/1947/12/inevitsoc.htm
36: Serge, 1963, and Serge 1972.
37: IS1/14 www.marxists.org/archive/sedgwick/1963/xx/serge.htm
38: Mike Kidron's comment on the article was: "This isn't a portrait of Serge, it's a portrait of Sedge."
39: IS1/17 www.marxists.org/archive/sedgwick/1964/08/2newlefts.htm
40: IS1/25 www.marxists.org/archive/sedgwick/1966/xx/pseudlr.htm
41: IS1/14 www.marxists.org/archive/higgins/1963/xx/10years.htm

around 1960 were contributing to the journal. Nigel Harris, who took over as editor in 1965, wrote among other things on the rise of Maoism, now a significant current on the left following the Sino-Soviet split of the early 1960s. In "Marxism: Leninism-Stalinism-Maoism" he concluded that "Stalin and Mao…have revised Marxism sufficiently to render it a contradiction of its original purposes".[42] "China: What Price Culture?" dismissed the Cultural Revolution (which was provoking great enthusiasm on some parts of the left) as "irrelevant to the poverty of the mass of the population" and a "battle…between different factions of an embryonic ruling class".[43]

Chris Harman's "Tribune of the People" (a history of the Labour left's weekly newspaper) provided a valuable critique of the mainstream Labour left which after the years of Bevanism was now largely capitulating to Harold Wilson.[44] He concluded sourly, "When the working class itself begins to solve its own problems, *Tribune* will no doubt…be looking the other way." For the 50th anniversary of the Russian Revolution in 1967 Harman wrote the much republished "How the Revolution was Lost",[45] which provided a historical complement to Cliff's work on state capitalism and answered frequently raised questions as to when and how Russia became state capitalist.

It is often claimed that *New Left Review* introduced the British left to a range of hitherto unknown foreign Marxists. This contribution was a real one, though some of its discoveries might have been better left undisturbed. But *International Socialism* also played a part. A proposal to translate Georg Lukács's *History and Class Consciousness* had to be abandoned for copyright reasons.[46] Erich Gerlach's essay on "Karl Korsch's Undogmatic Marxism" introduced an unknown thinker to a new generation[47] and Chris Harman's enthusiastic review article on Antonio Gramsci appeared at a time when the Italian communist was still little known in Britain.[48]

For those who have heard *International Socialism* derided as "workerist" and "economistic" it may come as a surprise to learn that in the Kidron-Harris years the journal often published poetry. There were poems

---

42: IS1/26 www.marxists.org/history/etol/writers/harris/1966/xx/marxism.htm

43: IS1/28 www.marxists.org/history/etol/writers/harris/1967/xx/culture.htm

44: IS1/21 & IS1/24 www.marxists.org/history/etol/writers/harman/1965/xx/tribune.htm and www.marxists.org/history/etol/writers/harman/1966/xx/tribune2.htm

45: IS1/30 www.marxists.org/history/etol/writers/harman/1967/xx/revlost.htm

46: IS1/24 & IS1/25 www.marxists.org/archive/lukacs/works/hcc-alt/orthmarx.htm

47: IS1/19 www.marxists.org/history/etol/newspape/isj/1964/no019/gerlach.htm

48: IS1/32 www.marxists.org/history/etol/writers/harman/1968/xx/gramsci.htm

by Hugh MacDiarmid (IS1/1), Adrian Mitchell[49] and Roger McGough (IS1/29) before they achieved their present eminence. More directly rooted in struggle were a selection of "Songs with Teeth",[50] several of them from the Scottish anti-nuclear movement and including Eric Morse's legendary "Worker's Bomb". An obituary of the surrealist poet André Breton[51] apparently persuaded the young David Widgery to join the organisation.[52] And one good reason to seek out the originals, despite availability on-line, is the magnificent series of covers designed by Reuben Fior.[53]

With the advent of the Labour government there was a rising level of industrial struggle and the group was able to make some small interventions especially around the 1966 book *Incomes Policy, Legislation and Shop Stewards* by Cliff and Colin Barker. The journal reflected this development with Barker's article "The British Labour Movement—Aspects of Current Experience"[54] and an analysis by Joyce Rosser and Barker of "A Working Class Defeat: The ENV Story"[55] telling the story of the organisation's first factory branch in north west London and drawing the lessons of the way trade union organisation there was eventually smashed.

The period after 1968 saw major changes in the organisation.[56] The membership grew amid a rising wave of industrial struggle that lasted until 1975. The role of the journal necessarily changed but its main aim was to provide a strategic framework for the organisation's activity. Chris Harman took over as editor; there would be no more poetry but a number of articles related to the tasks of the new period. Cliff's "On Perspectives" set out the economic analysis and political priorities for the coming years[57] while Harman's "Party and Class" provided a retrospective assessment of issues emerging from the fierce internal debate on internal organisation.[58]

At the beginning of the 1970s the journal published two major analyses of international perspectives for the coming decade, which were discussed at the International Socialism conference in spring 1970, and later

---

49: IS1/5 & IS1/28 www.marxists.org/history/etol/newspape/isj/1967/no028/mitchell.htm and www.marxists.org/history/etol/newspape/isj/1967/no028/mitchell2.htm
50: IS1/10 www.marxists.org/history/etol/newspape/isj/1962/no010/campbell.htm
51: IS1/27 www.marxists.org/history/etol/writers/birchall/1966/xx/breton.htm
52: Widgery, 1989, p xiii.
53: As I write, I learn that the indefatigable Einde O'Callaghan is now adding reproductions of the covers to the archive.
54: IS1/28 www.marxists.org/history/etol/writers/barker-c/1967/xx/labmvmt.htm
55: IS1/31 www.marxists.org/history/etol/writers/barker-c/1967/xx/env.htm
56: See Birchall, 2008.
57: IS1/36 www.marxists.org/archive/cliff/works/1969/04/perspectives.htm
58: IS1/35 www.marxists.org/history/etol/writers/harman/1968/xx/partyclass.htm

that year at an international conference the group sponsored along with the French organisation Lutte Ouvrière and the American International Socialists. Chris Harman wrote on "The Stalinist States", observing that Russia and its satellites were facing "a chronic crisis of slowing growth rates" and predicting that "the chronic crises of state capitalism will inevitably reach a nodal point at which the whole system is threatened".[59] Nigel Harris examined "The Third World" and concluded:

> What is centrally lacking in the backward countries today is a clearly expressed strategy to establish the dictatorship of the proletariat. Without this aim the sporadic involvement of workers in broader movements has no specific political implications except as a possible prelude to proletarian independence.[60]

In 1973 the journal moved to monthly publication under the editorship of Duncan Hallas. Initially this was not a success. Articles were limited to a maximum of two pages and the journal became an uneasy halfway house between a theoretical journal and a current affairs magazine. The only memorable contribution was a piece by Hallas, "Fourth International in decline", which broke the length rules and provided an account of the post-war degeneration of the Fourth International.[61] As the euphoria of 1968 faded some comrades were tempted by the formulations of "orthodox" Trotskyism. Hallas's article was a stern warning against any such reversion.

After an abortive attempt to bring Kidron back as editor Chris Harman resumed the editorship in the autumn of 1973. It was a stormy period for the left. The Chilean coup was followed by the 1974 British general election, where working class action brought down a Tory government. Central to the organisation's aims was the building of a rank and file movement in the unions. The general perspective on which such a strategy was based was set out in Andreas Nagliati's article "Towards a Rank and File Movement".[62] This began from the assumption that "we are at the beginning of a period of growing sharp conflict" and argued that revolutionaries must take "the greatest care…to involve broad support" but also "to put their more general political ideas across". In the following years

---

59: ISI/42 www.marxists.org/history/etol/writers/harman/1970/02/stalstates.htm
60: ISI/42 www.marxists.org/history/etol/writers/harris/1970/02/3rdworld.htm
61: ISI/60 www.marxists.org/archive/hallas/works/1973/xx/fidecline.htm
62: ISI/66, www.marxists.org/history/etol/newspape/isj/1974/no066/nagliati.htm

a number of articles addressed the question of rank and file organisation and the history of such movements. Pete Glatter, a working busman, contributed a piece on the London busmen's rank and file movement of the 1930s [63] drawing on rank and file papers from the period and recalling a bus workers' song to the tune of Clementine that asked, "What's the use of having a pension unless you are still alive?"

Another important piece from this period was Duncan Hallas's "White Collar Workers".[64] There had been a tendency in the International Socialists to identify the working class with manual workers but in the 1970s there was a rise in militancy from groups of workers with few previous traditions of struggle. By 1974 white collar workers constituted "around 42 percent of the workforce in Britain". Hallas concluded with a longstanding theme of the International Socialist tradition: the insistence that the main struggle is always that on one's own doorstep. "It is no use looking with vicarious pleasure at members working in a big car plant or a steelworks if you work in a civil service office. The job is to build in that office."

These years also saw a sharp internal struggle in the organisation about strategy and perspectives and a number of articles in the journal were thinly veiled polemics. Cliff's "Lenin's *Pravda*" (based on material for his later biography of Lenin) was part of his campaign to change the orientation and style of *Socialist Worker*.[65] Jim Higgins's "Now Let Us Praise Leon Trotsky" was a parting shot from a veteran comrade soon to be excluded from the organisation and can be read as a veiled polemic against Cliff's version of Leninism.[66]

In 1975 a special issue written by Cliff was devoted to "Portugal at the Crossroads".[67] This was rapidly translated into six languages. While the history of 1968 has been travestied and distorted the Portuguese Revolution of 1974-5, the biggest and most potentially revolutionary explosion of working class self-activity that Europe has seen since 1945, has been simply written out of history, and nowadays few people are aware of the events. Cliff's analysis is open to retrospective criticisms—he focused too much on the choice between socialist revolution and "extreme reaction" on the Chilean model and underestimated the threat posed by social democracy. But as a record of a memorable period of working class struggle it deserves to be read and remembered.

63: ISJ/74 www.marxists.org/history/etol/newspape/isj/1975/no074/glatter.htm
64: ISJ/72 www.marxists.org/archive/hallas/works/1974/10/whitecoll.htm
65: ISJ/67 www.marxists.org/archive/cliff/works/1974/03/pravda.htm
66: ISJ/80 www.marxists.org/archive/higgins/1975/06/trotsky.htm
67: ISJ/81 & ISJ/82 www.marxists.org/archive/cliff/works/1975/portugal/

Harman was succeeded as editor by Duncan Hallas and then Alex Callinicos. In 1977, to celebrate the journal's hundredth issue, Callinicos published contributions from all four former editors. Kidron's piece, "Two Insights Don't Make a Theory",[68] made a sharp critique of his own earlier work. It was effectively a farewell from the man who had once so brilliantly edited the journal.[69] Chris Harman's "Better a Valid Insight than a Wrong Theory" was a valiant defence of the young Kidron against his later self.[70]

The year 1977 also saw the Lewisham demonstration against the National Front following which the Socialist Workers Party (as the organisation had now become) was widely vilified.[71] The journal made no concessions but sought to arm comrades for the inevitable arguments with an article by Callinicos and Alistair Hatchett, brazenly entitled "In Defence of Violence", which concluded that "the only real answer to the violence of ruling class power is the organised power of the working class".[72]

At the beginning of 1978 the first series of *International Socialism* came to an end and was replaced by the monthly *Socialist Review* which in its early issues aimed to relate to the new milieu around the Anti Nazi League. The initiative to launch a new series of *International Socialism* came initially from a group of comrades outside the Central Committee but the new quarterly, edited for its first ten years by Peter Binns, rapidly took its place in the Socialist Workers Party's range of publications.

The new journal reflected many of the crucial arguments going on within the party. One heated debate concerned the relation of Marxism to feminism and in particular the role of the *Women's Voice* magazine in the party. Tony Cliff presented articles on Clara Zetkin (IS2/13) and Alexandra Kollontai (IS2/14), first drafts of chapters from his 1984 book *Class Struggle and Women's Liberation*, but containing additional material not in the book. There were sharp criticisms of his treatment of Zetkin from Lin James and Anna Paczuska, Juliet Ash and Janet Vaux (IS2/14). Irene Bruegel (IS2/1), Floya Anthias (IS2/2), Joan Smith (IS2/3), Barbara Winslow (IS2/4) and Lin James (IS2/7) presented a range of positions on the question of the family and women's oppression. Lindsey German's "Theories of Patriarchy"

68: IS1/100 www.marxists.org/archive/kidron/works/1977/07/insights.htm
69: Shortly before his death Kidron published one further article in *International Socialism*: "Failing Growth and Rampant Costs: Two Ghosts in the Machine of Modern Capitalism". It was marked with his customary wit and perceptiveness. IS2/96 http://pubs.socialistreviewindex.org.uk/isj96/kidron.htm
70: IS1/100 www.marxists.org/history/etol/writers/harman/1977/07/insight.htm
71: For details see Renton, 2006, pp69-70.
72: IS1/101 www.marxists.org/history/etol/writers/callinicos/1977/09/violence.htm

challenged ideas widespread in the women's movement by setting out to "show that it is not men who 'benefit' from the oppression of women but capital".[73] The continuing threat from the far right was covered in two articles by Colin Sparks on fascism and the working class: "The German Experience" (IS2/2) and "The National Front Today" (IS2/3).

There was also a broader debate about perspectives for the current period as the Labour government collapsed and Margaret Thatcher came to power. Chris Harman's "Crisis of the European revolutionary left" (IS2/4) was an informative survey of developments on the far left in Europe and also raised questions relevant to the difficulties which the SWP faced in this period. Steve Jeffreys' article "Striking into the Eighties" (IS2/5), which looked to a continuation of the current level of industrial struggle, drew a swift rejoinder from Cliff who, in "The Balance of Class Forces in Recent Years", set out his argument that the movement was now entering a period of "downturn".[74] This was Cliff at his best. His argument did not rely simply on statistics but contained extensive quotations from industrial militants speaking in their own voice about the changing situation in the workplace. Alex Callinicos's "The Rank and File Movement Today" (IS2/17) marked the abandonment of the rank and file strategy while insisting that such a perspective was "essentially correct—in the appropriate conditions".

The journal continued to respond quickly to events. When Jaruzelski's coup crushed the Solidarity movement in Poland in December 1981 a book length special issue, "Solidarnosc: From Gdansk to Military Repression", was produced within weeks by Colin Barker and Kara Weber (IS2/15).

The Great Miners' Strike of 1984-5 was central to the Socialist Workers Party's activity for a year. The story of the strike was told in another special book length issue, *The Great Strike* by Alex Callinicos and Mike Simons (IS2/27 & IS2/8), and Cliff analysed "Patterns of Mass Strike" from 1905 to 1985.[75] The strike also gave rise to an interesting covert polemic. Early in 1986 Paul Foot published a short pamphlet on the miners' leader of the 1920s AJ Cook.[76] Cliff responded with an article entitled "The Tragedy of AJ Cook" which never named Foot but was a direct attack on what Cliff saw as Foot's excessive sympathy for Cook (IS2/31). Cliff and Foot greatly liked and respected each other but there were real

---

73: IS2/12 www.isj.org.uk/?id=240
74: IS2/6 www.marxists.org/archive/cliff/works/1979/xx/balance1.htm
75: IS2/29, www.marxists.org/archive/cliff/works/1985/patterns/
76: Foot, 1986.

tensions between the two men. The polemic was doubly veiled for though the name was never mentioned by Cliff it was clear that the real subject of debate was not Cook but Scargill.

There were also lively exchanges on philosophical and cultural questions. Alex Callinicos's 1982 book *Is There A Future for Marxism?* provoked a debate between Binns (IS2/17), Callinicos (IS2/19) and Harman (IS2/21) showing that the party leadership was far from monolithic on philosophical questions. A critical review of Dave Widgery's 1986 work *Beating Time*, a history of Rock Against Racism (IS2/33) by myself drew a vigorous response from Widgery (IS2/35) in which I was categorised among "the sniffer dogs of Orthodox Trotskyism".

In 1988 John Rees replaced Binns as editor. The journal continued to produced a wide range of material on political and theoretical questions. There were special issues on the French Revolution (IS2/43) and the Frederick Engels centenary.[77] Rees's "In Defence of October" (IS2/52) provoked a wide ranging debate about Leninism and Stalinism eliciting responses from, among others, Samuel Farber, Robert Service and Robin Blackburn (IS2/55).

The collapse of "Communism" in the Eastern bloc was in some ways a confirmation of analyses developed by Cliff and others many years earlier but it also required further elucidation. In particular Chris Harman's article "The Storm Breaks" (IS2/46) attempted to show at considerable length how the state capitalist theory could explain the "contradictory development" in Eastern Europe. Despite dramatic political changes, he argued, "the central power of the ruling class was untouched". What had happened was that "the pygmy state capitalisms of Eastern Europe have cracked apart in the face of competition from the new giants of the world order".

The rise of New Labour during the 1990s produced a number of commentaries. Chris Harman's "From Bernstein to Blair: One Hundred Years of Revisionism" showed that while Bernstein and Anthony Crosland had tried to offer a "reformism of hope", all that Blair could promise was a "reformism of despair".[78] Lindsey German's "The Blair Project Cracks"[79] made a devastating critique of Tony Blair's record in power before his entanglement in foreign wars and her "How Labour Lost its Roots" described "disillusion and despair" among Labour Party activists.[80]

77: IS2/65 http://pubs.socialistreviewindex.org.uk/isj65/
78: IS2/67 http://pubs.socialistreviewindex.org.uk/isj67/harman.htm
79: IS2/82 http://pubs.socialistreviewindex.org.uk/isj82/german.htm
80: IS2/87 http://pubs.socialistreviewindex.org.uk/isj87/german.htm

The Seattle demonstrations of November 1999 gave rise to a new international anti-capitalist movement which in the post-9/11 world merged into a massive anti-war movement. The new challenges of the period were covered extensively in the journal. Chris Harman's "Anti-capitalism: Theory and Practice" stressed that "it is up to all of us to help build the new movement" but warned that "clarity of ideas is not a luxury in such cases".[81] Several other articles in the same spirit followed.

John Rees's "The Broad Party, the Revolutionary Party and the United Front" confronted some of the problems posed by united fronts and electoral alliances in a new phase of activity noting that "the most difficult struggles and the toughest decisions still lie ahead".[82] Paul McGarr's "Why Green is Red: Marxism and the Threat to the Environment" provided a valuable introduction to the emerging issues of environmental politics deploying extensive scientific knowledge in terms easily grasped by the lay reader.[83] His "Capitalism and Climate Change" gave an equally lucid account of 21st century barbarism's most menacing face.[84] He concluded grimly:

> The record of human history is that those who control societies have often been prepared to see the whole of society plunge into disastrous chaos and collapse rather than accept change which undermined their power. I see no reason to suppose the most powerful ruling class in human history, those who today head the giant global corporations at whose centre stand the fossil fuel corporations, will behave any differently to their predecessors whose societies' fate is witnessed only by ruined monuments.

When *Socialist Review* celebrated its 200th issue in 1996 Tony Cliff stated that he hoped there would not be another 200 issues, for he expected the revolution would come by then. Whether there will be another 50 years of *International Socialism* we do not know, and I for one am unlikely to find out. But at a time when capitalism is "an unconscionable time a-dying" and the prospect of what Marx called the "common ruin of the contending classes" is ever more likely, we need a Marxism like that of Cliff and Kidron that is unafraid to confront new and changing realities.

As the founders of this journal wrote 50 years ago in words still relevant today:

81: IS2/88 http://pubs.socialistreviewindex.org.uk/isj88/harman.htm
82: IS2/97 http://pubs.socialistreviewindex.org.uk/isj97/rees.htm
83: IS2/88 http://pubs.socialistreviewindex.org.uk/isj88/mcgarr.htm
84: IS2/107 www.isj.org.uk/?id=119

Marxism has a crucial role to play. A science of action, constantly assimilating and formulating the experiences of the international working class, it is the most biting weapon in the struggle against class society...

We present *International Socialism* as a small contribution to Marxist thought. Its function is to bring the traditions of scientific socialism to bear on the constantly changing pattern of class struggle, to help clarify its nature and, conversely, to keep the science of working class action a living one and not the compendium of quotations to which it is so often and so tragically reduced.

1 September 1958

References

Birchall, Ian, 1980, "The Autonomy of Theory: A Short History of *New Left Review*", *International Socialism 10*, second series (winter 1980).

Birchall, Ian, 2003a, Obituary: Michael Kidron, *Revolutionary History*, volume 8, number 3.

Birchall, Ian, 2003b, "Michael Kidron 1930-2003", *International Socialism 99*, second series (summer 2003), http://pubs.socialistreviewindex.org.uk/isj99/birchall.htm

Birchall, Ian, 2008, "Seizing the Time: Tony Cliff and 1968", *International Socialism 118*, second series (spring 2008), www.isj.org.uk/?id=426

Blackledge, Paul, and Neil Davidson (eds), 2008, *Alasdair MacIntyre's Engagement with Marxism: Selected Writings, 1953-1974* (Brill).

Foot, Paul, 1986, *An Agitator of the Worst Type* (Socialist Workers Party) www.marxists.org/archive/foot-paul/1986/01/ajcook.htm

Renton, Dave, 2006, *When We Touched the Sky: The Anti Nazi League, 1977-1981* (New Clarion).

Serge, Victor, 1963 [1951], *Memoirs of a Revolutionary*, translated by Peter Sedgwick (Oxford University)

Serge, Victor, 1972 [1930], *Year One of the Russian Revolution*, translated by Peter Sedgwick (Holt, Reinhart and Winston), www.marxists.org/archive/serge/1930/year-one/

Widgery, David, 1989, *Preserving Disorder* (Pluto).

Philadelphia Wobblies

John Newsinger

A review of Peter Cole, **Wobblies on the Waterfront: International Unionism in Progressive Era Philadelphia** *(University of Illinois, 2007).*

On 14 May 1913 longshoremen on the Philadelphia docks walked out on strike demanding a 10 cent an hour pay rise, a ten-hour day, time and a half for night work and double-time for Sundays. They enthusiastically signed up with the Industrial Workers of the World (IWW), the revolutionary syndicalist trade union known as the Wobblies, confident that this organisation would not sell them down the river. On 17 May "Local 8" (branch eight) of the IWW's Marine Transport Workers Industrial Union was formed. After a hard fought dispute, that saw violent clashes with police and scabs, the employers conceded most of the union's demands on 28 May. This began what was to be the IWW's almost decade long domination of the Philadelphia docks.

This success was achieved at a time when the IWW's organising efforts elsewhere in the eastern United States were ending in failure. The collapse of IWW organisation in both Lawrence, Massachusetts, where the great strike of 1912 was won, and in Paterson, New Jersey, where the great strike of 1913 was to be lost, demonstrated the difficulties the IWW faced. It led many strikes in the east, but, win or lose, it failed to establish stable workplace organisation. What Philadelphia showed was that this was not inevitable, that the difficulties could be overcome. According to Peter Cole in his *Wobblies on the Waterfront* Local 8 provided "a model for how the IWW simultaneously could advocate revolutionary ideals, while meeting the more immediate 'bread and butter' needs of workers". If the Philadelphia Wobblies could combine "IWW tactics and ideals, while also dealing pragmatically on issues like hours and labour supply—surely other IWW branches could have done just the same". Local 8, he argues, "seems to offer a 'path not taken'."

What was even more remarkable in the context of the time was the fact that Local 8 was also, as Cole insists, "arguably the most powerful mixed race union of its era". As he points out, at this time there were only a few unions that organised black workers and most of those were biracial, that is to say that black and white workers were organised into separate locals. This was not the case with Local 8. It was, in line with IWW philosophy, an integrated local and, moreover, insisted that black and white dockers worked in integrated gangs. Just over half of the 4,000 workers who walked out on strike in May 1913 were black, the rest Lithuanian or Polish immigrants and Irish Americans. In these circumstances the union had to satisfy the black workers' desire for equality and the IWW fitted the bill. Moreover, blacks "made up a majority of the leadership cadre" of Local 8—men such as Glen Perrymore, Alonzo Richards, Charles Caster, Dan Jones, Joseph White and, most especially, Ben Fletcher. Fletcher was, as Cole writes, "one of the great African Americans of his generation… He stands in the top echelon of black labour leaders".[1]

The IWW and black workers

From the time of its foundation in 1905 the IWW was formally committed to the organisation of black workers on equal terms with whites. Not until 1910, however, was it in a position to begin anything like a concerted drive to recruit black workers. According to Philip Foner:

> Leaflets and pamphlets were distributed by the thousands to convince the black man that he "has no chance in the old-line trade unions. They do not want him. They admit him only under compulsion and treat him with contempt. There is only one labour organisation in the United States that admits the coloured worker on a footing of absolute equality with the white—the Industrial Workers of the World."

One leaflet, "To Coloured Workingmen And Women", proclaimed, "If you are a wage worker you are welcome in the IWW halls, no matter

---

1:    Cole, 2007a, pp2, 3, 4, 5. Cole has also edited another valuable volume, on Ben Fletcher, Cole 2007b.

what your colour. By this you may see that the IWW is not a white man's union, not a black man's union, not a red man's union, but a working man's union. All the working class in one big union." The contrast with the American Federation of Labour (AFL) could not have been sharper. In 1910 eight AFL unions formally barred black workers from membership, while most of the other 50-odd affiliates kept black workers out by informal means. Some unions actually had higher initiation fees for black workers. For most black workers a strong union meant the closing down of job opportunities and even the sack if a closed shop was achieved by a union that barred black members.

Even in the South, where the Jim Crow laws enforced segregation, the IWW took an uncompromising stand in favour of equality, urging white workers to recognise that their class interests lay in unity with their black brothers. One IWW appeal asked white workers:

> If one of you were to fall in a river and could not swim, and a Negro came along who could swim, would you drown rather than accept his offer of aid? Hardly! That is the IWW position. Labour organised on race lines will drown. Only organised on class lines will it swim.

When white firemen on the Cincinnati, New Orleans and Texas Railroad went on strike in protest against the promotion of black workers to firemen the IWW unreservedly condemned them. Even when black workers took the strikers' jobs the IWW newspaper, *Solidarity*, warned that the strikers "are reaping the folly of unworking class conduct. They are getting what they deserved. Unity regardless of race, creed or colour is the only way out." As far as the Wobblies were concerned when black workers broke the strikes by AFL unions that had excluded them from membership and kept them off the job the AFL had "no one but themselves to blame".[2]

How successful was the IWW in recruiting black workers, in building working class unity? According to Sterling Spero and Abram Harris, in their *The Black Worker*, the IWW issued about 100,000 membership cards to black workers during what they describe as "the active part of its life".[3] Foner considers this an exaggeration but regardless of the exact figure a large number of black workers held IWW cards at one time or another.

2:   Foner, 1974, pp68, 73-74, 108, 109, 110. For racist firemen's strikes see Hammett, 1975, and for the 1911 Cincinnati, New Orleans and Texas Railroad strike see Arnesen, 2001, pp37-38. The Brotherhood of Locomotive Firemen did not drop its ban on black members until 1963.
3:   Spero and Harris, 1968, p331.

Nevertheless, for all its aspirations the scale of the problem that racism posed for the working class was too great. For most black workers racism remained the face of the white working class. Even those black workers who were allowed into AFL unions encountered insults and discrimination. When black dockers in Baltimore, members of the AFL-affiliated International Longshoremen's Association, had their offices remodelled they were expected to employ AFL carpenters and bricklayers whose unions barred black members.[4]

More serious was the East St Louis pogrom in July 1917 when white mobs killed 39 black men and women in an assault intended to drive black workers out of the city.[5] When the AFL convention met in the aftermath of the riot a resolution was proposed directing the executive council to work "to the end that all of the political, civil and economic disabilities so offensive and destructive to the rights of Negroes as human beings and American citizens be removed". The proposer apologised for bringing such an unsavoury resolution to the convention but excused himself on the grounds that he was obligated to because of the support his union had received from black workers in a recent dispute. The committee on resolutions refused to endorse the resolution and the convention voted to reject "the statements contained in the resolution". In effect, as one historian has pointed out, the AFL convention had countenanced "inequality and discrimination against the Negroes in America". The AFL, once again unlike the IWW, refused to condemn the lynching of black men in the South. AFL president Samuel Gompers made clear that this was a matter for Southerners to resolve without "meddlers from outside".[6]

Things were different on the Philadelphia waterfront. As one black longshoreman, James Fair, put it, "The IWW was the only union accepting black workers freely. They advocated just one thing—solidarity".[7]

4:　Spero and Harris, 1968, p194.
5:　In East St Louis the AFL unions were campaigning against black migration to the city, blaming black workers for the employers' attacks on wages and conditions. Instead of countering the employers' efforts to exploit divisions between black and white workers, the unions reinforced them. Eugene Debs, one of the leaders of the Socialist Party, condemned the riot as "a foul blot upon the American labour movement... Had the labour unions fiercely opened their door to the Negro instead of barring him, and forcing him in spite of himself to become a scab...the atrocious crime at East St Louis would never have blackened the pages of American history"—from Rudwick, 1982, p145. The use of strikebreakers to defeat a strike at the Aluminium Ore Company in April 1917 was widely seen as worsening relations between black and white workers, but as Rudwick shows "most strikebreakers at Aluminium Ore were white" (p19). Nevertheless black workers became a convenient scapegoat.
6:　Karson, 1965, pp76, 140-141. See also Foner, 1974, p139.
7:　Kimeldorf, 1999, p31.

On the waterfront

In the months following the 1913 strike Local 8 waged a low level guerrilla war against the employers, building up its strength and consolidating its hold over the docks. By 1916, according to Cole, with the exception of two docks, "Local 8 maintained job control on all the city's deep-sea piers." You did not work if you were not a paid-up IWW member. By the summer of that year the local had over 3,000 members. However, the union's revolutionary credentials were soon to be challenged. On 6 April 1917 the United States declared war on Germany and joined the bloodbath of the First World War. The American left was overwhelmingly opposed to the war, with the Socialist Party in particular taking a strong anti-war stance. Although most Wobblies were also opposed to the war, after some equivocation, the IWW decided not to campaign against the conflict. Such a stance would, it was felt, invite repression and compromise the opportunities that a war economy presented for building up the organisation. When the general executive board had discussed the issue it had been pointed out that if the union opposed the draft it would be destroyed. The chairman, Frank Little, made the point that they were likely to be run "out of business anyway... Either we're for this slaughterfest or we're against it. I'm ready to face a firing squad rather than compromise".[8] But no decisive stand was taken.

In Philadelphia the leadership went even further calling a meeting where a succession of union speakers, including Ben Fletcher, urged the need to support the war and to keep the docks working. The meeting, some 600 strong, voted not to strike for the duration. Members were encouraged to register for the draft and the union kept an "honour roll" of members serving in the armed forces at its headquarters. As the United States Shipping Board acknowledged after the war Local 8 members "loaded a large part of the munitions sent to Europe".[9]

What this highlights is the dilemma of revolutionary trade unionism in a non-revolutionary period. There was always a tension between the needs of revolutionary agitation and the fight to maintain organisation and improve wages and conditions. Outside of a revolutionary situation revolutionary ideas would only appeal to a minority of workers, while maintaining union organisation and winning on "bread and butter" issues required the

---

8:   Chaplin, 1948, pp208-209. Little was, of course, right about the IWW being the victim of repression regardless of what stance it took. He was assassinated by gunmen working for the Anaconda Copper Company in Butte, Montana, on 1 August 1917.

9:   Cole, 2007a, pp82-83.

support of all the workers. One of the reasons IWW locals so often collapsed, even after successful strikes, was that the activists were primarily
concerned with revolutionary agitation while the majority of workers
were still primarily concerned with better wages and conditions. As James
P Cannon, himself a former Wobbly, put it, one of the main reasons for
the failure of the IWW "was its attempt to be both a union of all workers
and a propaganda society of selected revolutionists". The IWW, he argued,
was "in its time of glory...neither a union nor a party in the full meaning
of these terms, but something of both, with some parts missing".[10] The
Philadelphia Wobblies, Cole believes, had found the way to overcome this
problem, building up a strong union committed to racial equality and class
solidarity on the docks. The war put this achievement to the test. To keep
the union strong the leadership effectively abandoned their internationalism. This was at a time, moreover, when the reformists of the Socialist
Party were taking a determined stand against the terrible slaughter on the
Western Front.

Cole, rather shamefacedly, apologises for Local 8's retreat over the
war. Certainly some in the leadership and most of the rank and file actually
supported it, but the revolutionaries kept silent. These were men who had
proven their credentials many times over, who had often been imprisoned
and brutalised by police and vigilantes, men who had made great sacrifices
and suffered terrible hardship in the cause. To keep the organisation they
had built in the docks intact they compromised their revolutionary politics.

With the declaration of war the United States was swept by a deliber-
ately orchestrated wave of patriotic fervour, of "100 percent Americanism".
In Philadelphia this saw German measles renamed "liberty measles" and
sauerkraut renamed "liberty cabbage".[11] Interestingly, Cole does not discuss
the efforts that were made by Philadelphia socialists to oppose the war.
In July 1917 socialists distributing anti-war leaflets were attacked in the
street: "People...began to beat and kick them. Before the police could
arrive to protect them, the mob had torn off their clothing and divided it
for souvenirs." Subsequent attempts at anti-war leafleting were stopped by
police arrests. On 26 August an attempt was made by the anti-war People's
Council to hold an anti-conscription meeting at the Archer Street Theatre,
but it was broken up by off-duty sailors and marines urged on by the press.
Two days later the offices of the Socialist Party were raided, literature was

---

10: Cannon, 1955. For Cannon's Wobbly years see Palmer, 2007, pp52-86. See also the
discussion in Darlington, 2008, pp212-217.
11: Abernathy, 1982, p560.

seized and the party secretary, Charles Schenk, was arrested. His opposition to the war cost him six months in prison.[12] And, of course, the pro-war stance taken by Local 8 did not save them from the repression that was about to engulf the IWW.

When the Wilson administration launched its roundup of the IWW leadership on 5 September 1917, Local 8 was not spared. Six of its leaders were arrested (Ben Fletcher, Walter Nef, John Walsh, Edwin Doree, Manuel Rey and Joseph Graeber). There were no protests, no walkouts on the docks. Even when Nef and Rey were finally sentenced to 20 years hard labour and Fletcher and the others to ten years in August 1918, there was no fight on their behalf. The focus on "bread and butter" issues had kept the union strong, indeed strong enough to survive the imprisonment of its leaders, but where were the politics?

After the war Local 8 maintained its dominance of the docks. This was a period of massive working class revolt throughout the United States, and the Philadelphia waterfront was not exempt. On 26 May 1920 the IWW called its members out on strike, "the largest this part of Philadelphia had ever seen, with close to 9,000 workers out at its peak…more than 150 ships were immediately idled on the Delaware River and another 100 were soon affected". Nevertheless the employers stood firm and after six weeks the union admitted defeat. When the employers followed up their victory, they were, according to Cole, assisted "by internal divisions and the insurgent challenge of Communism". He argues that what became known as the "Philadelphia Controversy" "was as detrimental to Local 8 and the IWW as any open shop campaign or federal raid".[13] This is not true: the ruling class offensive was decisive in driving back the whole US working class. Union membership fell from 5,110,000 in 1920 to 3,622,000 in 1922. This was a historic defeat in which the Philadelphia Wobblies unfortunately shared.

What of the "Philadelphia Controversy" then? In August 1920 Local 8 was expelled from the IWW because its members were loading the steamer *Westmount* with munitions destined for the White army fighting the Bolsheviks in the Crimea. *Solidarity* , the IWW newspaper, declared that the union "would rather face death and dismemberment than stand the disgrace of having its members render any assistance in keeping workers enslaved to the Moloch of capitalism". Cole is, however, sceptical that munitions were actually being loaded and instead sees the affair as a conspiracy by Communist sympathisers in the IWW out to weaken Local 8 which was

---

12: Peterson and Fite, 1957, pp31-32.
13: Cole, 2007a. p127.

an obstacle to their takeover of the union. This is a later invention because there seems to have been no doubt at the time that the allegation was true. James P Cannon, for example, writing at the time, had no doubt about it: "It seemed unbelievable that the IWW of Frank Little…could be engaged in this nefarious enterprise—this high treason to the international working class".[14] Howard Kimeldorf, in his account of the Philadelphia Wobblies, tells a more convincing story. According to Kimeldorf, the IWW general executive board ordered Local 8 to stop loading the *Westmount* after being approached by Soviet representatives. Ben Fletcher and another union official, Polly Baker, tried to persuade the gang doing the work to stop, but they refused and a meeting called to discuss the issue voted not to take any action. This precipitated Local 8's expulsion. Once they were expelled Local 8 finally voted to black the ship and was eventually readmitted in October 1920. Certainly this crisis intersected with increasing factionalisation within the IWW, but it can also be seen very much as Local 8 continuing the stance that it had taken during the war.[15] And there were many Wobblies who were not Communist sympathisers who were critical of Local 8.

Local 8 had introduced a $25 initiation fee that was in clear violation of IWW rules. When it was readmitted to the IWW in October 1920 it was instructed to reduce the fee. Refusal led to it being expelled once again in December 1920, an expulsion that was upheld at the IWW convention the following year by 774 votes to 96. As far as the great majority of Wobblies were concerned a $25 initiation fee smacked of the AFL. Eventually the fee was reduced to $2 and Local 8 was again allowed back into the union.[16]

By now it was facing a challenge from the AFL affiliated International Longshoremen's Association (ILA) which had the support of both the employers and the authorities. Presumably in an attempt to see off this threat in October 1922 Local 8 decided to impose the eight-hour day (they worked ten hours), starting work an hour late and finishing an hour early. On

---

14: Cannon, 1992, p72.

15: Kimeldorf, 1999, pp61-62. He quotes Local 8 veterans complaining that there were union members "breaking down every principle and rule established by the unions". See also Cole, 2007a, pp130-131.

16: John Gambs in his history of the IWW observed that, as well as Local 8, the IWW also suspended its New York bakers' local for having an initiation fee of $15. He wrote, "The principles involved far more than constitutional matters. It was a question of whether there was any place in the IWW for a group which maintained shop control by charging high fees, which had a relatively large treasury, which devoted its energies to the immediate welfare of a small group rather than to the emancipation of the working class"—Gambs, 1932, pp165-166.

16 October the employers responded with a lockout and set about smashing Local 8 with the full support of the ILA. By the time the dispute was over the ILA had supplied the employers with nearly 1,000 strikebreakers imported from New York. Local 8 was broken and, as is the way in these affairs, far from recognising the ILA the employers decided they preferred the open shop—that no union was even better than a scab union.

Without a doubt Local 8 won substantial improvements for its members, transforming work on the Philadelphia docks and uniting black and white workers, something particularly impressive given the racism of the time. Nevertheless, as a revolutionary organisation it failed to meet the challenge of war and solidarity with the Russian Revolution. These failures, as we have seen, were a consequence of the attempt to build a revolutionary trade union in a non-revolutionary period.

Class war in Philadelphia: the 1910 general strike

It is worth noting one other important weakness of Cole's book: his focus is so tightly on the Philadelphia waterfront as to completely neglect developments in what was one of America's major industrial cities. In 1900 there were over 700 factories in the city, employing 246,000 workers, principally in textiles, engineering and shipbuilding. The Baldwin Locomotive works was the country's largest manufacturer of railway engines, the Brill works was the largest manufacturer of streetcars and the Cramp shipyard had turned the Delaware River into "the American Clyde", "the shipbuilding capital of the United States".[17] Moreover, the city was the scene of a general strike in solidarity with striking streetcar workers, a strike that assumed the dimensions of "a mass uprising" according to one historian.[18] The 1910 general strike is not even mentioned by Cole.

Let us look at the development of the class struggle in Philadelphia in this period. In 1899 and 1901 strikes in the shipyards to secure a nine-hour day were defeated, in 1903 nearly 50,000 textile workers struck for shorter hours in "the most stunning effort yet made by Philadelphia labour" and in 1904 the building trades won "one of the most startling victories".[19] After this there was a period of retreat, but in 1909 shirt-waist workers in Philadelphia walked out in solidarity with those in New York who were striking ("the Uprising of the Thirty Thousand"), and Philadelphia's streetcar workers also went on strike. The streetcar workers won some

---

17: Harris, 2000, pp30-31.
18: Fones-Wolf, 1986a, p167.
19: Scranton, 1989, p216; Fones-Wolf, 1986a, p152.

improvements but not union recognition, and the company Philadelphia Rapid Transit (PRT) proceeded to set up a rival company union and victimise activists. On 19 February 1910 the PRT fired 173 union members and their union, the Amalgamated Association of Street Car and Electric Railway Men, responded by calling over 5,000 men out on strike.

Streetcar strikes in the United States were often accompanied by considerable violence and loss of life. Companies recruited scabs, often hiring strikebreaking detective agencies to keep a service going.[20] This involved sending vehicles through working class areas where the strikers and their families lived and where support for their cause was strongest. Inevitably the streetcars were attacked with pitched battles with armed scabs and police resulting. Philadelphia was to be no exception. When the PRT imported strikebreakers from New York and Boston violence was inevitable. On 21 February the *Philadelphia Ledger* reported the events of the previous day:

> Cars were smashed, then burned. A score of riots in which policemen, mounted and on foot, used revolvers and clubs, sent more than 100 men and women to hospital and impromtu infirmaries… Almost simultaneously, in widely separated sections of the city, crowds of men and boys began a determined effort to aid the strikers… Instances not unlike civil war marked the street disorders.

Over 10,000 people were on the streets fighting the police. Outrage at police conduct was so great that on 22 February there were spontaneous walkouts at building sites and textile and clothing factories across the city, involving some 30,000 workers. On the following day workers at the non-union Baldwin Locomotive works helped strikers demolish a tram during their lunch hour. They stayed to jeer the police who promptly opened fire, wounding two of them. The company's vice president, William Austin, wrote an incredulous account of what followed:

> The police ran the men back into the shop and then trouble began. Before anyone knew what started it we heard pistol shots. I looked out of the office window and saw a long line of policemen, about two dozen, lined

---

20: One of the most notorious of these detective agencies was run by James Farley, who "specialised in breaking streetcar strikes, which became endemic [in] the early 1900s"— Jeffreys-Jones, 1978, p80. Farley's notoriety was such that he actually gets a mention in Jack London's *The Iron Heel*. According to Farley, the way to break a streetcar strike was to let "the malcontents know that the cars are going to run, and that anybody who gets in the way is going to get hurt. That's all there is to breaking a streetcar strike"—quoted in Knight, 1960, p152.

up in front of the Willow Street Shop actually firing into the second and third storey shop windows. They were answered by a volley of nuts, bolts, washers, shaft hangers, iron rods, etc, some very heavy, and all calculated to kill if landed on the right spot. The police shot at least 200 shots into the shops. Fortunately no one was hurt on either side, but for a while it was a very serious business.[21]

The April 1910 issue of the revolutionary socialist journal the *International Socialist Review* actually printed a photograph of the police firing into the Baldwin works (along with another of "A Popular Bonfire" which showed a streetcar being burned by the strikers and their supporters).[22] One consequence of this incident was that large numbers of Baldwin's workers rushed to join the unions and many of them were to join the general strike.

State police and the National Guard were brought into the city to regain control of its streets. The streetcar workers' leader, Clarence Pratt, a Welshman, was arrested. In the face of this repression, with workers striking in solidarity, pressure built up for an official response. On 27 February the Central Labour Union (the equivalent of a trades council) called a general strike for 5 March if the PRT had not agreed to negotiations. A "Committee of Ten", including two Socialist Party members, was set up to manage the strike. On 5 March some 100,000 men and women stopped work and within a few days the number had risen to 150,000. There were 40,000 building workers out, 20,000 engineers (including over 3,000 Baldwin workers), and nearly 40,000 textile and clothing workers. Even piano movers downed pianos. Thousands of non-union men and women joined the strike and over 20,000 of them signed up with the unions. To deter the police and militia from carrying out a feared massacre the Central Labour Union president, John Murphy, warned that any such action would provoke "a carnival of riot and bloodshed that would startle the entire country". There were union men who "can shoot as straight as any trooper".[23]

Much of the city was effectively shut down and under police and military occupation. Demonstrations and meetings were banned. When

---

21: Brown, 1995, p217. See also Fones-Wolf, 1986b.
22: Cohen, 1910a, pp865, 868. *International Socialist Review* was very sympathetic to the IWW. Indeed Big Bill Haywood was on its editorial board and was a regular contributor. It provides a remarkable chronicle of class war America, right up until it was suppressed by the Wilson administration in 1918. For the *International Socialist Review* see Ruff, 1997.
23: Adams, 1966, p185.

Eugene Debs the Socialist Party leader spoke in the city he had to be smuggled in. The mayor even closed down a production of John Galsworthy's play, *Strife*, in the interests of "public order"—but really because the play advocated "arbitration" as the solution to industrial conflict. Streetcars were still run through the city but without stopping and with their scab crews shooting at anyone who came near.

Nevertheless, with the full backing of the mayor and of the city's business establishment the PRT still refused to negotiate. Inevitably the general strike began to crumble. Proposals to make it state-wide were abandoned when the Pennsylvania State Federation of Labour came under pressure from the AFL leadership. The Committee of Ten finally called off the general strike on 27 March leaving the streetcar strikers to fight on alone. Joseph Cohen, a Philadelphia socialist, wrote in the *International Socialist Review* that the "aftermath was the washing aside in all directions of hundreds of wage earners victimised for having quit work". He went on to observe that the general strike had been "the most unexpected affair Philadelphia had ever witnessed... It was the most magnificent performance ever achieved by the labour of the city." Nevertheless, a general strike confined to one city was always too likely to be "largely spectacular".[24]

By the middle of April the Amalgamated Association finally reached an agreement with the PRT. The company, on the verge of bankruptcy, guaranteed no victimisation, conceded a pay rise and acknowledged the right of the men to join the union. However, it still refused to recognise the union. In the course of the dispute over 300 of its streetcars had been wrecked, many of them totally destroyed. The dispute had been "one of the bloodiest and most destructive in the city's history". By the time it ended 29 people had been killed, "about half of them in the battles between strikers and scabs and policemen; the rest resulted from the dangerous operation of the cars by inexperienced strikebreakers".[25]

Without any doubt IWW members participated in these events and they were reported in the IWW press even though it was an AFL affair. The IWW newspaper, the *Industrial Worker*, pointed out quite correctly that an important factor in the failure to win a complete victory was the refusal of the power workers to support the general strike. As it pointed out, "The men who worked in the powerhouses, furnishing juice with which to run the cars, did more to defeat the striking motormen and conductors than the scab who manned the car." Nevertheless, Louis Duchez, writing in the

---

24: Cohen, 1910b, p981.
25: Abernathy, 1982, pp549-550.

paper on 26 March, still argued that even though it had failed the general strike had done more to teach "class consciousness and solidarity than a whole trainload of literature". From now on "the struggle…will be fiercer than it has ever been before…there will be a fight from now on".[26]

Some last points about the general strike. First of all it was, as we have seen, an AFL affair. A rank and file revolt, provoked by strikebreaking and police brutality, forced or enabled the Central Labour Union to call the general strike. Even the United Textile Workers president John Golden, a man hardly known for his militancy, was swept along by his members' fury. The general strike was, he proclaimed, "a splendid opportunity to preach the gospel of trade unionism" and indeed his union signed up thousands of new members.[27] This was the same man who two years later was to be immortalised by a Joe Hill song for his attempt to break the IWW strike in Lawrence ("A little talk with Golden makes it right, all right"). While the official leadership of the AFL was overwhelmingly collaborationist, anti-socialist, right wing and often corrupt, the rank and file clearly included many militants who were engaged in struggle not just with their employers but with their union leaders as well. The AFL unions were themselves the site of struggle. What also has to be recognised, however, is the shameful fact that the AFL unions in Philadelphia operated a ban on black workers.[28] Most of the AFL unions in the city had no black members. This, of course, makes the IWW's achievement on the docks, whatever criticisms one might have, all the more impressive.

26: Foner, 1980, pp162-163. Duchez was, unfortunately, over-optimistic. In 1913 a 13-week strike saw the unions cleared out of the Baldwin works with hundreds victimised. According to Fred Thompson, in his semi-official history of the IWW (Thompson, 2006, p43), there was a small IWW presence at Baldwin's at this time. It was made up of "dual card holders", militants who held both an IWW card and the card of their particular AFL craft union. These "dual carders" dominated the strike committee, but to no avail. Later, in 1921, as part of the post-war rollback of union strength, an eight month strike involving 7,000 workers at the Cramp shipyard ended in defeat, mass victimisation and the introduction of the open shop.
27: Weyforth, 1917, p35.
28: As late as August 1944 the Philadelphia Rapid Transit Union was to shamefully strike in protest against the employment of black workers as crew. One union leader proclaimed that driving a streetcar was a white man's job and that black workers belonged "on the roadway". See Winkler, 1972.

References

Abernathy, Lloyd M, 1982, "Progressivism 1905-1919", in Russell F Weighly (ed), *Philadelphia*, (WW Norton).

Adams, Graham, 1966, *Age of Industrial Violence 1910-1915* (Columbia University).

Arnesen, Eric, 2001, *Brotherhoods of Color: Black Railroad Workers and the Struggle for Equality* (Harvard University).

Brown, John K, 1995, *The Baldwin Locomotive Works 1831-1915* (John Hopkin University).

Cannon, James P, 1955, "The IWW", *Fourth International* (summer 1955), www.marxists.org/archive/cannon/works/1955/iww.htm

Cannon, James P, 1992, *James P Cannon and the Early Years of American Communism: Selected Writings and Speeches 1920-1928* (Spartacist), www.marxists.org/archive/cannon/works/earlyyears/earlytoc.htm

Chaplin, Ralph, 1948, *Wobbly* (University of Chicago).

Cohen, Joseph, 1910a, "When the Sleeper Awakens", *International Socialist Review* (April 1910).

Cohen, Joseph, 1910b, "When the Sleeper Wakes", *International Socialist Review* (May 1910).

Cole, Peter, 2007a, *Wobblies on the Waterfront: International Unionism in Progressive Era Philadelphia* (University of Illinois).

Cole, Peter, 2007b, *Ben Fletcher: The Life and Times of a Black Wobbly* (Charles Kerr).

Darlington, Ralph, 2008, *Syndicalism and the Transition to Communism* (Ashgate).

Foner, Philip S, 1974, *Organized Labor and the Black Worker 1619-1973* (Praeger).

Foner, Philip S, 1980, *The AFL in the Progressive Era* (International).

Fones-Wolf, Ken, 1986a, *Trade Union Gospel: Christianity and Labor in Industrial Philadephia 1865-1915* (Temple University).

Fones-Wolf, Ken, 1986b, "Mass Strikes, Corporate Strategies: The Baldwin Locomotive Works and the Philadelphia General Strike of 1910", *Pennsylvania Magazine of History and Biography*, volume 110.

Gambs, John, 1932, *The Decline of the IWW* (Columbia University).

Hammett, Hugh, 1975, "Labor and Race: The Georgia Railroad Strike of 1909", *Labor History 16*.

Harris, Howell John, 2000, *Bloodless Victory: The Rise and Fall of the Open Shop in the Philadelphia Metal Trades 1910-1940* (Cambridge University).

Jeffreys-Jones, Rhodri, 1978, *Violence and Reform in American History* (New Viewpoints).

Karson, Mark, 1965, *American Labor Unions and Politics 1900-1918* (Becon).

Kimeldorf, Howard, 1999, *Battling For American Labor: Wobblies, Craft Workers and the Making of the Union Movement*, (University of California).

Knight, Robert Edward Lee, 1960, *Industrial Relations in the San Francisco Bay Area 1900-1918* (University of California).

Palmer, Bryan, 2007, *James P Cannon and the Origins of the American Revolutionary Left 1890-1928* (University of Illinois).

Peterson, Horace Cornelius, and Gilbert Courtland Fite, 1957, *Opponents of War 1917-1918* (University of Wisconsin).

Rudwick, Elliott, 1982, *Race Riot at East St Louis* (University of Illinois).

Ruff, Allen, 1997, *"We Called Each Other Comrade": Charles H Kerr and Company, Radical Publishers* (University of Illinois).

Scranton, Philip, 1989, *Figured Tapestry: Production, Markets and Power in Philadelphia Textiles 1885-1941* (Cambridge University).

Spero, Sterling, and Abram Harris, 1968, *The Black Worker* (Atheneum).

Thompson, Fred, 2006, *The IWW: Its First Hundred Years 1905-2005* (Cincinnati).

Weyforth, William, 1917, *The Organizability of Labor* (John Hopkins University).

Winkler, Allan, 1972, "The Philadelphia Transit Strike of 1944", *The Journal of American History 59*.

Reviews

Practising Marxist archaeology
Neil Faulkner

Randall H McGuire, **Archaeology as Political Action** *(University of California Press, 2008),* £17.95

Archaeology is political. It can even provoke bloody confrontation. Over 3,000 people died during communal riots in India and Bangladesh after a Hindu nationalist mob destroyed the Babri Mosque in Ayodhya. The attack had been triggered by archaeological claims that in 1528 the first Mogul emperor had demolished an earlier Hindu temple on the site in order to build the mosque.

Archaeology is "at once trivial and significant": nothing that we find out about the dead can make any difference to them, but the claims we make about the past can be ideologically charged for the living. Nazi archaeologists claimed to have discovered an Aryan "master race" in the mists of German prehistory. Israeli archaeologists bulldoze Islamic levels to find substantiation of Zionist myths beneath. Ulster Unionists see a series of linear earthworks known as "Black Pig's Dyke" as an original Iron Age partition of Ireland.

Randall McGuire's book is a Marxist intervention in political archaeology. The author is one of a group of American archaeologists who consciously locate themselves on the side of the oppressed and seek to develop an archaeological theory and practice appropriate to their stance. This is to be welcomed. McGuire has no truck with the intellectually lazy and morally irresponsible argument that the archaeologist's job is to be "objective", "unbiased" and "apolitical". This is an exercise in self-deception, he argues, fraught with the dangers of triviality, complicity and unexamined prejudice.

A good recent example is provided by forensic archaeologists working on atrocity sites in Iraq. They deploy strong arguments: their work exposes human rights abuses, and it offers the solace of closure to the bereaved by recovering bodies and facilitating proper burial. What they ignore at their moral peril is the politico-military context in which they operate. They work sheltering under the guns of an imperialist army. The atrocities of the fallen regime are investigated; those of the invaders and their puppets are not. The crimes of the past are exposed; those of the present remain hidden—and archaeology becomes a purveyor of war propaganda.

A second example is the Battle of the Bean Field. The Stonehenge Free Festival had been established in 1974 to celebrate the summer solstice. Over the years it attracted growing numbers of hippies, travellers and young people. The Tories hated it and in 1985, claiming that archaeological sites around Stonehenge were being damaged, they decided to shut it down. The site was fortified with barbed wire, a trench was dug across the entrance and there was a full-scale police attack on the travellers. Scores were injured, hundreds arrested, and numerous vans, buses and cars were vandalised. There were archaeologists on both sides of the line: some backed the state and some faced the truncheons. There were occasional clashes in later years. Then in 1994 the Thatcher government passed a criminal justice act that greatly restricted travellers' mobility and rights. We learn that there is no such thing as "neutral" archaeology, but there is blinkered archaeology that cannot see beyond the end of an excavation trench. The great strength of this book is to say this loud and clear.

McGuire argues that archaeologists have to recognise that archaeology is inherently political, primarily through being "a powerful weapon in ideological struggles". We have to know this in order to be fully conscious of the potential impact of our work. Our aim should be radical practice—based on knowledge, critique and action—in which archaeology intervenes in the class struggle to advance the interests of the oppressed against the dominant, making its contribution to the struggle for human emancipation.

A good example from McGuire's own work is the Coalfield War Project, set up to study the site of the infamous Ludlow Massacre of April 1914, in which state militia and hired guns killed 19 men, women and children during an attack on a striking miners' encampment in Colorado. The material culture of the workers and their families, as revealed by excavation, has shed new light on how labour solidarity was forged in struggle among an ethnically diverse immigrant community. More widely, the project has involved archaeologists recovering "hidden history", building links with organised workers (the United Mine Workers of America have been key supporters of the project) and challenging some of the myths of classlessness that are so deeply embedded in popular perceptions of US history.

In standing with the oppressed, McGuire is clear that we can distinguish between good and bad ideas. He is insistent that some uses of evidence are illegitimate and some theories plain wrong, as, for instance, when archaeological data is hijacked in the service of nationalism and oppression. But his break with postmodernism— currently so fashionable in contemporary Anglo-American archaeology in the form of "post-processualism"—is only partial. Eager to be inclusive, McGuire embraces "alternative voices" and "multivocality".

"We also need to avoid totalitarian theories," he writes. "Social theories become totalitarian when they claim that their perspective identifies the determinants of social forms and thus serves as the way to engineer change in those forms. The feminist idea of entry point gives us a way to break this linkage by treating social theories as entry points to study social relations, with the recognition that, in any given case, multiple entry points will be possible and may give compatible interpretations that reinforce one another. A pluralistic praxis of alliance and common struggle can be built from these intersectionalities."

Here two quite distinct matters have become conflated. Let us proceed by example. We wish to understand women's oppression—past and present—and, armed with that understanding, to engage effectively in the struggle against it. There is a Marxist understanding of women's oppression as something rooted in class society and a socialist-feminist tradition arising from this that sees the struggle against oppression as an integral part of the wider class struggle. There is also a bourgeois feminist tradition, which explains the oppression of women in terms of "patriarchy", the implication being that all men benefit from women's oppression and therefore cannot be effectively enlisted as allies in the struggle against it. These two theories are incompatible, and they lead to very different political practice—and very different results. McGuire has failed to distinguish between the struggles of the oppressed, which as Marxists we seek to explain and support, and the non-Marxist theories that these struggles sometimes spawn—including theories which are false, politically disabling, and barriers to emancipation.

Underlying this "soft" post-modernism is an obsession with "the dangers of social engineering and the vanguard party", an obsession rooted, it seems, in an inability to distinguish between Bolshevism and Stalinism. Indeed McGuire appears to have no interest in trying to understand either the defeat of the Russian Revolution or the relationship between party and class: two issues absolutely fundamental to serious Marxist politics. Thus, all varieties of radical (and not so radical) "voices" are welcomed to the progressive alliance. But you cannot deal with differences of analysis and strategy—such as those between socialists and bourgeois feminists, or those between socialists and Third World nationalists—by blandly announcing that these are simply so many "entry points". McGuire wants us all to be nice to each other. But if the aim is to change the world, we have to base practice on clear understanding, and that means not fudging arguments with the people alongside whom we find ourselves fighting.

Zionism under the microscope
John Rose

Gabriel Piterberg, **The Returns of Zionism: Myths, Politics & Scholarship in Israel** (Verso, 2008), £14.99

This is an exhaustive analysis by an uncompromising Israeli scholar of many of the intellectual and literary documents, based on their original languages, that bind the Zionist project together. Hence it is a very important though not an easy read. Dense, complex and with too many loose ends, it is prone to a "Talmudic" style, with commentaries upon commentaries upon original texts. For instance, we have Piterberg on Anita Shapira, doyen of "liberal" Zionist scholarship, on Ben-Gurion on the Bible! (This particular argument will be familiar to readers of this journal.) But please persevere. Piterberg should join Ilan Pappé and Avi Shlaim as essential reading for Israel's opponents.

A good starting point is a confession in the diary of Theodor Herzl, Zionism's founder, that he wished he had been a Prussian aristocrat from the old nobility. Piterberg then shows how Herzl's late 19th century literary outpourings are positioned on this theme—not least his novel, *Altneuland*, his "prophecy" for a Jewish state in Palestine. A central theme in the novel brings an anti-Semitic Prussian Junker to accept the newly created paradise and stay.

Piterberg concludes that Herzl's "belief that having a successful colonial European-like venture in the East was the ultimate path to admission into the West was a genuine one". In other words, far from Zionism posing an alternative to assimilation of Jews into Europe, it was, and remains, assimilation "by other means".

This symbiosis with German right wing nationalist politics is explored to even more alarming effect in the case of Arthur Ruppin. Ruppin's role in the colonisation of Palestine is so pivotal that he is known in Zionist Israeli lore as the "father of Jewish settlement in the land of Israel". The main Jerusalem thoroughfare leading to the Israeli parliament is called Arthur Ruppin boulevard. Like Herzl, he was completely alienated from Judaism and knew little about it. He turned to Zionism because he felt rejected by bourgeois high society. But he did not reject the core values of that society, and when he looked at the Jews of Europe he did not like what he saw.

Ruppin saw his mission as nothing less than the transformation of the Jewish race. He absorbed all the contemporary "race science" claptrap peddled by charlatans such as Houston Stewart Chamberlain. One of the main tasks he set himself was the eradication of the Jews' "commercial instinct", responsible for their excessive fondness for Mammon. Ruppin's diagnosis was that the original Jewish *volk*, which had belonged to Indo-European tribes, deteriorated because of the increasing presence of the Semitic element in its body, in particular through intermingling with the Oriental type.

Yes, he really was saying that Arab types, including Jews from Arab countries, helped to degenerate "real" Jews with all this money business. He praised the superiority of European (Ashkenazi) Jews over the rest in "mathematics, hygiene and above all the Ashkenazi bio-mystic force called *Lebenszahigkeit* (roughly speaking 'life tenaciousness')."

Ruppin was one of the most senior Zionist officials responsible for immigration to Palestine in the early part of the 20th century. He developed a reputation for only selecting "fit" types by the kinds of criteria described above. He was explicit about adapting the German colonisation project for Posen and Eastern Prussia as his model. The "socialist" kibbutz commune type of settlement grew out of this, constructed on sites excluding Palestinian Arabs and only very rarely including Jews from Arab countries.

Several chapters demolish in forensic detail the so-called "Jerusalem school" of Zionist historians. This has been the seedbed developing the view that Jews had been in "exile" since the fall of the Second Temple in Jerusalem in AD 70 but had now "returned". The book's title and the chapters here play on this theme with great effect. The "re" prefix is exposed as an ideological fix—re-turn to the Land, re-turn to history, re-demption and especially re-storation—a product of the 19th century European Protestant imperial imagination and far more influential than the Zionists ever care to admit.

Gershom Scholem is the pivotal figure here. Scholem became Zionism's crowning authority on Jewish messianism in the Jerusalem academy of early 20th century Jewish-settler Palestine. He was also a contemporary and friend of Walter Benjamin, another expert on messianism, who was discussed in the previous issue of *International Socialism*. The struggle between the two of them over the Jewish "soul" caught the attention of George Steiner, who Scholem particularly loathed. Steiner, rightly, elevated the heroism of Benjamin, on the run from the Nazis, yet refusing to consider Palestine even as refuge. Benjamin was a symbol of European Jewry, tempted, yes, but ultimately unwilling to abandon "irreplaceable values...unwilling to exchange the legacy of Spinoza, Heine and Freud for that of Herzl".

Scholem was the authority on the strange figure of Sabbatei Sevi, born in Anatolia in today's Turkey, who proclaimed himself the Jewish messiah in the 17th century. He led a pan-European Jewish "messianic" mass movement after the double shock of the expulsions from Spain in 1492 and the gruesome Ukrainian massacres of Jews in 1648. Sabbatianism has been proclaimed as a proto-Zionist movement, and Jacqueline Rose, in her *The Question of Zion*, very effectively exposed the irrationality that carried from the proto-movement to the real thing.

Piterberg's chapter on Scholem requires especially close reading to get at the intellectual fraud at the heart of Scholem's system. This is based on something called the "mythology of prolepsis", where historical action has to await the future to grasp its full meaning. Scholem claimed that only someone like himself, a scholar, now at last "returned" with the exiled Jewish nation to "the land of Israel", could fully appreciate the embryonic Zionism within the Sabbatian mysticism.

Sabbatei Sevi famously shocked his followers by converting to Islam. Far from shaking Scholem's resolve, this fact too was incorporated into Scholem's very special "dialectics" as "redemption through sin". As Piterberg points out, a rather different approach is needed, highlighting the Ottoman Islamic context, with its own Islamic mystical movements intermingling with Jewish ones. Sabbatianism cannot be understood exclusively through the inner trials and tribulations of "exilic" Jewry. Its real history has still to be written.

A particularly brilliant subsequent chapter lays into more contemporary Israeli literary figures, and in particular Amos Oz, who is probably Israel's most famous novelist. Oz is accused of more or less personal responsibility for fabricating the international image of the "moral" Israeli soldier. Here's how.

After the 1967 war Oz became one of the chief editors of *Siah Lohamim* (*Soldiers Talk*). It was exactly that—soldiers recorded talking in the aftermath of war. It would become "one of the most effective propaganda tools in Israeli history, creating the image of the handsome, dilemma-ridden and existentially soul searching Israeli soldier, the horrific oxymoron of the 'purity of arms', and the unfounded notion of an exalted Jewish morality. It elicited some of the most self-righteous... pronouncements...'a sacred book...we are blessed to have such sons,' said Golda Meir, former Israeli PM." Below are just two of the countless examples of how the editorial mechanism worked.

In the first a commanding officer describes the feelings of his soldiers after they killed a Palestinian peasant in an ambush. The edited text reads, "What perhaps added to this terrible feeling was my impression of the soldiers who were lying in ambush and who as it happened killed that peasant." The original unedited transcript read, "What perhaps added to this terrible feeling was my impression of the enormous gaiety of the soldiers who as it happened killed this peasant."

In another example a manipulated soldier's report claims that the desires of soldiers to finish off a wounded Fatah fighter were thwarted by others with proper moral fibre. The original transcript ends in a rather different way: "Suddenly that man, who was so innocent and quiet, took his rifle and pointed it to the head of the Arab and killed him."

One description of the Israeli soldier

moral mindset reads simply "shooting then weeping".

In his opening chapter Piterberg poses the "conscious pariah" as the alternative to Zionism for dealing with the problems Jews were having with assimilation. Walter Benjamin, Bernard Lazare, a little known late 19th century anarchist writer and some time Zionist, and Hannah Arendt are considered as likely candidates. Piterberg is an expert on Arendt. His more general discussion of her in his book is strongly recommended, as is his excellent article in last November's *New Left Review*—"Zion's Rebel Daughter".

However, there are two problems with this concept. First, although Piterberg is at pains to place a distance between the German sociologist Max Weber's use of "pariah" for the Jewish condition and his own use of it, it remains a concept that Weber cultivated carefully and his association with it is difficult to break. Moreover it is an ugly concept and Weber's use of it, among other things, distinguished Jewish pariah "speculative" capitalism from a more wholesome Protestant sort of capitalism. (Abram Leon was misled by Weber on this matter.) The danger with this line of thinking should be obvious and no concessions should be made to it. But there is a stronger objection. It concedes the Zionist case that assimilation is not possible but instead poses a progressive alternative. While I'm personally sympathetic to this argument—though preferring Isaac Deutscher's formulation of "non-Jewish Jew" or even rootless cosmopolitan—I don't think it describes reality.

The response of millions of East European Jews just over 100 years ago to the failure of assimilation in the pre-revolutionary Tsarist Russian Empire was migration not to Palestine but to America. Today they form the largest Jewish population anywhere in the world. They are as assimilated into America as are the great grandchildren of all those millions of Irish, Italian, Polish, etc, etc Americans, if not more so—and, sadly, certainly more so than millions of black and Latino Americans.

Still, Piterberg may see the concept fitting his own condition. And if he wants to describe himself as a conscious pariah in relation to the Israeli state from which he is so thoroughly and brilliantly alienated, that certainly is his entitlement. And who will disagree with Lazare's formulation that Jews (especially in Israel 100 years later) should come out openly as a representative of the pariah, "since it is the duty of every human being to resist oppression".

Aid for Spain
Andy Durgan

Lewis H Mates, **The Spanish Civil War and the British Left: Political Activism and the Popular Front** *(Tauris Academic Studies, 2007),* £52.50

Few international events have had such an impact on British domestic politics as the Spanish Civil War. Despite the rich and powerful favouring Franco and the National Government backing non-intervention, by the end of the war, according to opinion polls, 71 percent of the population supported the beleaguered Republic.

What became known as the Aid for Spain Movement was based on hundreds of local committees and labour movement organisations. It not only raised thousands of pounds for the Republican cause, but sent over 200 medical personnel, 29 food ships and in May 1937 organised the reception in Britain of 4,000 Basque refugee children. Parallel to this was the recruitment of some 2,300 volunteers for the International Brigades.

Lewis Mates's study of the response to the Spanish Civil War by the labour movement in the north east of England sheds new light on two central facets of this solidarity: the exact nature and extent of "official" labour aid and the impact of the Communist Party's popular front policy.

The Labour Party and TUC leaders were loathe to organise effective solidarity with the Republic. The defeat of the 1926 General Strike and the Trades Disputes Act of 1927, along with the large majority in parliament for the National Government, were cited to justify this reticence. The supposed hostility of working class Catholics to the Republic was also used as an excuse for caution. However, fear of losing control of any mass movement was the real reason for such inaction.

Instead the official leadership supported the farce of non-intervention, arguing that, if effectively applied, this was the best way to avoid the war spreading. Meanwhile they sent humanitarian aid, but without ever raising the quantities collected by the "unofficial" campaign.

In October 1937, long after it became obvious that non-intervention was only a cover for abandoning the Republic, the Labour and TUC leaders reversed their previous policy. Rank and file pressure had played an important part in this change of heart. However, the leadership still baulked at taking any measures that could have forced the government to support the loyalist side in Spain, in particular industrial action.

Mates shows that, despite the conservatism of labour leaders, the party and union rank and file were far more active than has been assumed in supporting the Republic. While left wingers were prominent in both raising funds and opposing the leadership's initial support for non-intervention, mainstream labour supporters were also active over Spain. He also demonstrates that, in the north east of England at least, working class Catholics were more likely to follow their class instincts and support the Republic.

The labour leaders' caution opened the way for the Communist Party, already strengthened by its active involvement in anti-fascist mobilisations, to take the lead in raising support for Spain. The party trebled its membership in this period (from about 6,000 to 18,000), attracted into its orbit many prominent intellectuals and gained immense prestige due to the loss of some its most outstanding members fighting with the International Brigades. The creation of a British version of the popular front appeared a real possibility.

Yet, as Mates demonstrates, growth in Communist influence was more apparent than real. Many Labour Party members and trade unionists were active around Spain independently from Communist-inspired initiatives. Moreover, the popular front policy was opposed by most Labour activists who were hostile to forming any sort of alliance with the discredited Liberal Party—clearly the centrepiece to any British version of the popular front. Neither could they overlook that only recently the Communist Party had attacked Labour as "social-fascist".

By arguing that fascism was somehow independent from capitalism the Communists politically disarmed the solidarity movement. The popular front orientation of many committees and their emphasis on apolitical humanitarian aid proved a hindrance to building a strong campaign against non-intervention. Also attempts to collect funds in middle class areas, for instance, were largely a waste of time compared with the massive support offered in working class districts and workplaces.

Finally, the courting of a motley crew of vicars, Liberals and the occasional Tory not only put off many Labour supporters but also meant that the Communist Party could not defend the need for industrial action in support of the Republic, as this would have upset its would-be middle class allies. The signing of the Nazi-Soviet Non-Aggression Pact in 1939 finished off any lingering hopes that the CP could have had of seeing their popular frontist illusions become reality.

It would be wrong, however, to conclude that rejection of the Communist popular front line meant that significant sections of the labour movement activists understood what was at stake in Spain. Like the Communist Party, most Labour and trade union activists accepted that what was happening was simply a struggle between "democracy and fascism". References to the Spanish war being the result of a "foreign (fascist) invasion" or the absence of religious persecution in the Republican zone were two of the clearest examples of this distorted view. Unfortunately, only a small minority, most notably the Independent Labour Party, understood that only the deepening of the social revolution that had greeted the military uprising in July 1936 offered a strategy for victory.

The tragedy of Iraq's Communists

Anne Alexander

Tareq Ismael, **The Rise and Fall of the Communist Party of Iraq** *(Cambridge University Press, 2007), £50*

Early on the mornings of 14 and 15 February 1949 a macabre sight met the eyes of passers-by in Baghdad. Bodies dangled on public display from gibbets erected in three of the city's main squares. Notices posted nearby informed the general public that the three dead men were Yusuf Salman Yusuf, otherwise known as Comrade Fahd, secretary general of the Iraqi Communist Party (ICP); Zaki Basim and Husain al-Shabibi, two leading Communist activists.

Just over a year earlier Iraq had been shaken by a popular uprising against the imposition of a new treaty with Britain. School and university students, railway workers and the vast mass of the urban poor—migrants from the impoverished south who filled the mud shacks around Baghdad—combined in gigantic protests, forcing the regent to disown the treaty.

The ICP played a crucial role in the uprising and the wave of strikes which followed, although tragically the protests lost momentum in late spring 1948, allowing the pro-British politicians who ruled Iraq to weather the storm. The hangings in February 1949 were their revenge on the Communists, who had dared to challenge both the Iraqi monarchy and its imperial backers in Whitehall.

In the uprising of 1948 Iraqi Communists risked death to lead protests against a treaty that perpetuated the British military occupation of Iraq. How then could the leaders of the same Communist Party, who continued to lay claim to the legacy of Fahd and his murdered comrades, join the governing council set up by the US occupying forces in 2003?

Tareq Ismael's account of the rise and fall of the ICP attempts to answer this question. Using internal party documents, memoirs and interviews with leading Communist activists, Ismael traces the tragic history of Communism in Iraq from its earliest beginnings in the 1920s to the events of 2003.

Unlike in Hanna Batatu's influential study, *The Old Social Classes and Revolutionary Movements of Iraq*, which relied heavily on Iraqi police records, the voices heard here are largely those of Iraqi Communists themselves. Although some of these sources are well known to Arabic readers, Ismael's history is the first to give English speaking audiences the opportunity to follow the ICP's internal debates through the words of the party's leading activists. As a result it is an immensely valuable and rich history of one of Iraq's most important political parties.

Ismael argues that the ICP's subservience to Iraq's new occupiers is rooted in the crisis which engulfed the party after the revolution of 1958. The 1960s, in particular, marked the transformation of the ICP from a party of "vanguard activists", whose challenge to the existing political order was "mapped out onto a grassroots base" of Iraq's expanding urban poor (p318), into an organisation dominated by "rearguard opportunism", prepared to sacrifice any principle in order to forge a relationship with those in power.

The party's relationship with the USSR was a crucial factor in this process. Soviet support allowed the party to function in the face of terrible repression: party leaders could find sanctuary in the USSR; Soviet funds kept ICP publications going and helped the party's underground networks of activists to survive. However, in return the ICP was expected to display unquestioning loyalty towards its patrons in Moscow, even though the "Soviet leaders frequently neglected the real interests of their Iraqi comrades, sacrificing them on the altar of their own global political agendas" (p316). Following a classic Stalinist pattern, the ICP's leadership encouraged a "cult of personality" around the secretary general. As Ismael explains, the "dependent political culture" (p316) inside the party played a destructive role in encouraging and deepening splits within the organisation "which appeared to be the only avenue available for any questioning of ideology and praxis in this inflexible environment" (p316).

The most important of these was the rift between the ICP central committee (ICP-CC) and the ICP central leadership (ICP-CL), which solidified into a permanent split in 1968. The issues at stake in the split were profound: the relationship between the fight for national liberation and socialist revolution, the party's dependence on the USSR, the question of internal democracy and the role of armed struggle in the Iraqi Revolution. The first key problem concerned the party leadership's actions in the aftermath of the revolution.

The monarchy was overthrown in July 1958 by dissident officers led by Abd-al-Karim Qasim and Abd-al-Salam Arif, who invited the opposition parties (with the pointed exception of the Communists) into government. The birth of the Iraqi Republic struck a devastating blow to British influence in the Middle East and was seen by millions across the region as another sign that the era of colonial domination had passed. However, within a few weeks disagreements about the relationship between Iraq and the newly founded United Arab Republic (a union between Egypt and

Syria) caused a bitter conflict between Qasim and Arif. The ICP stood firmly with Qasim, opposing a headlong rush into unity with the United Arab Republic, while Arif was backed by various Arab nationalist groups, including the fledgling Baath Party. Against a backdrop of worsening conflict between Qasim and Arif, the ICP's influence grew massively as the trade union movement revived and the new regime began to enact important social reforms.

The peak of the ICP's power came in May 1959. The party had just played a pivotal role in derailing an attempted coup by Arab nationalist officers in Mosul. Hundreds of thousands of demonstrators took to the streets of Baghdad, calling on Qasim to invite the ICP into government. Yet Qasim outmanoeuvred the party leadership, making symbolic concessions but then purging Communist activists from the armed forces and government ministries.

The ICP's central committee quickly backed down from confrontation with Qasim and launched into a period of self-criticism (which some activists described as "self-flagellation"). As Ismael explains, the ICP-CL argued that the party missed a historic opportunity as a result of the leadership's failure to understand the nature of the Qasim regime: "Instead of taking the initiative to rally the masses against the ruling class's retreat from the revolution and reaction against the democratic gains it had brought, the ICP asked the masses to surrender submissively and stand behind the regime" (p216).

The ICP-CL was also bitterly critical of the ICP's dependence on the Soviet Union, and of the inability of the party's rank and file to hold the leadership to account for its disastrous strategy. Tragically, as Ismael points out, the ICP-CL was not able to build a viable alternative to the increasingly hollow structures of the ICP-CC. The ICP-CL

argued that Iraqi Communists should mobilise for "popular armed struggle", but attempts to organise guerrilla warfare against the second Baathist regime (which took power in 1968) were catastrophic failures. The ICP-CL ended up based in Kurdistan, isolated from Iraq's growing working class and dependent on the goodwill of the Kurdish nationalist leaders (p205).

Unlike the ICP-CL, the ICP-CC initially concluded an alliance with the Baath Party, joining the regime's National Patriotic Front in 1973. Despite the bitter experience of the 1950s and 1960s, the ICP-CC's leaders sacrificed what remained of the party's credibility as an independent political force with their enthusiastic endorsement of the Baath's "progressive" programme. But in the early 1980s the ICP-CC also fled to Kurdistan to launch an armed struggle against the Baathist regime, following another round of vicious purges and repression in the late 1970s.

Subsequent decades saw the ICP-CC, the ICP-CL and small groups that continually splintered from both becoming increasingly isolated from the party's former base inside Iraq. The only area where Communist activists could operate openly was in Iraqi Kurdistan, and this entailed negotiating a tricky path between the competing Kurdish nationalist parties. When the US invasion and occupation of Iraq in 2003 brought the Baathist regime crashing down, the ICP-CC's leaders threw their lot in with the occupying powers, following the path chosen by numerous other exiled opposition groups. The ICP, Ismael notes, "diluted its anti-capitalist rhetoric almost overnight. The outcome of this transformation was obvious: a seat on the governing council of Iraq and official political recognition for the party's leadership by the occupation authorities. However, the cost for the party was astronomical and involved its being cut off from the movement against the occupation forces, as many of the individuals engaging in active resistance came to see the members of the governing council, including the ICP, as 'collaborators'" (pp296-297).

Despite the weight of the ICP's tragic history, Ismael ends his account on a note of hope, arguing that the party's lasting legacy lies in its enrichment of Iraqi political thought through the politicisation of issues such as poverty and social injustice. The ICP's anti-imperialism has not been completely erased either, as this tradition still inspires networks of Iraqi activists such as Iraqi Democrats Against the Occupation.

Hidden histories of sexuality
Colin Wilson

BR Burg, **Boys at Sea: Sodomy, Indecency and Courts Martial in Nelson's Navy** *(Palgrave Macmillan, 2007), £50*

Neville Hoad, **African Intimacies: Race, Homosexuality and Globalization** *(University of Minnesota Press, 2007), £12.50*

Katherine O'Donnell and Michael O'Rourke (eds), **Love, Sex, Intimacy and Friendship Between Men, 1550-1800** *(Palgrave Macmillan, 2007), £16.99*

The past 30 years have seen an enormous growth in writing about the history of sexuality. A detailed and fascinating account is now available. This work began

in the 1970s with a desire to recover "gay history", though most historians now accept that sexuality varies between societies, and categories such as "gay" and "straight" are historically recent.

BR Burg's history of the navy makes this clear. He investigates trials for sexual misbehaviour between 1652 and 1866, when anal sex was often punished with hanging and other acts with extreme brutality ("500 lashes with the cat"). In the dozens of admiralty documents that Burg consults, no one suggests that some men desired sex with other males because they had a particular inclination to do so. They were not, in our sense, gay—they were "normal" but sinful and potentially rebellious. Sex with men was an offence, like drunkenness or insubordination, which any man might commit.

This attitude is reflected in the testimony of boatswain's mate William Brown at a court martial in 1815. Brown "said that god must have put it into men's hearts to commit the unnatural crime of buggery, and that therefore if god was to put it into his head to fuck a man he would as soon do it as fuck a woman". Sexual transgressions here went along with a general lack of discipline and morality. Brown told the court that he would bugger "not only the captain and the officers" but also "Jesus Christ if he was in his coffin".

Such cheerful contempt for authority was unfortunately rare. The courts martial reflect the deeply hierarchical nature of a ship's crew. The youngest and most vulnerable—boys as young as 11—were exploited, and their testimony often disbelieved. Senior officers seldom faced trial.

Katherine O'Donnell and Michael O'Rourke's collection of essays questions not only the distinction between homosexual and heterosexual, but wider concepts including friendship, sexuality and masculinity.

In one of the essays in the collection Alan Bray documents a tradition of deep and committed same-sex friendship between both men and women. In Westminster Abbey, Mary Kendall and Catharine Jones were buried in one tomb in 1710. Their monument records their "close union and friendship...even their ashes, after death, might not be divided". Such friendships, sealed with vows, were a lifelong commitment to another person, though they did not preclude marriage or have any effect on property.

Randolph Trumbach's essay describes the boisterous sexual life of 18th century London. Men followed each other through the streets and had sex in inns and coaches—as we know from encounters which went wrong and ended up in court. Other men crossdressed and were indistinguishable from female prostitutes. Some men were effeminate "Mollies" who used women's names but many who had sex with other men were not.

Some essays discuss when a "homosexual" identity first appeared—with the 18th century Mollies, or in the late 19th century? Choosing one date seems pointless. A whole series of changes happened. The growth of wage labour implied the development of a "private life", including sexuality, outside work. The expansion of London in the 17th century meant thousands of people lived outside traditional rural controls on sexuality and made the Molly subculture possible. Further changes happened in the 19th century as part of attempts to ensure the dominance of the family.

The broader point is that our commonsense ideas have no validity in this period.

Back then a man who had sex with many women did not demonstrate his virility because manliness was identified with self-control. Instead he would have been seen as effeminate. Sodomy was not a sexual crime but was associated with atheism, blasphemy, treachery and Catholicism. Even modern distinctions between friendship, sexuality and intimate relationships, around which we all organise our emotional lives today, worked in different ways.

In Neville Hoad's *African Intimacies* the history of sexuality combines with that of imperialism and African nationalism—a combination exemplified in the disgraceful story of Sarah Bartmann. Bartmann was a Southern African woman who travelled to Europe in 1810 and was exhibited semi-naked as "the Hottentot Venus". On her death she was dissected by one Baron Cuvier, who claimed that "her external genitalia recalled those of the orangutang". Bartmann's genitals were preserved in formaldehyde until 2001, when they were returned to South Africa for burial.

The association of Africans with ideas of uncontrolled animalistic sexuality played its part in imperialism. African sexual practices, according to European rulers, were proof of the "primitive" nature of those societies, justifying the 19th century "scramble for Africa."

In what became Uganda same-sex behaviour exemplified African barbarity. The first white people to arrive in the country were missionaries. Mwanga, the king, insisted that his pages submit to what the missionaries called his "unnatural desires": the pages, who had recently converted to Christianity, refused and Mwanga had 30 of them killed.

African nationalists rightly rejected any idea of "hypersexual" Africans. But many accepted an idea of sexual respectability introduced by the missionaries, who paved the way for imperialism. Many African leaders have dismissed homosexuality as un-African. In the words of President Museveni, "We don't have homosexuals in Uganda." In a further irony, the Anglican church in Europe and the US now sees tolerance of homosexuality as a key indicator of a modern, civilised society, once again marking Africans as "primitive".

Hoad's work addresses many of the same issues as examined, in an Arab context, by Joseph Massad, whose *Desiring Arabs* I reviewed in issue 118 of *International Socialism*. Hoad notes the—at best—political naivety of international gay organisations, which often seek to promote Western concepts of sexuality as the only way to liberation and so allow homophobic nationalists to claim that homosexuality is a foreign import.

At times Hoad is too much the postmodern academic to ask questions such as, "What really happened?" or, "Which of these accounts is actually true?" For example, while we should reject the idea that Africans are overly sexual or to blame for their own misfortunes, and while we should condemn the use of African people in dubious drug trials, Thabo Mbeki is still dangerously wrong when he suggests that HIV is not the cause of Aids. Similarly, O'Donnell and O'Rourke's collection is also heavy on postmodern academic jargon. Overall, however, these works contain fascinating insights that contribute to our understanding of the history of sexuality.

Taking the care out of social care
Helen Davies

Iain Ferguson, **Reclaiming Social Work: Challenging Neoliberalism and Promoting Social Justice** (SAGE, 2007), £21.99

This summer Wirral council announced it would shed up to 30 social worker posts because the "personalisation agenda" means these qualified social workers are no longer necessary. Presumably Wirral council is drawing this conclusion because service users are now becoming "co-producers" of their health and wellbeing as a result of personalisation. Some of the posts lost will be made up by employing non social workers instead. This practice may not be copied across the country—but most practitioners fear the worst.

In *Reclaiming Social Work* Iain Ferguson quotes Charles Leadbetter, the key figure behind the personalisation agenda. According to Leadbetter, the service users must behave as "active participants in the process—deciding to manage their lives in a different way—rather than dependent users" (p79). This "expert", Iain tells us, was formerly a financial journalist and consultant to British Telecom. Are these the credentials of someone you would look to in order to transform social care?

And so it goes on. This book lines up these fashionable theories, analysing the way in which social work is made to dovetail with economic theory and practice. I particularly enjoyed the way Iain discusses the sickening catchphrases that populate the world of social policy, such as "evidence based", of which "personalisation" is just the latest. The book is uncompromisingly

Marxist in outlook and will probably disappoint those still adhering to a post-modern view of the world. Its strength is that it describes a common set of goals with which I hope most people in the profession could identify. Iain articulates perfectly what is wrong—but it feels like we are a very long way from getting together to put it right. A first step would be to get people together to discuss the issues, and Iain writes about the successes so far in doing this.

This book is important reading for anyone involved in social services, social care or social work. It is a relief to realise that we are not alone in our absolute incomprehension of the absurdities the government thrusts upon us. Iain is able to give the history of these developments over the past 20 to 30 years and explain their "logic". His account is coherent and easily understandable, and his examples produced sighs and vigorous nods from my colleagues when I quoted them—they identify immediately with what he is saying.

A book on social work is bound to also be a book about the welfare state (or perhaps the "farewell state" as, in its current form, this state seems determined to absolve itself of any responsibility to anyone who is not responsible for a huge corporation and/or with a few million in spare cash). As such it may appeal to a wider audience than just those directly employed in social care. After all, sooner or later the vast majority of us will need the services of this sector either directly or indirectly as we care for someone who is in need.

Still fighting old battles
Andy Zebrowski

Jerzy Borzecki, **The Soviet–Polish Peace of 1921 and the Creation of Interwar Europe** *(Yale University, 2008), £35*

After 1917 it was not just the best known Bolsheviks who saw the October Revolution as the beginning of the international revolution—millions of ordinary people did as well. It was understood that for the rule of the workers' councils (Soviets) to survive in Russia the revolution had to spread. This was not just wishful thinking. The global impact of events in Russia was so colossal that it was felt way beyond Europe, from China to Argentina, from the United States to Indonesia. In 1919 the Bolsheviks organised the Third or Communist International which soon became a forum for strategy creation for the revolutionary parties springing up around the world.

Unfortunately, none of this makes its way into Jerzy Borzecki's book. The author is a patriotic Polish historian who has created a different context for himself. We are informed that the book is "a case study of the mode of negotiations between an emerging totalitarian state and a fledgling democracy". The negotiations referred to resulted in the Treaty of Riga of March 1921, following a war between revolutionary Russia and a newly independent Poland in the previous year. The war ended in the Bolsheviks' defeat at the Battle of Warsaw.

The offensive on Warsaw is often cited as demonstrating the "Soviet imperialism" of Lenin's "emerging totalitarian state". In fact it was predicated on workers rising up in the city. As Trotsky put it, "We tried to make a revolutionary offensive sortie into Europe with our march on Warsaw, but it did not come off. Why? Because the revolution had not matured. Not because such a sortie was wrong in principle, no, but because the revolution in Poland had not matured. In Italy the revolution had miscarried, and in Germany and Poland the preparatory period had not been completed." Counting on an uprising in Warsaw turned out to be a bad miscalculation but that it was a mistake was not a foregone conclusion.

An independent Poland was possible only because revolution had overthrown the three empires (German, Austro-Hungarian and Russian) that had ruled the partitioned country. At the end of 1918 the occupying German troops in Warsaw set up soldiers' councils and workers in the city did the same. Soviets were also created in various other Polish towns. In fact these organs of revolutionary democracy were set up before Poland became Poland so really Borzecki should talk about a "fledgling workers' democracy" in the country. In the mining areas of Silesia workers even organised Red Guard militias. The soldiers' councils were quickly terminated as German soldiers were sent back to Germany while the workers' councils were suppressed by the Polish government as late as summer 1919.

In Warsaw the Communist delegates to the Soviet were a substantial minority. In April 1919 Lenin declared that the "self-determination of the proletariat is proceeding among the Poles. Here are the latest figures on the composition of the Warsaw Soviet of Workers' Deputies. Polish traitor-socialists [ie traitors to the working class] 333, Communists 297."

In 1920, as the Red Army approached Warsaw, an embryonic provisional government was set up in eastern Poland and 65 revolutionary committees were organised. Soon after the 1920 war the Communist party made significant gains. Legally obliged to fight its first election in 1922 under another name (the Union of the Proletariat of Town and Country), it won two seats in parliament—obtaining its best results in Silesia and Warsaw, only two years after the war!

Borzecki's grasp of theory is weak. He says that the Riga Treaty forced Lenin "to embark on building socialism in one country". While this statement may be good news for followers of Stalin, as history it is laughable. Trotsky's analysis in December 1921 is more sensible and accurate: "The result of our military retreat from Warsaw—after sounding out our enemies and our friends—was a political retreat, not only by Soviet Russia but also by the entire revolutionary movement. What was the Treaty of Riga, for which we are now paying? It was part of our retreat. We are pulling back, cautiously and firmly, not yielding to the enemy any more positions than we have to." Trotsky added that the Communists were "now faced with a period of preparation—here, in Germany and in Poland". No sign of "socialism in one country" there.

In fact Trotsky (and most other Bolsheviks) felt international revolution was still on the cards in the not so distant future: "In Germany the preparatory period means waging a successful struggle to win the masses. In Poland it means the growth of the Communist Party: at the elections for the hospital-fund clubs the Communist Party won more votes than the Polish Socialist Party—that is a symptom of extraordinary importance."

Borzecki does not understand the revolutionary times he is dealing with. He mentions the Bolsheviks' intention to "sovietise" Poland without once explaining the revolutionary democratic nature of soviets. The reader is therefore left with the idea of "sovietising" in the Cold War sense of the term.

The war with Poland came towards the end of the horrendous civil war in Russia that followed the 1917 Revolution. The Bolsheviks saw the Communist International as the best way to spread revolution but they still had to operate as a state in a system of nation states and empires. Whatever concessions had to be made on the diplomatic front (including the Riga Treaty) the Bolsheviks' objective was spreading genuine revolution from below.

But the Polish side pursued more traditional goals. After independence Poland's future dictator Jozef Piłsudski was engaged in six border wars, aggressively trying to win out in the scramble for territory between the newly created nation states. The Bolshevik aims were of a different order entirely, which Borzecki does not understand. Nonetheless, once or twice he demonstrates this despite his intentions.

In July 1920 the Bolsheviks were planning to sign an armistice with Poland in the event that an offensive by counter-revolutionary General Wrangel made this necessary. But the terms demanded showed how different revolutionary Russia was from any other state. As Borzecki relates, "Within a month, the Polish army was to be reduced to 50,000 rank and file, and 10,000 officer and administrative cadres. Also within a month, all surplus arms and ammunition were to be turned over to the soviets, who would then use them to arm organised Polish "urban and industrial workers". Poland was to cease the manufacturing of arms and ammunition.

Here a state is demanding the arming of part of an enemy state's population—not on ethnic but on class lines. That is revolutionary diplomacy.

In Poland 15 August is marked as the date of the Bolshevik defeat. The televison news remembers "the miracle on the Vistula". It quotes the title of British diplomat Lord d'Abernon's book, which refers to the battle of Warsaw as *The Eighteenth Decisive Battle of the World*. But this claim is exaggerated. True, the battle forced a retreat for the international revolution. A revolutionary Poland would have helped spread the rule of workers' councils further west. But even without a revolutionary Poland the German revolution could have succeeded in 1923, if an uprising had been called by Communist Party leaders in November. This failure was much more crucial to the isolation of Soviet Russia and prepared the ground for Stalin's rule. The battle of Warsaw is stressed by mainstream historians because they are more comfortable dealing with battles than with workers' uprisings.

As for the non-revolutionary nature of Polish workers, as Borzecki would have it, it is worth noting that the day before the uprising was supposed to take place in Germany—7 November 1923—the workers of Kraków had disarmed and fraternised with the soldiers in the city and taken over. Only for one day it is true, but still.

A study in African resistance

Colin Barker

Leo Zeilig, **Revolt and Protest: Student Politics and Activism in Sub-Saharan Africa** *(Tauris, 2007), £47.50*

The revolutions in "Third World" countries in the three decades after 1945 posed some problems for Marxist theory. Leadership in those revolutions did not come from the "traditional" bourgeoisie. It proved quite as politically incapable as the bourgeoisies of Germany or Russia, whose behaviour in 1848, 1905 and 1917 provoked the initial formulations of the theory of "permanent revolution", first by Karl Marx and then by Leon Trotsky. The bourgeoisie's lack of revolutionary leadership was not unexpected. The age of the "classic" bourgeois revolution had ended before 1848.

What permanent revolution proposed, as policy and theory, was that the struggle for political emancipation—including national emancipation from imperial control—should and could be taken up and led by working class forces. By asserting their own independent interests and developing their own specific political forms (from workers' parties and militia to soviets) organised workers could, even while still a minority within underdeveloped capitalist formations, assert their political leadership over peasants and artisans, and so begin the process of socialist reconstruction of society under their own direct control.

However, no such scenario fitted the experience of the post-war revolutions in "backward countries". Certainly there were cases in which workers participated in the struggle for national independence. For example, in Nigeria, Senegal, Zimbabwe and Zambia general strikes preceded the actual struggle for the transfer of power from colonial authorities. But nowhere was the actual revolutionary process marked by the assertion of independent working class power and organisation. In many cases, indeed, the revolutionary transfer of power occurred without any significant working class involvement, as Tony Cliff recorded in his examination of the revolutions in China, Algeria and Cuba (see the article "Deflected Permanent Revolution", available from www.marxists.org).

Writing in 1963, Cliff offered a characterisation of the wave of Third World revolutions, offering the term "deflected permanent revolution". Given the weakness of independent working class organisation, leadership of a whole series of revolutions had fallen to a social force previously unexpected to play this role. A radical urban petty-bourgeois intelligentsia took the political initiative and set out to impose its own vision of societal development.

In sub-Saharan Africa, the focus of Leo Zeilig's study, this national intelligentsia was recruited from the small ranks of university educated graduates (many of them getting their degrees in the metropolitan centres, for the colonising powers had held back university development across Africa), from civil servants working in the colonial administrations and from the trade union bureaucracy. According to Zeilig, this group, mostly ex-students, came to see themselves as "the liberators of Africa and as uniquely representing the emergent nation" (p31).

If, commonly, they adopted a rhetoric of "socialism", theirs was a "socialism from above" marked by a concern to use the state as an agency of essentially national development. Cliff characterised their politics sharply: "They are great believers in efficiency... They hope for reform from above and would dearly love to hand the new world over to a grateful people, rather than see the liberating struggle of a self-conscious and freely associated people result in a new world themselves." Or, as Mahmood Mamdani was to write later, "Intellectuals...saw the state and not the class struggle as the motive force of development...socialism was turned into a strategy for economic development, and no more... From this perspective, it was difficult even to glimpse the possibility of working people in Africa becoming a creative force capable of making history. Rather, history was seen as something to be made outside this force, in lieu of this force and ultimately to be imposed on it" (cited by Zeilig, p33).

Across sub-Saharan Africa the situation after independence was ambiguous in its effects on students. They were commonly seen, and saw themselves, as the crucial bearers of a vision of national development. However, the expected benefits of independence were slow to arrive for the majority of the population. The regimes that emerged were commonly authoritarian and the gradually expanding university sector became an important setting for political struggle. As with student movements elsewhere in the 1960s and early 1970s, student politics was often explosive yet transitory and still marked by elitism.

Zeilig's study is focused chiefly on student movements in Africa in the subsequent period. From the mid-1970s the whole economic, political and social environment changed quite rapidly for the worse. The world recession had an especially catastrophic effect on Africa. States that relied chiefly for export income on a few primary products saw their prices collapse as the cost of their imports rose. Visions of national state-led capitalist development imploded as state debts rocketed.

Compelled to turn to the IMF and World Bank, they were to adopt "structural adjustment policies" involving varying degrees of economic liberalisation and privatisation. These, if they benefited international capital, did little or nothing to improve the lot of the majority of sub-Saharan Africa's peoples. Those majorities bore the brunt of "adjustment" in rising food prices and falling employment.

Those popular majorities provided the social basis for a wave of "street demonstrations, marches, strikes and other forms of public action" during the late 1970s and 1980s. These rocked the regimes and provided an important precursor to the anti-globalisation movement today (p52).

In the early 1990s the scale and extent of popular protest activity expanded rapidly, compelling many governments to introduce reforms and to hold democratic elections. Though insufficiently noticed, African countries played a key part in the wave of "democratic transitions" that, of course, included those in Eastern Europe and the former USSR. But the democracy produced has been weakly developed, not least because popular resistance to state policies of "economic liberalisation" has remained powerful: "While the demand for economic liberalisation may have weakened formal democratic structures, in some cases it created an extraordinarily explosive cocktail of social forces" (p58).

That cocktail included African students. If in the immediate aftermath of independence students were an actual or aspiring elite, the same world capitalist forces that drove down popular living and working standards across the continent also pulled them down. Zeilig provides a graphic account of the problems afflicting Africa's higher education institutions, from physical decay of buildings to the slashing of library book and journal stocks, from spiralling student fees and living costs to overcrowded classrooms and inadequate teaching. Behind these developments lie World Bank policies, themselves close to what one critic termed "academic exterminism". In the process "university students have seen their status collapse, along with every other social class. These are general processes that have seen the decimation of classes previously regarded as privileged—teachers, university lecturers, civil servants and white collar workers" (p78).

It is this changed context of social breakdown that makes Zeilig's account of recent student activism across Africa so interesting. Given the variety of conditions across the continent, any generalisation must be very provisional. Yet it is clear that students regularly played a significant role in democratisation processes. To that we must add that they were most effective when their own activism succeeded in forcing a wider political opening up, even where they themselves lacked a clear alternative strategy. As Mamdani commented, "Its possibilities depended far more on the character of forces that student action succeeded in mobilising than its own internal energies" (cited, p90). That conclusion, of course, fits the French events of May 1968 quite as much as it fits modern Africa.

From being an elite group, set apart from and "over" society, students—and the unemployed graduates that many go on to become—have become an important part of the popular classes themselves. Here too there are significant parallels with the "proletarianisation" of students that recent European commentators have recorded. No longer a tiny "transitory" group awaiting jobs in government, African students have at once expanded their numbers but have also been "pauperised, converging more and more with the wider urban poor—the social groups

they historically saw as their responsibility to liberate" (p91).

This is not to say that student politics have been purged of all elements of elitism, but now they are tempered by the realities of campus poverty. African students, however, retain the ability, noted in other parts of the world, to mobilise and organise more quickly and effectively than many other social groups. If they cannot by themselves remake politics, they can and do play a specific energising role in oppositional politics which has regularly brought them into conflict with their various regimes.

At the core of Zeilig's book are two substantial chapters based on extensive interviews detailing student activism in Zimbabwe and Senegal. In 1991 in Zimbabwe Robert Mugabe's government introduced its first full structural adjustment programme, producing a rapid rise in unemployment accompanied by a cut in exports and growing inflation. Although it took several years for organised resistance to mobilise large-scale forces, by the mid-1990s mass strikes, student demonstrations and food riots began to coalesce against a notoriously brutal police regime.

There were growing calls on the Zimbabwe Congress of Trade Unions, led by Morgan Tsvangirai, to form a labour party. But these calls were soon joined by other, middle class voices. In 1999 the Movement for Democratic Change (MDC) emerged, but rapidly dissociated itself from its labour base by supporting further privatisation, with the union leadership acting to contain and stifle widespread protest activity.

From the second half of the 1990s Zimbabwean students' formerly privileged economic position was speedily reduced under a second wave of structural adjustment policies that slashed grants, expanded loans and privatised food and accommodation just as prices were soaring. Student economic demands now coalesced with demands for political reform, drawing them into links with the trade unions and the formation of the MDC.

The contradictions and tensions were considerable. Students were fighting the privatisation of education at the same time that the MDC, the party they supported, was advocating more of the same. It was in this context that the small International Socialist Organisation worked to develop some ideological and practical clarity, as Zeilig documents at some length. Zimbabwe's campuses were rocked by protests, to which the regime responded with brutal force.

As Zeilig shows, however, a new force now entered the scene, in the shape of international NGOs, who poured in money to the opposition, producing what activists termed the "commodification of resistance", funding expensive conferences and scholarships, and distorting the structures of indigenous opposition. Students found themselves isolated and subjected to violent assaults when they demonstrated on the campus. Zeilig's whole chapter is invaluable for anyone trying to make sense of the current situation in Zimbabwe.

Students in Senegal had their own, less known, "May events" in 1968 when student protests coincided with widespread strikes. As their material situation worsened, economic and political issues also became intertwined with their waves of protest action. Their most notable recent role in Senegalese politics occurred in the years 2000 and 2001. To many observers, Senegal after independence had looked like a one-party state under Senghor and his nominated successor Diouf. In 2000, however, Abdoulaye Wade, himself a former student activist, succeeded in capturing the levers of state power in a hotly contested election. In that election, conducted under the slogan *Sopi* (change), students played an indispensable role, fanning out across the country to mobilise the vote in their towns and villages of origin.

Wade, like the MDC in Zimbabwe, saw his role as continuing "structural adjustment" policies. Within a year those policies brought him into sharp conflict with the very students who had campaigned for him in 2000. A student campaign of strikes and demonstrations, which involved the death of a law student, compelled Wade to reverse his previous support for World Bank sponsored cutbacks in university spending. Wade's regime, having conceded, then broke the back of the student movement by buying off its leaders with overseas scholarships in a local variant of "commodification of resistance".

If in the countries of advanced capitalism the distinct status of students has declined, making them a "student mass" (Stathis Kouvelakis) within the workers' movement rather than a distinct class, across most of Africa students are still a much smaller proportion of the population. If many of their previous material privilege have withered, Zeilig suggests they retain some privileged autonomy as political actors. Their concentration on the campus and their unique social situation between two very different social worlds give them a degree of freedom to act collectively (and be beaten up!) when other sections of the oppressed are shackled.

Nonetheless, the international collapse of the old post-colonial project of state development and the dominance of structural adjustment programmes have converted them into "more modest agents of social change" (p239). Their autonomous role as agents of transformation often appears in the early stages of popular mobilisation, but is accompanied by their inability, alone, to carry through significant social and political transitions. Student militancy appears most effective when it is directly connected with struggles by unions and other popular movements—a process that reduces students' special significance.

The collapse of state development projects, along with the ideological certainties that the Stalinist regimes used to provide, has generated widespread uncertainty in the realm of radical ideas. There is a significant dialectic at work here. In Senegal, where student resistance was less connected than in Zimbabwe to vibrant popular movements, the level of political analysis among students was also less developed (p243). Across sub-Saharan Africa, as in the rest of the world, the left is struggling to develop new theoretical accounts of the world and new forms of political practice that can pose real alternatives to the failures of both state capitalism and global marketisation. Leo Zeilig's book helps capture many of the dilemmas and possibilities that are emerging.

The rise of the modern state
Pepijn Brandon

Heide Gerstenberger, **Impersonal Power: History and Theory of the Bourgeois State**, translated by David Fernbach (Brill, 2007), £139.10

Heide Gerstenberger's *Impersonal Power* is an ambitious book. It tries to give an explanation for the form and content of the bourgeois state, rooted in a wide-ranging description of over 1,000 years of English and French history. If this review is critical in tone, this is not out of a lack of appreciation for the wealth of historical knowledge and detail displayed in its almost 700 pages.

The problem of the state has always caused much debate among Marxists. The famous description in the *Communist Manifesto* of the state as "but a committee for managing the common affairs of the whole bourgeoisie" provides little more than a pointer as to how the state functions and why.

In order to come closer, Gerstenberger borrows a concept from Marx's youthful critique of Georg Hegel's *Philosophy of Right*. In this complex and unfinished piece of writing, still heavily influenced by the Young Hegelians, Marx provides a number of valuable insights into the rise of modern politics. Among other things, he draws a sharp distinction between the close relationship between social classes and the state in medieval times and the modern "separation between the state and civil society". Put schematically, in the Middle Ages exploitation was organised primarily through violence or the direct appropriation by the ruling classes of part of the surplus product from the direct producers by "political" means. This also meant that social relations were immediately political. In such conditions there is no separation between state and civil society, or as Marx puts it, "In the Middle Ages, there were serfs, feudal goods, guilds, scholarly corporations, etc, that means, in the Middle Ages property, trade, society, human beings [are] political; the material content of the state is determined by its form; every private sphere has a political character or is a political sphere, or politics is also the character of the private sphere."

By contrast, under capitalism exploitation is primarily an economic process. State and civil society become separate entities, in which the state ceases to be the direct tool of individual members of the ruling class and becomes the general overseer of society. However, far from liberating the state from the particular interests of the economic ruling class, as Hegel implied, the state thereby came to be based more firmly on the institution of private property, since private property became the guiding institution of the society on which the state rested.

In the 1970s many Marxists went back to those ideas to argue against mechanical interpretations promoted by Stalinism, which explained the class nature of the capitalist state merely from the hidden dealings of individual members of the bourgeoisie. Against this highly personalised and simplistic explanation of class rule they posed the idea that the capitalist state is a form of "impersonal power" or, in the original German title of this book, "subject-less violence".

Although a welcome counterweight to mechanical interpretations, this concept is itself not unproblematic. For one thing authors basing themselves on it tend to overestimate the autonomy of the functioning of the state from prevailing class relations.

The strange jump by Gerstenberger in the last lines of her book from describing the inherent inequalities and limitations of bourgeois democracy on an international scale to suggesting strengthening of international law as a (partial) solution to the problems created by the system can be seen as·one expression of this.

However, the heart of Marx's argument was to expose the falseness of all universalist claims by bourgeois state and law. Instead he showed how these are rooted in capitalist society even when they appear to exist as completely independent entities. The realities of class rule are all the more easily forgotten by proponents of the concept of "impersonal power", since it operates on such a high level of abstraction. The real state is, of course, made up of real people who in real historical circumstances apply highly subjective violence.

To be fair, Gerstenberger does try to avoid some of those traps. Indeed already in the 1970s she criticised the ahistorical nature of much of the so-called "state derivation debate", and in a way this book can be seen as a major attempt to give the concept of "impersonal power" a more historical underpinning.

The main part of this book, then, consists of a historical description of the making of the bourgeois state in the two countries that are traditionally at the centre of discussions on the transition from feudalism to capitalism: France and England. Gerstenberger argues that the history of state power in both countries can be divided into three successive stages. The first was that of the highly personalised, divided power at the high point of feudalism, when "the state" consisted of a conglomerate of sovereignties of often competing feudal lords.

The second phase is one of "generalised

personal power" in which kings managed to subject the competing lords to their rule and started to build more centralised state machines. This Ancien Régime, which roughly coincides with the period between the 16th and the 19th century, is often described as the age of absolutism. It saw the integration of the rising merchants, bankers and bourgeois professionals into a power structure that, in the eyes of Gerstenberger, was still decidedly non-capitalist, being based on estate privileges defended by the personal rule of the monarch.

Only when those estate privileges themselves started to disintegrate, she argues, could the state transform from a form of generalised personal rule into the impersonal realm of class rule, the third stage in the process. Capitalism arose out of the Ancien Régime, rather than the Ancien Régime being a response to the rise of capitalism.

The transitions between the three phases mentioned were not automatic. Particular events, such as the bourgeois revolutions, played a role in the process. But Gerstenberger denies that they were in any way the crucial turning points. According to her, after the "Glorious Revolution" of 1688, which she sees as more important than the (much more revolutionary) civil war of the 1640s, it took over 100 years before the Ancien Régime really started to disintegrate in England. And Gerstenberger manages to find traces of the Ancien Régime well into the 20th century.

The importance Gerstenberger attaches to the prevalence of aristocratic political practices derives from her denial of any primacy for economic developments. Legal reforms, changing cultural or religious practices and political shifts within the ruling aristocracy seem to be as important to her as the underlying shifts at the base of society. Her approach comes close to the "political

Marxism" of writers such as Robert Brenner, Ellen Meiksins Wood and Benno Teschke. Gerstenberger tries to find the roots for the changes within the feudal state apparatus in the power relations stemming from particular modes of exploitation. But like those other writers she tends to cut off the forms of exploitation, and more particularly the forms of political rule, from the changes in the forces and relations of production.

This weakness is of great consequence to her general approach. While she traces in great details the complex mixture of feudal, Ancien Régime and bourgeois forms of government over a large span of time, the complete transformation of economic life between, say, the year 1000 and 1789 receives only scanty attention. The social content of the political, juridical, ideological and religious practices she describes therefore remains unclear.

This methodological weakness also helps explain why Gerstenberger treats the Ancien Régime almost like a separate form of class rule, non-feudal and non-capitalist in nature, while refraining from determining more precisely the nature of the prevailing mode of production during this phase. Now, the choice to treat this period as a completely separate phase rests on a real difficulty facing historians of the transition. Anyone who tries to come to terms with the 17th and 18th century basing themselves on a set list of what is feudal and what is capitalist will run into serious problems. In most societies, at least the ones under investigation, an intricate mixture existed between the old feudal forms in strongly adapted new guises and the new capitalist ways of dealing which were deformed by the feudal straitjackets in which they arose.

Further complicating the matter, no state was allowed to quietly work out "its own transition" since permanent warfare forced them to constantly adapt their internal structures and copy successful practices among neighbouring states. The international nature of the rise of capitalism, and especially of the process of state formation, should therefore preclude any attempt to fit the transition onto the Procrustean bed of narrowly defined national models.

Unfortunately, this is precisely the road that Gerstenberger takes. If we simply take the modern state form as our ideal type, all 18th century states will indeed fail the necessary requirements to be called capitalist. The mistake lies in the attempt to define the social content of the state from its form.

Judging superficially one could say that those states that had gone through a successful bourgeois revolution (such as the Netherlands and England) and those that had not (such as France) had many more common features than differences. All were primarily geared at raising taxes in order to pay for war. All more or less improvised a state bureaucracy in order to fit those demands, leaning both on existing aristocratic ties and on merchant wealth. All allowed for widespread corruption and the intermingling of state and private interests as long as the money needed for war kept coming in. And all to a certain extend stimulated the growth of manufacture and trade in order to be able to compete internationally.

In many aspects, the warring mercantilist states of the 18th century were so symmetrical that this seems to warrant speaking of a particular type of society. However, doing so means glossing over the very real differences in the way those states related to the acceleration of capitalist development within their domains, despite similarities in forms of rule or specific policies. While in France capitalist interests always remained subsumed under the dynastic aims of the feudal state, the Dutch and English states were to a far larger extent willing to set the forces of accumulation free. It is by their successive attitudes to the interests of capitalist accumulation that the class nature of early modern states should be judged.

Of course, in a book of such scope one can find much to learn from despite disagreeing with the general direction of the argument. Many of Gerstenberger's arguments are challenging and refreshingly undogmatic. Unfortunately, there are other weaknesses to add to the ones already mentioned. The most important of those is inaccessibility.

There is the issue of the book's price, but readers who are interested can always try to find a university library willing to order it for them. However, even when overcoming this problem many readers will find the style of the book disheartening. The structure of the argument is overburdened by the many side-roads taken, and some ruses in the construction of the book were necessary to save the theoretical argument from collapsing under this weight of detail. Often the author does not bother to explain how much importance is to be attached to various factors or what selection criteria led her to expound on those rather than others.

In all, the book does not manage to escape from the primary weaknesses of the state derivation debate of the 1970s. Its composition remains highly academic. The historical argument seems to be built around a set of theoretical ideal types, instead of the theoretical model being rooted in critical historical investigation. And finally, the models that are chosen are in essence national, ignoring both the international nature of the transition to capitalism and the international dimension of capitalist accumulation and state formation. Gerstenberger's book grapples with important questions. But after 700 pages she leaves us wanting.

William Morris designed wallpaper; along with furniture, ceramics, stained-glass windows, tapestries, and carpets. He was a painter, he wrote novels, poetry, and translated Icelandic sagas, he wrote on politics, architecture, and the state of art under a growing industrial capitalism and what possibilities existed for life in the future. The ravages of industrial capitalism, imperialism and war, the destruction of the environment, and above all, the enslavement of human labour to the machine appalled him.

As the nineteenth century progressed he become more political, and realised that reviving the methods of arts and craft from the Middle Ages could not end exploitation and oppression for the mass of people, so he took a giant step across the 'river of fire' and became a revolutionary socialist. *Hassan Mahamdallie* shows that the socialism of Morris grew out of his view of the past and his hatred for a system of 'shoddy' production and that during the last decades of his life, Morris threw all his energy into the struggle to change the world.

www.redwords.org.uk

Crossing the 'river of fire' : the socialism of
William Morris

by Hassan Mahamdallie

ISBN: 9781905192328
£7.99

A REVOLUTIONARY PORTRAIT

REDWORDS

available from Bookmarks
www.bookmarks.uk.com
& all other good bookshops

Pick of the quarter

This has been a bumper quarter for Marxist analysis that complements articles which have recently appeared in this journal.

The July-August *Monthly Review* was a special issue on capitalism's ecological crises. John W Farley spells out in detail the scientific case over climate change, while Minqi Li argues that its effects are likely to be more rapid than is suggested even by the books of George Monbiot. Fred Magdoff shows how dishonest and dangerous is the agenda pushing biofuels as an answer and John Bellamy Foster draws together the most recent evidence on "peak oil"—the point at which oil output worldwide will stop rising. The articles are available online at www.monthlyreview.org

Coming to very much the same conclusions as *Monthly Review* is a recent piece by Mike Davis, "Living on the Ice Shelf: Humanity's Meltdown". This article is available at www.tomdispatch.com/post/174949/mike_davis_welcome_to_the_next_epoch

Readers will find Tsering Shakya's "Tibetan Questions" in the May-June *New Left Review* (which arrived in early July) a very useful supplement to Charlie Hore's piece for *International Socialism 119* on a question which is contentious among some on the left (www.newleftreview.org/?page=article&view=2720). Also in the same issue is a critical but favourable review of Chris Wickham's book on the *European Early Middle Ages*. The book was hailed as a major breakthrough in Marxist history when it came out two years ago. Wickham himself writes on the logic of the feudal mode of production in *Historical Materialism 16.2*, in the process replying to points made in the review of his book (by Chris Harman) in *International Socialism 109*. In the same issue of *Historical Materialism* Jeffrey R Webber provides the first part of a fascinating account of Bolivian society and politics; Alex Callinicos looks at the different approaches of Marxists in Britain and France towards Muslims, questioning some of the formulations of Daniel Bensaid; Alexander Anievas criticises the notion of a new transnational ruling class; and Lise Vogel provides a succinct summary of the 30 year old discussion within Marxist political economy of domestic labour.

Events in Venezuela are of immense interest to socialists everywhere in the world. The summer issue of the *Review of Radical Political Economics* contains an informative article on structural change and planning in its economy by Paulo Nakatani and Rémy Herrera.

The Olympic games focused attention on Chinese nationalism. Au Long Yu, writing in the September issue of *Against the Current*, analyses the impact of this, including its impact on what is often called the "Chinese new left" (www.solidarity-us.org/node/1886).

International Socialism contributor Mike Haynes has written a fascinating piece in the *History Teaching Review Year Book* on attempts to calculate the numbers killed in wars. He points to the hypocrisy involved in lots of pro-Western or pro-colonial estimates, before finishing with a summation of the appalling toll of Iraqi dead as a result of war, sanctions and occupation. (http://pers-www.wlv.ac.uk/~le1958/war.pdf)

You would not normally expect us to refer to the *British Journal of Dermatology*. But it recently contained a fascinating article on something often used to make fun of Karl Marx—his notorious carbuncles. The article suggests, in fact, that they were the product of a discomforting and debilitating disease, *hydradenitis suppurativa*, which caused pain around his groin and posterior more or less continually from 1862 to 1874 with "only a few periods of freedom in between". These were, of course, the years when Marx completed volume one of *Capital*, wrote *The Civil War in France* and was at the centre of the First International. But they were also the years in which he failed to turn his manuscripts for volumes two and three of *Capital* into finished works (a task which Engels had to take up after Marx's death). The clinical diagnosis suggests this is not something for enemies of Marxism to mock at, but an effect of an ailment which would have prevented most other people from doing anything.

JC and CH